P9-DUR-367

FALLING OFF THE EDGE

FALLING OFF THE EDGE

TRAVELS THROUGH THE DARK HEART OF GLOBALIZATION

ALEX PERRY

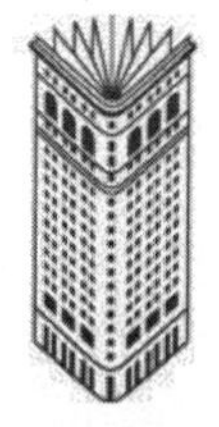

BLOOMSBURY PRESS
New York Berlin London

For information address Bloomsbury Press, 175 Fifth Avenue, New York, NY 10010.

Published by Bloomsbury Press, New York

All papers used by Bloomsbury Press are natural, recyclable products made from wood grown in well-managed forests. The manufacturing processes conform to the environmental regulations of the country of origin.

LIBRARY OF CONGRESS CATALOGING-IN-PUBLICATION DATA
Perry, Alex.
Falling off the edge : travels through the dark heart of globalization/Alex Perry.—1st U.S. ed.
p. cm.
Includes bibliographical references and index.
ISBN-13: 978-1-59691-526-8 (alk. paper)
ISBN-10: 1-59691-526-9 (alk. Paper)
1. Globalization—Political aspects—Asia. 2. Globalization—Social aspects—Asia. 3. Crime and globalization—Asia. 4. Terrorism and globalization—Asia. I. Title.

JZ1318.P457 2008
303.48'25—dc22
2008025998

First U.S. Edition 2008

1 3 5 7 9 10 8 6 4 2

Typeset by SetSystems Ltd. Saffron Walden, Essex
Printed in the United States of America by Quebecor World Fairfield

For Tess

'Only the dead have seen the end of war.'

Inscription at the entrance to the
Imperial War Museum, London, credited to Plato.

CONTENTS

PROLOGUE

In the days before *iinen*, says En-mei, before jeeps and bananas and medical – before road – there was the world. The world had jackfruits, jungle roots and honey bees, monitor lizards, civet cats and jungle pigs and white ants big enough to eat; and in the sea, fish, snakes, clams, robber crabs and big, lazy turtles to roll over on the beach and roast whole, upturned in their shells. Sometimes, *iinen* came to the world, to fish or cut trees or take pigs, and the elders would fight them. But most of the time, and sometimes for generations, the people were alone. 'It was good,' says En-mei. 'Sometimes I went with my friends Eingane, Toepel, Ten-mei and Eiantho to collect fruit from the jungle. But most of the time, I never used to do anything.'

En-mei is vague about how he came to leave the world. But the *iinen* who knows him best, Indian anthropologist Vishvajit Pandya, says En-mei fell in love. En-mei is a Stone Age Jarawa tribesman from South Andaman Island, a tiny speck of volcanic rainforest and white beach rising out of the middle of the Bay of Bengal between India and Thailand. As a teenager, he set his heart on a Jarawa girl from the Middle Andaman tribe. But the Middle Andaman Jarawas considered themselves superior to the southerners, and the match worried the girl's father. In early 1997, En-mei went to see the man to plead his suit. The pair argued and the father, stronger than En-mei, took the boy out into the forest, broke his leg and left him to die.

It was too far to crawl home. En-mei's only hope was a tiny medical clinic on the edge of the forest that administered to Kadamtala, a small town of settlers from the Indian mainland. So it was that he dragged himself out of the jungle, through the clinic's doors and into the history books. An astonished trainee doctor at Kadamtala telephoned his superiors in the island capital Port Blair to tell them he had made the first friendly contact with a Stone Age tribe lost to civilization for 50,000 years.[1]

Though En-mei was the first Jarawa to leave the forest willingly, the tribe was not unknown. Savage legends have been spun about the Jarawa since almost the beginning of recorded time. In Hindu myth, the Andaman and Nicobar archipelago is known as Kalapani, or 'black waters', a lost world in a sea of Styx from which no man ever returns. In the second century BC, the Alexandrian scholar Ptolemy wrote of 'islands of cannibals'. In AD 1290, Marco Polo described the inhabitants as 'no better than wild beasts ... [with] heads like dogs, and teeth and eyes likewise ... they are a most cruel generation and eat everybody they can catch, if not of their own race.'

British colonizers claimed the islands in 1789. There was a natural deep-water harbour at Port Blair and the islands' isolation later made them an excellent site for the notorious Cellular Jail, where the British held and executed India's freedom fighters. But it was not a prized posting. Malaria was rife, and those who did venture into the forest were often met with a barrage of Jarawa arrows. Nevertheless, the British succeeded in capturing a handful of Jarawa tribesmen and in the late 1850s, one was taken to Calcutta by Frederic John Mouat on HMS *Pluto*.

'Joe Abraham' drew huge crowds. People were amazed. The Andamans are in Asia. But the Jarawa were African pygmies. More than a century later, DNA analysis would confirm the Jarawa had been isolated for tens of thousands of years and are direct bloodline descendants of Early Man, from northern Kenya and southern Ethiopia. Anthropologists speculate they migrated east from Africa during the Ice Age, perhaps 100,000 years ago, walked across the vast frozen plains of what is now the Indian Ocean and, when the ice began to melt and the waters rose around them, retreated to the highest ground they could find, the Andaman and Nicobar mountain range. Later expeditions would discover the islands were home to five other tribes, African and Asian, almost as though, as the great flood advanced, a Noah's Ark of Stone Age men sought shelter there. Cut off from the world and repelling all intruders for tens of thousands of years, the tribes had not changed. For scientists, they are the First Man. For Christians, they are the closest living relatives to Adam and Eve.

For the islands' visitors, they were a menace. The Jarawa fought the British, the Japanese in the Second World War and, after India achieved independence in 1947, Bengali settler families from the mainland. Then En-mei slithered out of the forest and suddenly the Indians had an opportunity to kill the Jarawa threat with kindness. For six months, they plied En-mei with every luxury and privilege the islands could provide. They gave him electricity, air conditioning and television in a private room at Port Blair's hospital; bananas, coconuts and curry; a chauffeur-driven car; even a visit from the then prime minister, Atal Bihari Vajpayee. And it seemed to work. En-mei lapped it up. On his miraculous return to the forest in autumn 1997, he told his astounded tribesmen: 'The outside people are good. No one attacked me. And there are lots of them.'

Within days, scores of Jarawas appeared on the road demanding food and, shrieking with laughter, riding on the roofs of buses into town. The people of Port Blair were told to let the naked tribesmen wander freely. The authorities would pay stallholders for whatever they took. The wild men of the Andamans were finally being tamed.

Except they weren't. Rather, says Samir Acharya of the Society of Andaman and Nicobar Ecology, they were being decimated. 'Contact with the outside brought infection from diseases for which they had no immunity,' he says. 'Measles, mumps, diarrhoea. Around 30 per cent contracted hepatitis B. I believe the entire elder generation was wiped out.' The situation became all the more alarming when a new best estimate put the total Jarawa population in Middle and South Andaman at a mere 264. A storm of international protest blew across Port Blair.

En-mei, however, was prospering. When he left the forest, according to Acharya, he had not only been rejected by the Middle Andaman tribe, he had also been 'effectively excommunicated' by his own South Andaman group for a wilful nature that, in his teenage years, had become petulance and given him a violent temper. Returning so spectacularly from the dead, and with tales of other-worldly adventure, he was suddenly a star. 'People came,' says En-mei. 'A lot of them came. To see me.' En-mei quickly capitalized on his new celebrity, holding court with the surviving elders and taking younger Jarawas on guided tours of the modern-day wonders of Kadamtala and Port Blair.

And then, two years after he left the forest, En-mei vanished. His guided tours stopped. Small groups of children still gathered by the roadside to beg and Jarawas continued to travel to the medical station at Kadamtala for treatment. But the remarkable burst of contact between the Stone Age and the modern world fizzled. En-mei, the environmentalists' champion, the man with whom the administrators felt they could finally do business, the anthropological find of a lifetime, disappeared.

It took almost a year to work out what had happened. Finally Pandya tracked him down. The anthropologist discovered En-mei's elevated status had culminated in the realization of his oldest and dearest ambition: marriage, not to the girl he once loved, but an arranged match to Chailla, an eminent Jarawa girl from South Andaman. As soon as he got what he wanted, the tours stopped. All the married En-mei wanted to do was hunt.

I caught up with En-mei on one of his rare excursions from the forest.[2] He explained that when he was growing up, the Jarawa attacked outsiders because they were afraid. 'When we first saw these people, we were scared. *Sahibs* used to come in large numbers and frighten us with guns. They used to kill deer, set traps. That's why we attacked. We used to think, "Why are these people coming here? No one should come to our house."' Despite the way he had profited from his time in the outside world, En-mei had mixed feelings about it. 'Port Blair [had] buildings and lights and tables. Everything is nice. But I did not enjoy myself. I did not see my people.' The modern world had not overwhelmed him.

Rather, he developed an ambivalence about what outsiders called progress. When I asked about the Andaman Trunk Road that had been cut through Jarawa territory, he replied: 'It's good. Buses and jeeps are good. And cutting trees can be good. It cleans the place. But they should not clean in far-off places. If you clear forest inside the jungle, there will be no rain and we won't get water. And now people use the road to come here and take pictures of us. It's not good. I snatch the camera and break it.' Finally, after perusing everything the developed world had to offer, En-mei had rejected it. 'The jungle is good,' he said. 'I don't feel like going outside now. We will stay in the forest. In the forest, there is a nice breeze.'

When I visited Pandya at his research offices in Ahmedabad in eastern India in 2004, he said that even if the Jarawas survived the onslaught of disease and the challenges of the road, the damage was done. 'You can't expect these guys just to forget everything they've seen and go back to Eden,' he said. 'En-mei may be happy back in the forest, but others won't be. You can't wind the clock back. The Jarawas, as they are, are doomed.'

And yet, added Pandya, En-mei's adventures were not without worth. Before he left our world and returned to the forest, En-mei left behind a profound human truth. 'This guy crossed a creek of 80,000 years and saw the world,' said Pandya. 'But instead of staying in wonderland, he went back. Why?'

Pandya said his studies had uncovered a Jarawa culture of sophisticated and exotic ritual. But he had come to understand that it would be a mistake to regard the Jarawa only as unique and distinct. Perhaps the first men to venture out from Africa's cradle of life, the Jarawa were also the first to set in motion an essential human process – exploration and migration – that today culminates in what we call globalization. En-mei's behaviour also showed that the Jarawa were 'smart, adaptable, political human beings'. Polo's 'wild beasts' would sometimes kill to get what they wanted. But by going back to his old life, En-mei had also demonstrated a more sophisticated side. He 'knew he couldn't live in a holiday forever,' said Pandya, and when 'he saw an opportunity to get on in life' – marriage to Chailla – 'he took it.'

Pandya was breathing shallowly. He paused to catch some air, then leant forward with the manner of someone passing on a revelation. 'You see, for many years I was looking at the differences between them and us,' he said. 'I was missing the point. It's not the differences between us that are so remarkable. It's the similarities.' En-mei 'handled the culture shock of entering the modern world no problem at all,' said Pandya. He used his trip to further his own ambitions. How and why was he able to do that? Because the same essential rules of human behaviour applied in the outside world as among the Jarawa. In other words: a violent, selfish schemer, driven to exploit distant lands? It's who he was. It's who we've always been.

PART ONE

INCOMING

CHAPTER 1

BOOM, THEN BANG

On 24 November 2001, a bright autumn Saturday, 8,000 Taliban soldiers who had fled the American bombardment of Kunduz, their last stronghold in northern Afghanistan, laid down their weapons in a vast natural rock amphitheatre in the desert a few hours to the west of the ancient Bactrian Silk Road city of Mazar-i-Sharif. They surrendered to Northern Alliance General Abdul Rashid Dostum, who crowed that his forces had achieved a 'great victory'.

In earlier episodes of Afghanistan's wars, Dostum was reputed to have killed his enemies by tying them to the tracks of his tanks.[1] But outside Mazar, Dostum decided to make a gesture of reconciliation to unite Afghanistan's warring tribes. Thousands of Afghan Taliban were free to return to their farms. Only the few hundred foreigners would be kept captive. They were taken on flat-bed trucks to Qala-i-Jangi, a sprawling mud-walled nineteenth-century prison fortress to the west of Mazar, where Dostum stabled his horses and which contained a large dungeon. The prisoners were led down the steps into their new jail, a succession of small underground cells on either side of a dark, earthen corridor. They were not searched.

The next morning was clear and cold. Two Americans

arrived at Qala-i-Jangi. They were Johnny Michael Spann, thirty-two, a CIA paramilitary operative who had been parachuted into Afghanistan at the war's beginning, and Dave Tyson, a CIA officer operating in central Asia. Their mission was to identify any members of al-Qaeda among the prisoners. They decided not to interview their charges one by one. Instead, they asked for all the men to be brought out and made to kneel, with their hands tied behind their backs, in lines in a large enclosed courtyard in the south-west of the fort. There, overseen by a handful of Alliance guards, the two Americans walked the lines, examining the fighters, prodding them, asking questions. The prisoners, trussed and cramped, began wailing with pain. Prisoners and captors also had little language in common, and the interrogations suffered as a result. Spann used loud English. Tyson tried Russian, the language of Afghanistan's hated former invaders.

The last men were being brought out of the cells when there was a shout. One prisoner had a grenade. He threw himself at Spann. There was an explosion. Other prisoners lunged forward, at Tyson, at the guards. More men launched themselves at Spann, scrabbling at his flesh with their hands, kicking and beating him. The Alabaman was said to have killed three men with his pistol and AK-47 before he became the first American to die in combat in Afghanistan.

Other Taliban fighters quickly overpowered the Alliance guards, killing them with their own weapons. Tyson grabbed an AK-47, opened fire and ran. When he reached the fort's north wall, he paused, borrowed a satellite phone from a German TV crew to call in news of the uprising to his commanders and stayed put to figure out how to extract Spann's body.[2] That was not going to be easy. A few hundred yards to the south, the prisoners discovered the courtyard they now controlled also held Dostum's armoury. They ransacked it for AK-47s, grenades, mines, rocket launchers, mortars and thousands of rounds of ammunition.

The Taliban held the south-west of the fort. The Alliance held the south-east and the north. A vicious exchange of fire ensued across the open ground between. Two ancient Russian tanks now in the possession of the Alliance were driven up the ramparts on to the north wall and started firing on the Taliban. High in the sky, an American B-52 began to circle.

All this happened before I arrived. I had been in Mazar for a fortnight after slipping over the border illegally from Uzbekistan, and that day I had hired a rusty Lada cab and set off south from the city with my fixer, Najibullah Quraishi, to investigate a story about the assassination of a renegade Alliance commander. We made it to the city's southern outskirts before the ancient Russian car gave up. I got out for a cigarette and, in the quiet of the desert, I could hear the distant 'pop, pop, pop' of gunfire. After five minutes under the bonnet, the driver managed to start the car. We turned around and followed the noise of weapons through Mazar and out to its western edge. It became clear we were heading to Qala-i-Jangi. As we got closer, we began to see signs of combat. At one point, a car sped past us carrying a badly wounded man. A few hundred yards further on, men were out in the street, looking excited and frightened. Then the fort appeared and our driver refused to go further.

Najib and I walked up the track to the fort's entrance. A junior Alliance commander came out to greet us. 'There's nothing happening here,' he said. A rocket-propelled grenade split the air between us at a little over head height and exploded a few hundred yards away in a mud cloud. The embarrassed Alliance man let us pass. We skirted the bodies of three Islamist fighters who had apparently tried to escape, neat and precisely placed diamond-shaped holes in their foreheads indicating close-range executions. Inside the fort, we met some more senior Alliance commanders, who told us what we had missed.

At 2 p.m. two minivans and a pair of open-sided white Land Rovers mounted with machine guns pulled up outside the fortress gates. From the minivans jumped nine American Special Operations men wearing Oakley sunglasses and baseball caps, carrying snub-nosed M-4 automatic rifles. The Land Rovers disgorged seven British Special Boat Service soldiers armed with M-16s and dressed in jeans, sweaters, Barbour jackets, Afghan scarves and *pakuls*, the distinctive woollen hats of the Afghan mujahideen. The Americans and British quickly convened a conference with the Alliance leaders. 'I want eyes on, and I want satcom[3] and JDAMS[4],' said the American commander, Major Mark Mitchell. 'Tell them there will be six or seven buildings in a line in the south-west half. That's where they're getting their weapons and ammunition. If they can hit that, then that would kill a whole lot of these motherfuckers.'

A bearded American in a Harley-Davidson cap and mirrored sunglasses raised Tyson on his radio. 'Shit . . . shit . . . OK . . . Shit . . . OK. Hold on, buddy, we're coming to get you,' he said. Then, cutting the radio, he turned to his commander: 'Mike is MIA[5]. They've taken his gun and his ammo. We have another guy. He managed to kill two of them, but he's holed up in the north side with no ammo.' As a hurried discussion of tactics began, Harley-Davidson went back to his radio. Then he cut in: 'Shit. Let's stop fucking around and get in there. This guy needs our help.' Pointing to the sky, he added, 'Tell those guys to stop scratching their balls and fly. We have a guy in the north, enemies in the south-west and friendlies in between.'

Outside the fort, Alliance soldiers began pouring out of the north-east battlements, sliding over the walls and down the ramparts. The wounded were whisked away in commandeered taxis. A firefight raged inside the fort through the afternoon, the occasional rocket or mortar spinning out over the walls. Two American fighter planes began circling the area. Inside, the Americans' translator fled. They ordered Najib up on to the parapets where they had set up a command post and told him to translate between them and their Afghan allies. I went with him.

On the roof, Alliance General Majid Rozi told the Americans and the British that their warplanes needed to hit the armoury, a pink single-storey building inside the Islamist area. Najib translated and the visitors spotted the target for the planes far above. 'Thunder, Ranger,' said an American radio operator, speaking to the aeroplanes above. 'The coordinates are: north 3639984, east 06658945, elevation 1,299 feet.' He turned to his comrades. 'Four minutes.'

'Three minutes.'

'Two minutes.'

'Thirty seconds.'

'Fifteen seconds.'

From the sky, a great, arrow-shaped missile appeared, zeroing in on its target a hundred yards away and sounding like a car decelerating in high gear. The spotters lay flat. Alliance commanders and soldiers leaned into the mud walls. A warplane flew overhead. Then the missile hit. CRACK-WHOOMF! Lungs emptied. Minds blanked, rebooted. The building bounced, a dust cloud flew into the air and shrapnel whistled by. The Alliance soldiers burst into applause. A US soldier picked up a piece of fallen metal. 'Souvenir,' he grinned.

Six more strikes followed before the British SBS commander re-established contact with Tyson, just as night began to fall. Some of the attacks were on target. At least one was a mile wide, landing on houses nearby. The Alliance soldiers yelled at Najib. He blamed the foreigners. 'Somebody should be criticized,' he said indignantly. At 4:25 p.m. the sun set over the hills to the west.

That night, I broke the news about the battle and Spann's death on *Time*'s website and in a live interview with CNN. Overnight, around a hundred more journalists arrived. They included *Time*'s contracted photographer Oleg Nikishin and two freelance cameramen friends, an American, Dodge Billingsley, and a Frenchman, Damien Deguelde.[6] Fighting was constant overnight, with red tracers shooting off into Mazar city.

The next morning, Monday, I took a cab, picked up Oleg, Dodge and Damien at 6 a.m. from their hotel and took them to the fort. We scrambled up the side of the north wall until we reached Alliance commander Mohammed Akbar, who was guiding mortar and tank fire on to Taliban positions in the south-west. We watched for an hour or so before Akbar threw us out. I later discovered Akbar was acting on a request from an unusually skittish Najib.

Dodge, Damien, Oleg and I took up a new position on a road outside the fort. Around 10 a.m., four more Special Operations soldiers and eight men from the US 10th Mountain Division arrived to join us. A jet pilot circled overhead, radioing instructions to the spotters.

'Be advised,' said the pilot to the soldiers in the fort, 'you are dangerously close. You are about a hundred yards away from the target.'

'I think we're perhaps a little too close,' came the spotter's reply. 'But we have to be, to get the laser on the target.'

Pause.

Bomb spotter: 'We are about ready to pull back.'

Pilot: 'We are about to release.'

Spotter: 'Roger.'

Then suddenly, spotter: 'Be advised we have new coordinates: north 3639996, east 06658866.'

Pilot: 'Good copy.'

Spotter: 'Two minutes.'

At 10:53 a.m. a 2,000-pound missile slammed into the north wall, a direct hit on Akbar's command post and exactly where Najib and I had been standing half an hour before. His nerves had saved our lives. Much more powerful than previous strikes, which had been 500 pounders, it sent clouds of dust 1,000 feet into the air. 'No, no!' Alliance commander Olim Razum yelled at the 10th Mountain soldiers. 'This is the wrong place! Cut it! Tell them to cut it!' The men around us froze with incomprehension. How many Alliance soldiers were dead? How many Americans and British? A Special Ops soldier standing next to me glanced up at a tower of rocks and shrapnel thrown up by the explosion and saw what was about to happen. The debris was mushrooming into a giant fog and speeding towards us like a tornado. 'Incoming!' he shouted. 'Get down!'

It took a second. Then we were inside it.[7,8,9]

This is a reporter's book. It was born out of the slow realization during the years that followed 9/11 that – sometimes by chance, sometimes by design, but always because it was simply my job – I was often *there*; and, what surprised me: very few others were. It is a reassertion of that old tenet of beat reporting: if you want to know, go.

As the years passed and my experience increased, I began to wonder about the absent. In particular, I began to question how they viewed the world. My travels made some of their ideas – often those that originated inside universities and strategic studies institutes or banks and newspaper offices in London or New York – feel increasingly unsatisfactory. Few people now think we are living in a time when history is ending, but it seems to me that the world is not peacefully flattening either. Instead we are entering a new era of war. This book also rejects the idea that militarism and ignorance in American foreign policy are the sole reason why global war is the legacy of the Bush era – though they certainly played an important part. My encounters across Asia, Africa and the Middle East made me believe that this is primarily a story about global economics, and the rising inequality that results. The shared truth that links conflict zones as distant as the Himalayas and the Sahara is this: globalization starts wars.

Globalization, like terrorism, is of course a word that overuse has made so elastic, it has almost lost definition. I aim to rescue globalization from some common misunderstandings and rediscover its meaning by viewing it in the context where it is best understood – at close quarters, in the developing world.

Narayan Murthy, the Indian offshoring pioneer, describes globalization as 'securing capital from where it's cheapest, talent from where it's available, producing where it is most cost effective and selling where the markets are.' That's globalization in a purely economic sense, what *New York*

Times columnist Thomas Friedman calls 'flattening the world'. But when we're talking broad human development – about progress – we need to consider globalization in a wider sense, as a political, cultural, humanitarian and even environmental phenomenon.

An American soldier charged with bringing democracy to Iraq personifies political globalization. The worldwide release of a Hollywood blockbuster is cultural globalization in action. The World Food Programme is a manifestation of humanitarian globalization. Global warming is an unfortunate instance of environmental globalization, in which a few of us have produced enough pollution to heat the world. Though these are all recent examples, it's worth noting that Indians drank Italian wine in the second century BC. Globalization is a new word, but the phenomenon has deep roots.

All these examples share a common trait: an element of dominance by a powerful country or philosophy, or even a movie star. Globalization is global governance without global government. In an unregulated environment, the ideas of our more powerful national governments – or philosophers or companies or pop groups – tend to dominate. Globalization describes standardization in the image of the elite.

This is what opponents of globalization object to – and why, since the champions of our world are so often Western or American, anti-globalization activists are frequently anti-Western and anti-American. As Joseph Stiglitz writes in *Making Globalization Work*: 'Globalization should not mean the Americanization of either economic policy or culture, but it often does – and that has caused resentment.'[10] The antis say that for the poor majority, globalization means being pushed around. They argue that, like a kill-or-cure, globalization fortifies the strong but impoverishes the weak. It makes might right, and want wrong. Moreover, they say, the elite works to keep it that way. 'The critics of globalization accuse Western countries of hypocrisy,' writes Stiglitz, 'and the critics are right. The Western countries have pushed poor countries to eliminate trade barriers, but kept up their own barriers, preventing developing countries from exporting their agricultural products and so depriving them of desperately needed export income.'[11] The anti-globalization movement is a world collective that regards itself, or others, as victims. Or, to borrow Friedman's metaphor again, the problem with a flat world is that people fall off the edge.

That is why a growing movement rejects globalization and fights to be non-standard – to be different. And that applies not just to economics, but to anything from arms control to fast food, and is as true for an Iranian nuclear scientist as it is for an Amazonian Indian worried that logging will ruin his way of life or a French farmer who sprays cow dung at a Kentucky Fried Chicken outlet.

Or a terrorist. After 9/11, some argued terrorism was a distraction from globalization. But if globalization is standardizing the world, and anti-globalization is resistance to that, then terrorism is a subset of the anti-globalization movement. Albeit a prominent, bloody subset. At Qala-i-Jangi I saw American and British commandos and barefoot Afghan soldiers courageously and skilfully slaughter 300 of their enemies in the single bloodiest battle of the Afghan war. I saw an Alliance fighter split a Talib's head with a rock. I stepped over the giant white intestines spilling from the stomachs of Dostum's dead horses. I slipped and fell in another man's brains.

But Qala-i-Jangi was about more than death. It was also

about two visions of life. It was a fight between a dominant Western way of living and a more ancient Eastern one. The West wanted conformity to what it considered to be the universal norms of law and democracy. The Taliban wanted to be different, and al-Qaeda had demonstrated the forcefulness of that objection in New York.[12] A mud fort in Afghanistan was about as far as you could get from the famed global village. And yet here, on the edge of the world, was a war that, at root, was about globalization. It was a fight between those who believed in integrating the world and those who demanded a separate space in it – and who would start a world war to get it. Afghanistan was nothing on the scale of the First or Second World Wars. But in the era of globalization, the world was shrinking, and Afghanistan was one of a new kind of local conflict that had global ramifications. There were many others. In Iraq, American soldiers fought to fold that country into a democratic world community, against insurgents who refused the idea that outsiders could impose any politics, however ostensibly benign. In Somalia, US-backed Ethiopian soldiers fought to crush an al-Qaeda offshoot that espoused the most extreme end of Islamic exceptionalism. In Nepal, the US backed the losing side in a fight between a government and Maoist rebels who saw globalization not as a harmonizing phenomenon, but an elitist conspiracy. Since these conflicts shared similiar causes – and since almost all took place in the developing world – you could plausibly call them a collective Third World War. But comparing today's vexed battles with yesterday's more straightforward fights against tyranny is dubious. Better to describe them simply as small world wars for an increasingly small world. American soldiers in Iraq, British soldiers in

Afghanistan, US-backed Ethiopian soldiers in Somalia were globalizers. The Taliban, the insurgents of Iraq and Somalia's rebels were anti-globalizers.

Qala-i-Jangi also demonstrated how these new wars would be truly international fights. In a small corner of northern Afghanistan, soldiers from the US and Britain, aided by northern Afghans, Uzbeks and Tajiks, faced off against Pakistanis, Chechens, Bangladeshis, Uzbeks, Tajiks, a Central American, a Russian, a German and 'American Taliban' John Walker Lindh. The battle also showed how, faced with overwhelming odds, globalization's opponents might choose death before surrender. When the fighting finally ended after six days, the toll was at least one dead American, scores of dead Northern Alliance and 300 dead Taliban.

So, war and terrorism cannot be separated from progress and globalization. They are often flip sides of the same story. According to John Gray in his short, angry and influential tract *al-Qaeda and What it Means to be Modern* the separation of globalization from terrorism derives from a common misconception. Dating back to the Enlightenment, this is the idea that as democratic capitalism spreads, 'a universal civilization will come into being, and history will come to an end.'[13] The same nebulous thinking underscores the perception that since the end of the Cold War, the developed world has been on a more or less linear path to progress, at worst suffering brief periods of stasis or recession before resuming an inevitable upward path to prosperity. All the poor world has to do, so the thinking goes, is get with the programme.

At first glance, this has some merit. Nearly all of us are living longer, wealthier, healthier and more comfortable lives than we would have two hundred, a hundred or even fifty years ago. And it seems reasonable to give capitalism, the system under which most of us live, the credit. As the *Wall Street Journal*'s motto says: 'Free markets and free people.'

But there are problems here. Progress is not inevitable. Many of the most advanced civilizations have collapsed. Where are Thebes, Machu Picchu, or Angkor Wat now? Nor is globalization a one-way ticket to prosperity: markets go down as well as up. And like communism and Nazism, radical Islam is modern. Though it claims to be anti-Western, it is shaped as much by Western ideology as by Islamic traditions. Like Marxists and neo-liberals, radical Islamists . . . 'are convinced they can remake the human condition,' declares Gray.[14] Though their eventual utopias are anathema, Marxism and Islamism share the same dynamic. Both believe mankind is enslaved by an uncaring, dominant elite. Both prescribe revolution as the solution.

That brings us to freedom – and the reason why the outcome of this debate is so crucial to our idea of ourselves, and so contentious. One of the outgoing US president's favourite pieces of rhetoric, and the one most ridiculed by his opponents, is that the 'war on terror' is a war to defend freedom. Perversely, perhaps, I'd argue Bush was on the right track. Freedom is at the heart of the debate over globalization, and terrorism.

Both sides claim freedom as their own. The pro-globalization crowd argue their values are all about freedom. What's oppressive about democracy, free markets and freedom of expression, they ask? What's more free than a free-for-all?

Almost anything, according to the anti-globalizers, who argue that freedom of expression in the West all too often means freedom to insult. Western democracy is a members-only club, they add: look at the long list of dictatorships and repressive regimes backed by Europe and the US. Likewise to call it the 'free' market is disingenuous: in reality, it means freedom for the mighty, and slavery for the weak – and a global free market only exacerbates those positions. Globalization even allows multinational giants to overcome restrictions placed on them by national governments. Globalization is capitalism beyond control.

But these arguments are flawed, too. The anti-globalizers say that to be different is to be free, and a good thing – the world would be a poorer place if we all ate, thought and loved the same way. That seems reasonable. Until the pro-globalizers point out that one man's cultural preservation is another man's bloody intolerance. One reason Indonesian Islamic militants killed 202 people at a nightclub in Bali in October 2002, for example, was to signal disapproval of the dangerously catchy idea of letting women out at night.

The debate hinges on different ideas of freedom. Globalizers and most Westerners (at least since the Enlightenment) believe in 'freedom to'. Active freedom. Freedom to express yourself, freedom to marry, freedom to drink and dance all night on an Indonesian island paradise. Anti-globalizers, Islamists and much of the European Left, limit themselves to 'freedom from'. This is passive freedom, which zeroes in on the absence of subjugation, rather than active choice. It's a more pessimistic view of the human condition and assumes that everyone, to some extent, is oppressed.

So who's right? Advocates of globalization are correct that the process has raised average productivity and national wealth – and therefore freedom – across the world. According to the World Bank, the proportion of people living on less than $2 a day fell from 67 per cent in 1981 to 47 per cent in 2004.

Globalization has also created a market for luxury in almost any country you care to name. This is all the evidence many pro-globalizers need. They point to increases in average per capita income and conclude this is irrefutable evidence that hundreds of millions of people have been lifted out of poverty.

But average height has always been a poor means of describing a tall person and a short one. Globalization's opponents note that you can obtain a healthy-sounding median from averaging the rocketing income of one very rich man and the falling incomes of ten poorer ones. A rise in a nation's overall wealth says nothing about equality *within* that nation. 'Globalization might be creating rich countries with poor people,' writes Stiglitz.[15]

The facts support the anti-globalizers. A 2004 report by the World Commission on the Social Dimension of Globalization found 59 per cent of the world's people were living in countries with growing inequality, while 5 per cent were in countries where inequality was declining.[16] Income inequality inside Western countries is now at heights unseen since the roaring 1920s.[17] The rich have also reaped disproportionate rewards in the Asian tigers – Singapore, Taiwan, South Korea and Hong Kong.[18] In December 2006, the World Institute for World Economics reported that 1 per cent of the world's adults owned 40 per cent of all global assets and the richest 10 per cent owned 85 per cent; the poorest half, meanwhile, owned less than 1 per cent.

Underneath the elite, the picture is one of stagnation. In the West, it's becoming clear that one of the biggest effects of globalization is not just the loss of jobs to Asia. It is also the *threat* of jobs moving east in a vastly expanded global labour market – one in which, with the addition of China, India, the former USSR, South East Asia, Africa and South America, the labour force has doubled from 1.46 billion to 2.93 billion.[19] The result is depression of wages at both ends of the migration, and the first boom since the Second World War in which real wages have failed to rise. [20]

Globalization has nurtured even greater disparity in the developing world. India now has 40 million more destitute people than it did in 1993.[21] China's southern coast has rocketed into the twenty-first century in the last two decades. But inequality across the country has also increased: the Gini co-efficient, the standard index of income disparity, is now greater in communist China than ex-communist Russia or the freewheeling US. Millions of Chinese, like their Indian counterparts, are actually worse off. An analysis by World Bank economist Bert Hofman found the real income of the poorest 10 per cent of China's 1.4 billion people – 140 million people – actually fell by 2.4 per cent in the two years to 2003, a period when China's economy was growing by at least 10 per cent a year. Beijing-based economists Louis Kuijs and He Jianwu found the wage share of GDP in China fell from 53 per cent to 41 per cent from 1998 to 2005.[22] The same pattern can be observed around the world.[23] In its 2003 report *Making Global Trade Work for People*, the UN Development Programme found that because population growth often outstrips economic growth, even as percentages of people living in poverty are falling, the absolute number living in poverty is rising. In Africa, for example, the numbers living on less than $1 a day doubled between 1981 and 2001, from 164 million to 316 million.[24]

The growing gap between haves and have-nots strikes at the heart of globalization. Globalization was supposed to be the tide to lift all boats. But millions of boats seem to be not merely missing the tide, they seem to be sitting on the bottom of a different ocean. Capital is assimilating. Labour is not. Globalization is not about integrating the world. So far, it is about integrating the rich.

The rich prosper through the conventional economics of trade and the cumulative exponentials of investment returns. The poor do not integrate and do not prosper. Why? Because they have no money to invest. They do not have the means to send email or call international – even if they had someone to communicate with. Aside from the few million poor families working in global commodity industries like coffee and flowers, easier world trade means nothing to the poor. What do the trade talks in Doha have to do with a subsistence manioc farmer in Zimbabwe? Isolated by their poverty, billions are left to fester.

Economists will recognize this as the age-old problem of economic theory: how it crumbles when assumptions of perfect knowledge, rationality and functioning markets are confronted by a real world of asymmetries, irrationality and inefficiency. In layman's terms: we do not all live in the same world. A New Yorker may live in the same shrinking 'village' as his counterpart in Tokyo or London or Johannesburg, enjoying a life that is at once instantly recognizable to, and seamlessly connected to, his counterparts. But don't mistake these rarefied links for a connected world. There's millions more villages out there. They're made of mud and straw roofs and have no running water. People walk miles to connect with their neighbours. The world remains over the horizon.

If for hundreds of millions of people, globalization is a story of enduring poverty and widening segregation, it's easy to understand why the overriding experience of it is not one of a rising sense of well-being, but an accelerating sense of injustice. Globalization has winners and losers. It can boost development. But it can also accentuate inequality and squash individuality. And that can lead to violence. Boom, then bang.

Look at a key symptom of globalization: labour mobility. What impression of the outside world flows back to India, Pakistan and Bangladesh via the 700,000 South Asians who build the roads and the high rises of Dubai and Kuwait? What conclusions do they draw from the comparisons between their hardscrabble lives and the indolent rich around them?[25] Or look at the global standardization of television. The fruits of rising world prosperity may have failed to trickle down, but *Friends* is everywhere. As a result, the poor no longer even have to travel to learn that they are missing out. They can see precisely which cars, gadgets, clothes, food and liquor they lack by tuning into *Girls of the Playboy Mansion.*

The result is an angry suspicion, gathering strength around the world, that the ordinary, the poorly connected, the non-elite are being left behind. Angel Gurria, secretary general of the Organization for Economic Cooperation and Development (OECD), acknowledged the phenomenon when he released a report in June 2007 that showed internal inequality increasing from Poland to South Korea. 'Millions are benefiting from globalization,' he said, 'but at the same time, there's a feeling that something's wrong with the process.'[26] Or, as Alan Greenspan, former Federal Reserve chairman told *Newsweek* in late 2007: 'Despite this set of extraordinary gains, capitalism has not yet gotten closure.'[27]

This sentiment finds diverse expression, even inside a single country. Take India. In the election of spring 2004, the ruling Bharatiya Janata Party (BJP), buoyed by the country's new worldwide economic prominence, ran on a platform that declared 'India Shining' – the country had never had it so good. The campaign took its lead from the established wisdom about India, that it was a country on the rise, a new power, a place whose time had come.[28]

To the BJP's profound shock, India disagreed. The party lost to an alliance led by Sonia Gandhi, whose central pledge was a promise to help the rural poor. Underlining how badly the BJP got it wrong, Gandhi was backed by the Communist Party of India, who won sixty-two seats, their greatest tally ever.

Resentment over India's growing economic divide finds less peaceful ways of expression. Riot police quelled days of uproar in Delhi in 2004 when the authorities began bulldozing slums that were home to 100,000 people to make way for a riverside mall. In the last few years, migrants moving from poor eastern India to the richer west have been targeted in mob attacks, attacks that have claimed hundreds of lives.

And there is organized violence too. Unnoticed by much of the world, the dirt-poor central and eastern hinterlands of India are the home ground of a rebel army that in a few years have become some of globalization's most ferocious opponents – a 10,000-strong band of Luddite, Marxist warriors who have declared war on the new India and global capitalism. Government figures show the Naxals – as they are known, after a 1967 communist uprising in the eastern Indian town of Naxalbari – killed 653 people in 2004, 892 in 2005 and 749 in 2006. They hold up trains, rob banks and ambush columns of policemen. In one attack in November 2005, 700 guerrillas overran an entire town in eastern India, broke into its jail and freed 400 prisoners. In another in July 2006, 250 fighters held up an express train, Wild West-style, and robbed the passengers. The Delhi-based Institute for Conflict

Management says the Naxals now operate in 182 of India's 625 districts, a vast red corridor stretching thousands of miles across central India and touching the outskirts of tech meccas like Bangalore and Hyderabad. So alarmed is the government by the rebels' rise that in April 2006 Prime Minister Manmohan Singh called the Naxals 'the single biggest challenge' to internal security ever faced by India. And in a context of Kashmir, Bhopal, plague, terrorism, a tsunami, several earthquakes, countless deadly riots and the assassinations of three Gandhis, that is saying something.

The revival of revolutionary communism in South Asia is mirrored across the world. Marxist armies are fighting the state in the Philippines, Turkey and Bangladesh. In Nepal, they have taken power. Leftist populism once again dominates Latin America, in Bolivia, Brazil, Chile, Ecuador and Venezuela. In China, Vietnam, Laos and North Korea, communism never went away.

This resurgence in left-wing revolution is often overlooked in discussions on globalization. For one thing, it's a hard story to report (more on that later). For another, it runs against conventional thinking.

One of the central arguments in favour of economic integration is that it has nothing to do with rebellion. It is meant to be just the opposite: a force for peace. Peace was the central reason for the economic integration of Europe after the Second World War. It is also one of the main motives for the United States to construct ties with China and India. It's a prime reason for the Doha Development Round of discussions on global free trade, and the main cause of the anxiety over their failure to secure an agreement. The idea is to smother the poverty and discontent that fuels war under a blanket of interdependent prosperity. You bind nations together so tightly that they come to depend on each other for their continued advancement. War becomes unthinkable. If you attack your enemy, you end up attacking yourself.

The same idea, albeit with less intellectual rigour, underpins the perception that the world is entering a golden age of peace and prosperity. After the end of the Second World War and then the collapse of the Cold War, so the thinking goes, there were no more enemies. Globalization, in that sense, is the name we give to the process of adjustment that has happened since – in which everyone signs up to the same economic system, the same values, laws and international organizations.

There's a practical problem with that scenario: reality. A glance at the headlines on any one day suggests the dawn of a new era, sure, but less one of peace and harmony than one beset by a bewildering diversity of hostilities. Bombings from Oklahoma to Jakarta, war from Niger to Kashmir, civil conflicts from Sierra Leone to the Solomon Islands. Around 5.4 million people are estimated to have died in the Democratic Republic of Congo in the last decade – a greater number than in any conflict since the Second World War. People died three times as fast in the 1994 Rwandan genocide as in the Holocaust. Twice as many people have died in tiny Sri Lanka's civil war – 70,000 people – as were killed there by the 2004 tsunami. As it entered 2007, the International Crisis Group, an independent watchdog of world conflict, said it was sending missions to fifty-seven countries to research war, and monitoring tension in forty-five others. In the past four years, conflict has declined in one of the world's most war-torn areas, southern Africa. But the general trend is clear: more war than ever before.

Not all conflict stems from globalization. But in a world where conflict is rising as globalization gathers pace, it seems fair to ask if there is a connection. Common sense suggests that there could be. After all, most great changes in history are accompanied by tumultuous violence.

There is, however, an intuitive logic to the idea of peace through inclusion. It worked in Europe, after all. This is a place that suffered more wars than anywhere else in the world, but since the integration of Europe, there's been nothing a little subsidy or a referendum couldn't cure. But Europe is a partnership of equals, more or less. What happens when we try to integrate an uneven world? How do you ensure the stronger partners don't dominate? (And should you, given that the stronger partners probably got something right?)

Added to which, if you accept the idea that peace comes through inclusion, then does the opposite – war through exclusion – hold true? And what does *that* mean next to mounting evidence that much of the world is excluded by globalization? Does it mean global war?

The short answer is: not yet. But as we shall see, many of today's wars suggest the beginnings of something like that. An increasing number of conflicts are about globalization – or rather, about being excluded from its benefits. Another common trait is whereas once they might have been obscure civil fights in forgotten parts of the world, now the wider world is precisely what the rebels have in their sights. They share an insight about globalization's great flaw – that it boosts the dominant, the rich and the few, but leaves the rest of the planet relatively worse off. Most also subscribe to the idea that the ultimate enemy is the global economic system and its leader, big business.

That's also a view held by an increasing number of (mostly) peaceful groups. On a very rough scale of descending levels of violence, they include G8 protesters, European anti-immigration parties, the Democratic Party in the US (which fights those parts of globalization that cost domestic jobs) and neo-statists in Japan, 2 million of whom have bought copies of Fukiwara Masahiko's lament for a nation lost to globalization, *The Dignity of the State.*

And it's a view endorsed by the most violent of revolutionaries. It is worth repeating Gray's point here: Islamic terror is not just about religion. The idea that al-Qaeda is merely following the evil plan of some crazy genius to take the world back to a medieval caliphate ignores other dynamics at work. At root, Islamic terror is also like all rebellion: a reaction to oppression, bad governance, injustice and alienation, in this case from the feudal regimes of the Middle East and their backers in the West. Globalization raises the sense of exclusion – and the stakes, by expanding the target list. Religion adds (considerable) spiritual justification.

Viewed this way, the twenty-first century can sometimes seem like it is running to a nineteenth-century script. Karl Marx and Frederick Engels described the age of globalization with uncanny precision 160 years ago. In 1848, in the *Communist Manifesto*, they wrote:

> The need of a constantly expanding market for its products chases the bourgeoisie over the whole surface of the globe ... All old-established national industries have been destroyed or are daily being destroyed. They are dislodged

> by new industries, whose introduction becomes a life and death question for all civilized nations, by industries that no longer work up indigenous raw material, but raw material drawn from the remotest zones; industries whose products are consumed, not only at home, but in every corner of the globe ... In place of the old local and national seclusion and self-sufficiency, we have intercourse in every direction, universal inter-dependence of nations ... The intellectual creations of nations become common property. National one-sidedness and narrow-mindedness become more and more impossible, and from the numerous national and local literature there arises a world literature. The bourgeoisie ... compels all nations, on pain of extinction, to adopt the bourgeois method of production; it compels them to introduce what it calls civilization into their midst ... In one word, it creates a world after its own image.[29]

Could it be that rather than being outdated, Marx and Engels were simply ahead of their time? Perhaps. They're not right on everything. Their prediction that local and national grievances would melt away, and with them the distractions of patriotism and religion, are as far-fetched today as they were in 1848.

But Marx's and Engels's vision of global revolution reveals an important point. In a connected world, it is no longer enough to hit your immediate enemy. You also have to strike at what you perceive as its underlying origins, even if that's half a world away. You can also use the same logic – as the Naxals do – to justify killings closer to home: you're not killing families from the next-door village, you're eradicating agents of a sinister world order.

Thus a movement with its origins in nineteenth-century India and Saudi Arabia, or that takes its inspiration from a twentieth-century Chinese dictator, feels it has to target New York, or London or Madrid, even a nightclub in Indonesia. What was September 11 if not a demonstration of how globalization transforms local fights into world wars? Globalization even assisted the attackers. The new international mobility eased their travel, and the impact of their attacks was multiplied by worldwide live TV.

The problem for academics and pundits is that much of this is taking place in the most remote corners of the world and they don't have ringside seats. The gathering era of global war is happening in the developing world. Why? First, because it's big. Four fifths of humanity lives in the developing world, and two thirds in Asia. Just two countries – India and China – account for more than a third of the world. Consider their size, the forces at work inside them and the impact they will have on the rest of the world – and then remind yourself that they just joined the world economy. This is a human laboratory unprecedented in history. Chinese economic growth is hovering at around 10–12 per cent, doubling the size of the economy every seven years, and India is not far behind with 8–10 per cent. Predictions are that the Chinese economy will be the world's second largest by 2020 and India's the third soon after. Asia is the supercharged continent, the land of the moment, and it is hip, from Ayurveda to the *Art of War*, Bollywood to open-air Balinese bathrooms. When I interviewed him a few weeks after he was appointed, Indian Prime Minister Singh said the biggest kick he got from his new job was the idea of running the world's biggest democracy as it merged with the world. 'India's development is unique,' he said. 'It's the biggest experiment in world history.'

India and China are part of an eastern arc of rising wealth that stretches from the palm-fringed islands of the Philippines to the fake giant palm islands of Dubai. This is the engine of the new global economy, where offshoring thrives and where new Silicon Valleys spring up in places like Bangalore and Shenzhen. Some talk about New York and London as being the centres of the global economy, but are they? They are the bases of the finance industry, and to the extent that bankers control the world, New York and London do too. But where is the economic activity on which such derivative industries are founded? It's there on the labels: Made in China, Made in Thailand, Made in Indonesia. Put it another way: who do you know who's offshoring to New York?

Moreover, the developing world is not just a place where globalization is happening. As we saw above, it's also where its results are most extreme. India and China and the rest of the developing world are not the gilded edges of globalization. The more you look at them, the more they look like its dark heart.

To students of history, the idea that the world increasingly turns on an Eastern axis will come as no surprise. It has done before. As recently as the eighteenth century, China's GDP was bigger than that of the US and at the end of the eighteenth century, China's per capita income was seven times that of Britain. Millennia ago, along with the Nile Valley, the North China Plain and the Indus Valley were the cradles of our early civilizations, where fire was harnessed, tools invented and animals domesticated. The Chinese shared a common culture for longer than any other group on earth.

Chinese writing dates back 4,000 years. China invented cast iron, paper, whisky, pasta and gunpowder and discovered the circulation of the blood. Chinese mathematicians invented the decimal system, the planetarium and the seismograph. The imperial dynasties lasted from 221 BC to 1911 – the equivalent of the Roman Empire stretching from Caesar to the present day.

India has also long been a crucible of progress. It is also one of the great staging posts of history – almost every imperial army since Alexander the Great has passed through India. And it is a home to all the world's religions and the birthplace of three of them – Buddhism, Hinduism and Sikhism. From Einstein to Thoreau, the West has credited India with teaching the world to count, to talk (Sanskrit, the mother of most European languages), to learn (the world's first university was in Taxila in 700 BC), to heal (Ayurveda) and to play chess. In *Following the Equator*, Mark Twain wrote: 'India had the start of the whole world in the beginning of things. She had the first civilization; she had the first accumulation of material wealth; she was populous with deep thinkers and subtle intellects; she had mines, and woods, and a fruitful soil. It would seem as if she should have kept the lead, and should be today not the meek dependent of an alien master, but mistress of the world, and delivering law and command to every tribe and nation in it.'[30]

Today China, India, and much of Asia are host to the new twin drivers of our age – trade and technology. They are redefining our idea of economic growth. They are also the authors of much that ails the world: the worst pollution, exploding AIDS populations and Deobandism, the fundamentalist creed of the Taliban, to name but three. The point is: if you want to know about globalization, if you want to know about mankind, if you want to know where we're heading, then you have to go where things are changing. The clue's in the name: the *developing* world.

CHAPTER 2

SPEED BUMPS IN SHENZHEN

Living in Hong Kong at the dawn of the millennium was an exercise in schizophrenia. When Britain relinquished its last Eastern outpost of empire in 1997, capitalist Hong Kong became part of communist China under an arrangement known as 'one country, two systems'. Some surface differences between Hong Kong and the mainland had narrowed in China's two-decade flirtation with capitalism. But Hong Kong Island was still separated from the mainland by more than mere water. Hong Kong had its own distinct political system that allowed limited democracy, an independent judiciary and a largely free press. English was an official language in Hong Kong, and the hundreds of thousands of Western expatriates and Filipino maids gave the city a far more cosmopolitan air than the monolithic mainland. The skyscrapers of the island remained a focus of global commerce and wealth, a steel-and-concrete forest of banks, million-dollar apartments and Tiffany boutiques. If Hong Kong and China were family once again, Hong Kong was still something of a distant relation. It had more in common with those other centres of capitalism's old order – New York, London and Tokyo – than the cities springing up along China's southern coast. For, like any succeeding generation, they were emerging as entirely different creatures.

Nowhere was that more apparent than when you crossed from Hong Kong into the border city of Shenzhen. In 1980, the then Chinese leader Deng Xiaoping inaugurated Shenzhen as China's first Special Economic Zone and invited the people of Hong Kong to make something of the 3.5 square-kilometre stretch of fishing villages and rice paddies just over the border. By 2001, Hong Kong's businessmen had poured $15 billion into 70,000 firms in the border province of Guangdong, much of it for the manufacturing that once drove the Hong Kong economy.[1] Investors from Taiwan and the rest of the world soon followed. From a few hundred in 1980, the population had grown to 4 million by 2001 and to 15 million by 2007 – or 25 million if you included the adjoining city of Dongguan. Shenzhen's economy was soaring by 31 per cent a year. Exports from its port hit $200 billion in 2006. The city became the world centre for the kind of light manufacturing that powers the consumer age, turning out iPods, McDonald's toys, Gap jeans and mobile phones. In hindsight, Deng's experiment can be seen as a pivotal moment in history, a move that prefigured the opening up of the Soviet Union and India, and the shift of Western manufacturing to places like Brazil or Vietnam. Shenzhen is where the modern era of globalization began.

But a visit to Shenzhen also revealed heavy hints that globalization would be taking the world down a new, unruly path. The city was less a copy of Hong Kong than its parallel universe. It had the same energy, the same get-ahead ethos and the same towering respect for a buck. But thanks to loose laws, loose women and dirty officials, it was an unregulated free-for-all. You could get anything you wanted: cheap labour, knock-off Prada handbags, pirate DVDs, ecstasy pills, one-night stands. A number of restaurants specialized in endangered species, such as pangolin, bear and turtles. (The gulf between East and West is perhaps never more neatly summed up than by their opposing attitudes to rare wildlife. 'There's only a few left' implied a duty to preserve in the West. In Shenzhen's restaurants, it meant get them while they're hot.)

Once inside this looking-glass world, nothing was quite the genuine article. The Louis Vuitton bags were fakes made in sweatshops in the surrounding state of Guangdong. Many of the impressive skyscrapers were empty. Two-thirds of the population didn't have a residency permit.[2] The women were often stunning, but that beauty might have been bought from Shenzhen's army of plastic surgeons. Shenzhen was a city of beggar syndicates, drug traffickers and restaurants serving lobster sashimi to Triad bosses dressed in fake Versace. Even the money, Shenzhen's raison d'être, was suspect: local buses alone were collecting $160,000 in fake coins every year.[3] The city was Hong Kong's twisted sister, a place where Hong Kongers went to make illicit love and illicit money, and a magnet for hustlers and chancers from all over China. Tijuana, with Chinese characteristics.

It took just a few steps to pass from the old world into the new. Coming from Hong Kong, the visitor passed through immigration at Lo Wu, walked across a narrow bridge spanning a stinking, black canal and stepped directly into a six-storey shopping complex that was a monument to China's status as the world's counterfeit capital. Shops displayed perfect replicas of Armani suits, Gucci handbags, Nike trainers, Rolex watches, Cartier jewellery, as well as racks of pirated videos and discs. Televisions in shop windows aired graphic advertisements for clinics that offered breast enlargements and other cosmetic surgeries. In one of these street-side clinics Dr Cao Mengjun told me his Fuhua Plastic and Aesthetic Hospital saw more than 2,000 people a year, half from Hong Kong. Cao was the proud inventor of 'Amazing Gel', an enlarging agent not dissimilar to mason's putty that he injected directly into the body. He offered everything from freckle-removal and teeth-whitening to 'maidenhead recovery'. His most popular procedure was the most requested operation in Shenzhen: eye-widening. The city's 1,600 surgeons were making almonds out of 8,000 pairs of pine nuts a week. The look was mixed race, cosmopolitan, indeterminate – global, in fact.

Much of the city was tailored for women, and unsurprisingly: there were at least five women to every man.[4] Millions of women worked in the sweatshops, stitching sneakers and footballs. Hundreds of thousands of others had followed the money to the nightclubs, bars and brothels that had popped up all over town. Still more had come to be concubines close to Hong Kong businessmen wanting a conveniently located partner. In one part of the city, I visited an entire apartment complex – several tower blocks, housing thousands of women – that was known as '*er nai cun*', or 'second wives block'. Another suburb was inhabited almost entirely by prostitutes. By 2001, Shenzhen's second wives and Hong Kong's errant husbands had produced what the Hong Kong government estimated was 520,000 illegitimate children, thousands of whom were fighting for Hong Kong residency. The All China Women's Federation described the situation as 'a time bomb'.

Inside this illicit world, a new form of ultra-free-for-all economics was emerging. Zhang Jin saw the female population solely in terms of competition. She was a second wife to a sugar daddy who was rich – and tantalizingly old. When he died, Zhang, twenty, said she stood to inherit half his wealth (the rest would go to the legal wife across the border). Zhang claimed her Hong Kong man's wife knew all about her: 'She is very open, she doesn't mind.' But during the long stretches when her man was away, Zhang said she was bored, staying at home playing mah-jong with other second wives and banking the $2,000 a month he gave her. 'He is old,' she said. 'No energy. Like my grandfather.' Hedging her bets, three times a week she slipped on a miniskirt and headed out to the basement Moonlight Club, looking for someone younger and richer.

But Zhang had also used her two years in Shenzhen to educate herself. A Mandarin speaker from Qingdao on China's east coast, she learned Cantonese from her Hong Kong motor executive 'husband' as well as some Japanese, Korean and English from other clients. The languages would come in handy, she said, when she opened her own border beauty parlour. She was giving herself ten years to save enough money. But competition was tough. The Moonlight's chain-smoking madam, Zhou Min, boasted 200 girls on her books, and Zhang said she was able to charge just $40 for an hour in a nearby hotel. 'Hong Kong men come to Shenzhen to find girls because they're cheap,' explained Madam Zhou flatly. 'For 10,000 yuan ($1,250) a month they can have a place and another wife.'

Law-breaking was integrated into every part of this new economy. And as with the second wives, the most lucrative scams had an international flavour. For years Gavin Zheng, thirty-two, had been part of a thriving liquor-smuggling operation in the city. One of his special skills was re-labelling cheap French red vin de table as upmarket brands. Customs knew what he was up to: it oversaw the whole operation and took a cut. 'No one got caught,' says Zheng. His gang would also transport Hennessy brandy or Bordeaux wine from Hong Kong to the border at Lo Wu, whisk them through the state-run duty free store, and wheel half of the consignment straight into the city without paying the mandatory 180 per cent duty. Other gangs ran cigarettes into Shenzhen, or – going the other way, into Hong Kong and beyond – heroin, methamphetamine ('ice'), fake designer gear, cellphones, endangered species and forged credit cards. And, of course, there was the trade in illegal immigrants, who cross at Lo Wu or cram into cargo containers that take them to Hong Kong, the busiest port in the world.

When I met Zheng in early 2001, he told me smuggling had become dicey. China was making a very public effort to crack down on corruption: the former head of Shenzhen's customs, Zhao Yucun, had been executed for taking $1.2 million in bribes. At the same time, Chinese mafia gangs – Triads – were muscling out independent operators. Working both sides of the border, these gangs owned perhaps half the nightclubs and bars in Shenzhen, often reportedly in partnership with senior officers of the People's Liberation Army and the Public Security Bureau. They were into anything that paid: car theft, gambling, prostitution, kidnap for ransom. The bulk of the bribes received by convicted customs chief Zhao came from smuggling gasoline. Zheng explained how the racket worked. A tanker would anchor in international waters off southern China and wait for buyers' motor launches to gather round. An auction followed at sea, and the buyers smuggled the fuel to shore in barrels to sell to the nearest state-run station, no import duty paid. 'The whole of southern China is running on smuggled gas,' said Zheng. 'And half the time, the government is controlling it.'

Another doctor, 'Huang', told me about another racket run more or less openly by the state, which depended on China retaining its tight grip on human rights as it opened up the economy. Huang was a transplant specialist. And in the run-up to Labour Day on 1 May, the authorities were planning to execute an array of criminals. That year they were taking aim at violent offenders and Triads. Huang said the busy schedule meant a bumper crop of kidneys, livers and hearts for transplant. Getting a kidney from death row might sound merciless, Huang said. But it was undeniably efficient. Patients could be matched to donors in advance, and a bullet to the brain caused no damage to other organs. As a result, organ transplants were another of Shenzhen's booming global businesses. Around half of Huang's customers were foreign. Anticipating rising demand, he said many execution grounds had recently built organ extraction clinics on-site.

Satisfaction was hardly guaranteed, however. Wiwijaya, an Indonesian-born ethnic Chinese, told my *Time* colleague Wendy Kan the story of his brother, who was suffering from renal failure. His brother ordered a replacement kidney for $25,000 and, as a twenty-six-year-old, made the journey to southern China from Medan in 1996. The transplant was successful, but when he returned for an internal check-up four years later, something went terribly wrong. His stomach swelled up, his new kidney collapsed and he fell into a coma. A second transplant was ordered. 'But the doctor had another plan,' said Wiwijaya. 'He wanted to give the best kidney to whoever paid the best price.' Wiwijaya said his brother was given a lesser match. He died in January 2001, a skeleton on a dialysis machine. 'The doctor took his life,' Wiwijaya said.

'Everybody in that hospital wants a fee for everything they do. They're like vampires.'

One of the biggest new industries was drugs. By 2001, southern China's Triads were running a virtual narcotic conveyor belt from South East Asia's Golden Triangle via China to Hong Kong – and then on to anywhere in the world. In mid-April 2001, Vancouver customs officials found 42 kilograms of heroin with a street value of $64 million stuffed inside cans of pineapple chunks. (The contraband had been canned in Guangdong and shipped through Hong Kong.) Meanwhile every weekend night, tens of thousands of Hong Kong nightclubbers were ripping through an ever-expanding number of Shenzhen dance halls where ecstasy, ketamine and methamphetamine were freely available and thrillingly cheap. Ecstasy was selling for $10 and tranquillizer pills, which cost $4 in Hong Kong, could be bought for 10 cents. Since 1998, seizures of these drugs had risen tenfold. In a single weekend in March 2001, police in Hong Kong, Macau and Guangdong jointly raided 10,000 bars and nightclubs, arrested 1,411 people and seized 307 kilograms of methamphetamine and 47,747 ecstasy pills. The Hong Kong police conceded they were unable to stop the flood of illegal drugs from across the border, often smuggled across by teenagers to pay for their weekends. 'The sheer volume at the border crossing provides opportunities for traffickers,' said Paul Lewis, a senior inspector in the Hong Kong narcotics bureau.

Some in Shenzhen were alarmed at how the city's conscience was lagging its economy. He Qinglian, a forty-seven-year-old Shenzhen economic researcher and journalist, had written a pamphlet in March 2000 that detailed state corruption. She had since been banned from publishing and was being watched day and night by police. Nevertheless, she was continuing her research, and was increasingly focusing on the widening gap between rich and poor, and its corrosive effect on morality. 'Rich people are getting richer and the poor poorer,' she said. 'The poor have no rights and are forced into crime, killing, stealing and hijacking to make money. I've met families who are selling their babies – $750 for a boy and $250 for a girl – to rich families who want more. How desperate do you have to be to sell your own child?'

Attorney Zhou Litai was also dealing with the fallout of the Shenzhen way of business. He shared his crumbling four-storey home in the down-at-the-heel suburb of Longgang with forty of his clients. All were amputees who had lost arms or legs in machinery at local factories set up by Hong Kong and Taiwanese firms. None had an artificial limb and all had received derisory compensation, generally a one-off payment of around $1,000. In 2001, official figures showed there were 13,000 serious work injuries each year in Bao An, a district of Shenzhen. Zhou, a former brick factory worker who was then forty-six, had taken on 600 cases since 1997, winning pay-outs of up to $99,000. It was dangerous work. Two other Guangdong lawyers doing similar work had been murdered. And it had left Zhou tired, bitter, and $25,000 in debt from handouts and unpaid fees. 'Places like Shenzhen are built on sweatshops,' he spat. 'Old machinery, no training, 14 hours a day, 450 yuan ($56) a month, ineffective safeguards – that's the secret of China's economic "miracle". The government knows this. So the government protects the bosses and does not enforce the law.' The result, he said, was a rising swell of anger directed at the government and the Communist Party. One of Zhou's housemates, Lai Nilang, nineteen, slapped the scarred stump of his right arm, crushed four days into his new job at a computer-chip factory. 'The government doesn't care about us,' he murmured. 'They only care about money. People hate them.' Zhou studied his young client, gauging his loathing. 'If you neglect the people, then the balance of society is upset,' he concluded. 'It's a very dangerous situation.'

What was happening in Shenzhen was happening all over the world. One view of the 1990s is that it was the decade when the US won the world. The Cold War ended, America emerged as the sole superpower and free market democracy became the way of the world. Borders and barriers to trade came down, technology surged, elections multiplied and the price of every kind of connection, from flights to international telephone calls, tumbled. Proof of the supremacy of the Western way of doing things was the longest bull run in stock market history. To the victor, the spoils.

But as Moisés Naim wrote in 2005 in his incisive book *Illicit*: 'There is the story we know. And then there is the other story.'[5] The other story is the rise in smuggling, trafficking, and counterfeiting that accompanied globalization. Global drug seizures doubled between 1993 and 2003, according to the UN Office for Drugs and Crime. In 2006, the UNODC found the second most common crime after drugs was human trafficking – enslaving 2.5 million people in 137 countries around the world. Music piracy, meanwhile, has been legitimized as a cultural phenomenon.

Some of the surge in crime had direct implications for war. The illegal arms trade was given a once-in-a-lifetime boost by the selling of the Soviet Union's weapons stock on the open market. Russian-made RPGs and AK-47s have since turned up in fifty conflicts around the world.[6] And dirty money – laundered, untaxed cash needed to fund these purchases and pay rebel armies – has risen from an average 12.7 per cent to

16.7 per cent of GDP for the twenty-one countries of the OECD, according to a 2004 study by Peter Reuter and Edwin M. Truman.[7] As this last figure suggests, this new criminality is pervasive and diffuse – from the way conflict diamonds are mixed in with legitimate stones to the corrupt African ministers who keep their stashes in respectable banks in London and New York.

But the new global criminality has its focuses. As the birthplace of globalization, Shenzhen was one. The sex industry, for example, was far bigger than the hundreds of thousands of second wives. The seedier corners of the city offered a whole world of women: Russians, Filipinas, Nigerians, Indians, Peruvians and Burmese. Many were children.

The trade in child slaves is one of the most pernicious aspects of globalization. Across Asia, hundreds of thousands of children are being peddled into servitude each year. Some toil with their families as bonded labourers on farms. Others are sold by their parents – or tricked by agents – into servitude as camel jockeys in the Middle East (mainly Bangladeshis), fisher boys in Indonesia or beggars in India (often Nepalese). In Burma, some were being kidnapped by the state and forced to become soldiers.

But the big trade was sex. The International Labour Organization's best estimate is that there are 1 million child prostitutes in Asia. Thailand, India, Indonesia and the Philippines are the hubs: each exports and, in Thailand and India's case, imports tens of thousands of children. In the age of AIDS, virgin children are most profitable: a girl's virginity sells for as much as $3,500 in Bangkok. The number of child prostitutes in Thailand was at least 60,000 in the early years of the new millennium, though estimates went as high as 200,000. It was a growing problem, fuelled by the uneven pattern of

Asia's development, which across the continent had produced a yawning gap between poor countryside and rich city, isolated hinterland and wealthy, connected coast. To escape deprivation, whole villages became complicit in the sale of their children. Sompop Jantraka was a leading Thai activist who had saved thousands of girls from brothels. He said the recruiters might be the wives of village heads, or even teachers. Sompop had seen whole truckloads of girls being picked up directly from school; policemen were often at the wheel. The phenomenon had a name: *tok keow*, or green harvest. 'This is a war,' said Sompop. 'A war for our children.'[8]

When I'd lived in Hong Kong from 1999 to 2002, Shenzhen's seediness was on open display, safe in the lee of general world wonder at Chinese economic prowess. By the time I returned in late 2007, that was changing. China was hosting the Olympic Games in Beijing the following summer and was determined to make a good impression. It was proving to be an uphill task.

Some things had changed for the better. Despite exploding in size to make a continuous urban band around the Pearl River delta, Shenzhen was tidier. But that good impression was clouded – literally – by pollution now so thick the sun seemed to be permanently setting. And wealth and scandal were still roaring ahead hand in hand. Real estate prices had risen 50 per cent from January to May, according to local press reports. In August, Shenzhen's stock market hit a record high. City mayor Xu Zongheng was asking his subjects not to buy any more cars as Shenzhen could no longer cope with the 200,000 new vehicles appearing on its roads every year.

But Shenzhen's dark side was also thriving. Hong Kong's *Mingbao* newspaper was reporting a growing trade in giant rats served up by Shenzhen's restaurants.[9] A group of fifty women were suing Dr Mengjun and his Fuhua Plastic and Aesthetic Hospital for the predictably ugly results of 'Amazing Gel'. Competition among prostitutes was now so fierce that they greeted foreign visitors a few steps after customs, trying to usher them into waiting minibuses to whisk them directly to a nearby massage parlour. Perhaps evening the score with their men, Hong Kong women were now also looking for Shenzhen toy boys, besieging the city's dating agencies. Fakes were still the backbone of the retail economy. China's biggest ever piracy bust happened between 6 and 16 July 2007, when the Chinese police and the FBI seized $500 million worth of counterfeit software – 290,000 Microsoft and Norton programs – and busted two gangs, one of them in Shenzhen.

Grabbing the lion's share of headlines, however, was a scandal over poor quality manufacturing. Barely a week was passing in the summer of 2007 without some fresh alert over the shoddy and sometimes dangerous output of Shenzhen's factories. Warnings were sounded about a range of Chinese exports, from spinach to toothpaste to fruit juice to drugs to car tyres to pet food. In July 2007 alone, Europe announced half of all the defective goods recalled that year were made in China. The US banned imports of Chinese catfish, dace, shrimp and eel and withdrew six products from sale, including ovens whose doors had trapped dozens of children's fingers and remote control aeroplanes that were exploding. Elsewhere, South Africa's pineapple growers had to ditch half their crop after cadmium was discovered in a Chinese-made pesticide they used.

Beijing accused its Western customers of xenophobia. But it was also taking stern action, introducing a raft of new safety measures and executing the former head of its State Food and

Drug Administration, Zheng Xiaoyu, in June 2007 for taking bribes in exchange for approving substandard pharmaceuticals, including an antibiotic blamed for the deaths of at least ten people, and Dr Mengjun's 'Amazing Gel'.

In Shenzhen, there were more signs that the authorities were worried by the scandal. Red and gold banners signed by the 'Local Authority Propaganda Department' were hung along the central reservations of main roads announcing: 'We will fully investigate food and product safety', 'Producers and manufacturers of products are the sole responsible persons for product safety and quality', 'Make sure we win the war on food safety and product quality'.

It was another slogan that caught my eye. 'Let us be like a social orchestra and make harmonious music.' Shenzhen had begun showing serious signs of discord. Suicides were rising: a new, favoured method was leaping from the new high-rises. And a crime wave was washing over southern China. In Longgang, muggings, carjackings and kidnappings of the rich had become commonplace. The suburb was no longer safe to walk around at night.

There were more organized forms of violence too, ones that hinted China's economic miracle might be coming unstuck. In the years I'd been away, I'd read about a series of angry workers protests that had erupted in and around the city. Many were squashed by baton-wielding security services and private goon squads hired by factory managers. On more than one occasion, demonstrators had been shot dead. The picture was mirrored nationwide. China was being swept by a tide of worker unrest. Though the authorities don't release figures for the numbers of protests and other incidents of protest in China, the *Economist* said one official source told it there were around 23,000 'mass incidents' in 2006, a slight decline from 26,000 in 2005. The magazine admitted, however, that 'the reliability of these figures and the definition of what constitutes such an incident remains open to doubt – other official sources put the number of mass incidents in 2005 at 87,000.'[10] The *Blue Book of China's Society*, an official social research publication, put the number of protests as rising from 8,709 to 60,000 from 1993 to 2003 and the number of participants as rising from 0.73 million to 3.07 million.[11]

The reason? As Zhou Litai had said five years before, China's boom was built on sweatshops. The balance of society was being upset. One of my first stops once I arrived back in Shenzhen was to see Zhou once more.

Zhou's opinion of local government and state enterprises in China hadn't changed in the five years since I'd seen him last. 'They are willing to sacrifice the workers – their health, their bodies – in the name of development,' he said. 'The law is there. But the rule of law is absent.' And the boom meant there was more work than he could cope with. Zhou had opened new offices in Shenzhen, two more offices in southern China and now employed a total of fifty-three staff. His firm had handled a total of 7,000 cases to do with migrant labour. He had met scores of journalists, visiting politicians and trade union activists. He had even been feted on a twenty-one-day tour of US universities. But periodically the government would try to shut him down – and occasionally succeed – and, plagued by clients who didn't pay their fees, he was now several hundred thousand dollars in debt.

Zhou also had competition. I met several other lawyers now specializing in migrant labour. Xiao Qing Shan, forty, was a former welder and migrant labourer who had taught himself labour law to fight for his own rights when he was twice summarily sacked and had gone on to found a law firm,

Qin Tian Law Consulting Services. Based in Dongguan, he had handled 800 cases in two years. He had been beaten unconscious by police and arrested – and had discovered Dickensian levels of squalor. He had yet to meet a worker who was being paid the legal minimum of 690 yuan ($93.49) a month. One case concerned four children of fourteen and fifteen who were working thirteen hours a day for 29 US cents an hour. Xiao agreed with Zhou: 'There is no law at all. The big picture is that globalization is the big problem, and there is a big disconnection in information. Foreign companies who invest here might even pay extra to ensure everything is OK with their workers, but the bosses never pass the money on.' In the case of the children, he said, two girls – one fourteen, the other fifteen – had told him the only training they received was coaching in how to lie about their ages and working conditions to visiting foreign investors.

Liu Kaiming, a native of Shenzhen, and an economist, journalist and director of the Institute of Contemporary Observation, had charted how migrant labour had exploded in China. There were two reasons why Shenzhen was now the 'factory to the world', he said. Foremost was the attraction of 'not having to comply with worker or environmental law'. Second, 'so much cheap labour'. China accounted for 22 per cent of the global labour force, he said. The bulk of that was migrants. Liu estimated the local population in Shenzhen at 300,000; migrant workers numbered 15 million. The proportions in Dongguan, which had a population of 10 to 15 million, were the same. The Chinese state media said there were 'more than 120 million' migrant workers in China who had left the countryside for the cities.[12] Liu said the figure was more like 200 million, with 50 million of them in manufacturing. It wasn't often a pretty picture, he admitted.

'There is no support for the people,' he said. 'All the money goes to the rich and the government.' Shenzhen might be 'the world's model of globalization'. But 'if the government cannot solve the problem of migrant labour – their work conditions, their poor pay – then development will not be sustainable. There will be more and more social unrest, more strife, and more collective action against the government.'

In places, China's economy was even built on slave camps. As I was planning my return to China, a series were uncovered in the provinces of Shanxi and Henan. More than 570 workers, including 41 children, had been forced to work in scorching brick kilns, working before the ovens had cooled down as the owners tried to maximize production and meet demand from China's booming construction industry. Pictures on Chinese television showed many of the workers were emaciated and suffering burns to the feet and body. Accompanying reports said they endured beatings, were guarded by dogs and some became mentally ill as a result. Many had also been kidnapped. A total of 160 people were arrested for their part in the scandal; 53 had been jailed and one, camp guard Zhao Yanbing, was sentenced to the firing squad for beating one worker to death.

The picture I was uncovering was of a gathering tide of unrest aimed directly at the state. China was the new heart of the global economy. The turmoil it was experiencing added up to more than the odd palpitation. Two protests in particular stood out as examples of how China's boom was unravelling.

According to contemporaneous accounts in the *Mingbao* and other dailies such as the *Ta Kung Pao*, the *Wen Wei Po* and the *Sing Tao*, on 18 January 2006, Shenzhen's authorities moved in on Shazui Village (literally 'Mistress Village'), an area of nightclubs, karaoke bars, saunas, massage parlours, hostels, apartments and gynaecological clinics just inside the Hong Kong border at Futian. In a joint operation between Shenzhen's public security bureau and its fire, commerce and cultural administration departments, several hundreds of these places were shut down for being unlicensed or violating fire regulations.

At 6 a.m. the following morning, a crowd began to gather outside the offices of the Shenzhen City Government. By 8 a.m., there were 600 people, by 9 a.m., 2,000, and by 10 a.m., 5,000. For the authorities, the numbers were bad enough. More shocking was the protesters' appearance. First, they were nearly all women. Second, despite it being a chilly winter's morning, the women were wearing school uniforms, micro-skirts, sauna towelling robes and, according to one paper, 'other sexy outfits'. Then there were their slogans: 'We want to eat! We want to live!'.

Soon after 10 a.m., around 1,000 riot police, with helmets, shields and attack dogs, began to surround the demonstrators. A truck mounted with water cannons was driven up. The riot officers attempted to divide the crowd into smaller groups. There were scuffles and four women were arrested. 'What you are doing now is affecting social order and breaking the law,' one of the commanding officers said over a loudhailer. 'You must leave immediately or you will be held responsible.' Some demonstrators left at that point, but witnesses told the papers that around 1,000 stayed. At 11 a.m., the police took the remaining protestors away in twenty buses. Some twenty-five people were detained for fifteen days and criminal charges were laid against one.

A Shenzhen city spokeswoman said the drive against prostitution was part of a three-month campaign 'to improve

Shenzhen's social order and to reform villages such as Shazui'. And, indeed, the January raids turned out to be only the first crackdown on the sex industry. Later the same year, on 29 November, the authorities held a public parade of prostitutes in Shenzhen, hauling around a hundred sex workers and their clients through the streets. Handcuffed and wearing yellow prison tunics, the parade attracted a crowd. Once sufficient numbers had gathered, police revealed the names, home towns and dates of birth of the prostitutes, and sentenced them to fifteen days in prison.

For Shenzhen, this was a step too far. 'I think the parade is a violation of human rights,' said Ai Xiaoming, a professor at Sun Yat-sen University in nearby Guangzhou. 'The public humiliation may frighten people, but it is not a good way to resolve problems. And it is not fair. Why are only sex criminals paraded in public? What about people guilty of graft and corruption?' The All-China Women's Federation filed a protest with the Ministry of Public Security. Yao Jianguo of the law firm Shanghai Promise complained to the National People's Congress that the police had violated human dignity.

A mass protest was alarming for a Communist Party that valued harmony above all else. Then again, a bunch of sex workers were hardly likely to start a revolution. What was truly worrying were the events described in an article in the spring 2007 edition of *China Security* by Yu Jianrong, professor and director of the Rural Development Institute's Social Issues Research Center at the Chinese Academy for Social Sciences in Beijing (which published the *Blue Book*).[13] Detailing what he said was a 'pathological' avoidance of discussion of social conflict by the Chinese leadership, Yu went on to argue that soldiers demobilized from the 2.3 million-strong

Chinese army, the People's Liberation Army, were acting as a 'bond' to bring together the disaffected. Yu estimated the numbers of ex-servicemen at 20 million and argued they had the 'social capital, organizational, networking and mobilization capabilities to be the bridge between workers and peasants'. With poor retirement packages, they also had the motivation. Soldiers had been at the forefront of a series of protests in rural China, as well as one highly unusual mass protest in Beijing outside the army's General Political Department in April 2005. In the southern province of Hunan, meanwhile, Yu said veterans had also formed an 'anti-corruption brigade' including laid-off workers, peasants and intellectuals of 100,000 members. Yu postulated that the soldiers would be the catalyst and leaders to a general protest movement. Because of rising inequality, he said, 'in the next decade or two, China will likely enter a period of frequent social conflict'.

I'd returned to Shenzhen in part to test Yu's theory against reality on the ground. If the Communist Party was having to face down discontent in its own army, that took things significantly closer to full-scale rebellion. A short cab ride from Lo Wu took me to a housing block for retired soldiers. There, as the clack-clack of mah-jong games echoed down stairwells and out into the street, several residents described how they were part of 20,000 PLA men ordered to Shenzhen in 1982, organized into five construction companies and told to build the new city. With little more than their bare hands, they worked day and night, flattening mountains, felling bamboo jungles and building housing blocks, roads, bridges and the city's first skyscrapers. More than 300 died in the process, falling from scaffolding or crushed by heavy loads. They were paid 120 yuan ($16.26) a month and lived in tents or with their pigs in sties. In 1983, their families were allowed to join them. In 1992, they were finally given houses. They kept building and building until well into their fifties when, in 2005, without warning, the construction companies laid them off.

That was when the problems started. Pension money had gone missing and, while wages and payments had risen with inflation, they were still asked to live on 2,000 yuan ($271) a month. A promised one-off retirement payment of 37,000 yuan ($5,012) also failed to materialize. Many of the unemployed soldiers were struggling to make ends meet. They met their old bosses and demanded the money they were owed, and took their protests to the labour authority. Nothing changed. So in November 2005, a few thousand ageing PLA veterans left their cramped apartments, formed up into their old companies and marched on the government. When they arrived at Shenzhen City Hall, they sat down in Shennan Boulevard, the city's main thoroughfare, and blocked the traffic.

The authorities' reaction was predictably intransigent. They cut all Shenzhen's phone lines, blocked Internet access and mayor Xu refused to come out of his city hall office to meet them. The next night, the soldiers marched again. And again the next night. And again for a fourth night. By then, word of the protest had spread through the veterans' ranks and their numbers had swelled to the full 20,000. On the third night, they chose Yang Shibao, a forty-six-year-old worker and anti-corruption activist, to be their representative and put their demands before the government.

Hours after his selection, Yang and his wife were arrested. That enraged the soldiers. On the fourth night, they refused to go home until they had spoken to Xu. The mayor, still hiding out in his office, finally emerged to promise to investigate the missing money. The soldiers demanded he also release Yang and his wife. When Xu tried to drive off in his limousine, they blocked his motorcade. But Xu was adamant: Yang would have to be punished. The soldiers, who until that point had displayed the discipline of their profession, allowed their anger to spill over. Several police cars were overturned, the riot police moved in and the protest was dispersed.

Nothing came of Xu's promise to investigate. Yang and his wife were convicted of inciting social unrest and – incredibly – plotting to poison the city's reservoir and set off bombs around Shenzhen. Yang's wife was released after ten months, Yang himself after a year. Friends said Yang had long been a thorn in the side of the authorities because of detailed research he conducted into official corruption. During his year in jail, he was beaten and tortured by policemen who would turn the air conditioning to maximum, then pour cold water on him. Meanwhile, the biggest soldiers' construction company – now renamed from Shenzhen Construction Company No 1 to the Jiang Ye Construction Group – announced assets of 200 million yuan. Some soldiers I spoke to claimed the real figure was 2 billion.

By late 2007, the PLA protests were over and Yang and his wife were released. But the anger remained. 'This city is founded on our labour,' said one soldier. 'But when we got old, we were just abandoned and forgotten. The young kids running the companies say we are a burden on profits.' Another said street cleaners received a better retirement package than soldiers. All stressed that they remained committed to the ideals of the Communist Party, and many felt the top national leadership had their interests at heart. But local party bosses and company heads were betraying the promise of communism and stealing from the people. The soldiers saw themselves as the vanguard of a movement to rectify the mistakes and corruption of local leaders, and restore China to its true communist path. They were counter-counter-revolutionaries. 'When I was in the army, I wanted to serve my country,' said one. 'I wanted to contribute. I gave my life to building this city. Now I know the law and the constitution is a joke, just beautiful words on pieces of paper.' Another swore he would keep fighting the local government even if it cost his life. 'I don't see any reason to keep on living this way,' he said. The government was aware of the simmering tension. It issued an open letter to the former soldiers, insisting that 'the government pays attention to people's concerns', but advising protesters to 'keep their minds clear and rational. Do not listen to rumours and strictly preserve national enterprises and social stability. Use legal channels to report complaints.' Some protesters had already stopped listening, however. Across southern China, reports of soldiers kidnapping their bosses for ransom, even murdering them, were on the rise.

Modern China was founded on revolution. Could these protests be the seeds of a second? The poor, disenfranchised and disaffected were challenging their rulers' totalitarianism and demanding globalization be allowed to give them political freedom as well as the free market. As unrest grew alongside the economy, the central question for China was whether it could keep the lid on one while unleashing the other. It had squashed the previous mass challenge to its authority on 4 June 1989, when students demanding democracy staged weeks of sit-ins in Tiananmen Square. But now there were tens of thousands of little Tiananmens erupting across China every year. Where was it all leading? Yu was clear: 'A collapse of China's social institutions will loom in the future if it fails to provide an effective channel of expression for the grievances of disadvantaged groups in society or fails to establish a mechanism to balance diverse social interests as the gap between the rich and poor continues to widen. If China's problems of socioeconomic equality are left to fester, revolution may indeed be unavoidable.'[14]

One of the soldiers I spoke to said Yu's conclusions were too cautious. 'This is not a crisis of the future,' he said. 'This is a crisis now. Where is equality in China? Where are our rights? Chinese people are very practical. They don't want to make trouble for the government. They just want to live their lives. But things have become so bad, what choice do we have but to fight? This is about survival.'

On my last day in Shenzhen, there was yet another protest. Thousands of workers from the Aigao Electronics factory blocked a highway outside the factory gates in Dongguan in protest at their bosses' decision to raise the price of the food it supplied them, from 79 cents to $1.02 a day. It was the latest in a long list of complaints. The workers lived sixteen to a small dormitory; food was terrible, as well as expensive; pay was 690 yuan ($93.47) a month, or 500 yuan ($67.73) after deductions for food and board.

The authorities sent more than 1,000 riot police and dozens of police dogs to battle the protesters. More than ten workers were beaten and arrested. One who escaped the police was a 'Ms Shen'. She said: 'The police are even worse than the goons. They beat women and trampled on them.' She returned to the scene of the protests the next day. There were thousands with her.

CHAPTER 3

WAKING UP IN BOMBAY

The day the world's fifth largest city[1] collapsed, dawn brought little warning. Grey squalls were rumbling in off the Arabian Sea and rattling slums, buffeting offices and scattering early-morning walkers along the seafront. But that was nothing for Bombay[2] in monsoon and the city went about its business with practised adjustment. In the harbour, shrimp fishermen moved rusty trawlers into deeper water. In the markets, fruit sellers tied umbrellas to their wooden carts. In the doorways of a million one-room shacks, housewives put out cheap plastic *chappals* – sandals – for their men to wade through the puddles on the way to work. Wine maker Rajeev Samant glanced at the traffic crawling past his office gates and added an extra thirty minutes to make his shuttle to Delhi. Slumlord Brij, a migrant from the eastern state of Bihar, shrugged on a plastic mac and set off on his rounds, hopping between dripping shanty overhangs, collecting protection and dropping off sweeteners for the police. 'I felt pretty good,' remembers Brij. 'It was a good day to be out and earning in Bombay.'

By the time Rajeev landed in Delhi, Bombay had fallen apart. Heavy showers overnight – 25–26 July 2005 – and a steady downpour since mid-morning made almost a metre of rain in twenty-four hours. Drains, sewers and rivers burst. The floods swallowed roads, railway tracks and runways. Power lines and telephones went dead. Desiccated colonial-era home and office blocks soaked up the water like sponges. Scores crumbled. Whole shantytowns were washed away. In hours, a city of 21.6 million ground to a halt. Television pictures showed a third of the metropolis underwater. A caramel-coloured lake stretched from horizon to horizon where hours before a dense patchwork of tiles and metal sheeting had designated one of the most thickly populated places on earth. Commuters on stranded buses headed out single file into the chest-high water like D-Day soldiers, mobile phones and briefcases held over their heads.

I was with them. After finishing an interview downtown in the late afternoon of 25 July, I'd spent twelve hours fording rivers and lakes of sewage before I made it back to my hotel 30 kilometres away. In the streets around me, 435 people died; 25 drowned in their cars.

Even in a city so big, no one was unaffected. Thousands were hospitalized with leptospirosis, a virus caught by wading downstream of the city's markets just as 1,200 buffaloes and 15,000 goats, drowning on their tethers, emptied their bladders in panic. Rajeev's flat was flooded by two feet of water and his midtown office, headquarters of his Sula Vineyards empire, cut off. Thirty-six hours passed before his twenty staff could leave. Worse hit was Brij. 'I have 55 bodies in the water and 15,000 homeless,' he said when I saw him the next day. 'That's just one slum. The place is five metres underwater. You can't even see the roofs. When we drive in tankers of fresh water, they float away like balloons.'

That was Tuesday. On Wednesday, twelve rig workers died when the unusually high seas slammed a support ship into the Bombay High platform 100 miles offshore, sparking a fireball that crippled the source of 14 per cent of India's oil consumption. On Thursday, eighteen shoreline slum-dwellers died in a stampede started by rumours of an incoming tsunami. The airport reopened on Friday, only to close again on Saturday when an Air India 747 to Chicago skidded off the wet runway. By the following Monday, with floods still covering much of the city, aviation minister Praful Patel said all airlines should still stay away. Three weeks later, Bombay's health authorities announced 160 more people had died in the aftermath. As well as leptospirosis, 5,500 had contracted malaria, gastroenteritis, dengue fever, hepatitis and typhoid. Further catastrophe struck on 23 August when a weakened hundred-year-old apartment block crashed to the ground, killing eleven. Five days later another block collapsed, killing five. Around this time, the state government of Maharashtra unveiled its new disaster management plan: a ban on plastic bags, whose drain-clogging properties it held solely to blame for the catastrophe. Total damage estimates varied from a government figure of $1.3 billion to the $3.5–4 billion put out by analysts and business associations. Unknown was the cost of 52,000 refugees, millions of dollars in lost wages and insurance claims, the toll on the city's mammoth black economy and the fall in foreign investor confidence.

The morning after the floods, I made my way across the city to the disaster epicentre. Word was that 150 people had been killed in a landslide in Saki Nagar, a slum under the flight path into Bombay airport. I stood on a roof at the edge of a large pile of rocks and rubble with teenager Mohammed Afzad, watching the firemen work through the debris. Mohammed had lost his parents, three teenage sisters, three nieces and twelve-year-old brother when the 30-metre cliff face behind the family home collapsed, pulling twenty-five shacks over the precipice and crushing another twenty-five underneath.

You hear the kind of dreamy talk that had brought the Afzad family to Bombay everywhere in India today. India will be the next China. India will be the next Silicon Valley. If you're looking to the future, you've got to be in India. As India's business capital, Bombay is the cradle of those hopes. And it was with an eye on the main chance that the Afzads moved from their village hundreds of miles away to the slum of Saki Nagar fifteen years before. It didn't matter that the family had merely swapped growing vegetables for selling them. Although ten people were crowded in a two-bedroom shanty, they had television and electricity and a telephone, and the aeroplanes that skimmed Saki Nagar's rooftops were a reminder that Bombay was a destination of opportunity. 'It was a good place,' said Mohammed blankly.

Since arriving in India in early 2002, I had struggled to square the bullish analysis of the country, so popular among government ministers and Western economists, with my everyday experience. India's business leaders liked to paint a picture of a nation that had arrived overnight. Trade officials, bursting with pride after decades of the country enduring a reputation as a basket case, claimed to be presiding over the instant emergence of one of the great twenty-first-century powers. Western economists too hailed India's rise as proof of the benevolence of an integrated world economy, globalization you could reach out and touch.

I could see how, if you heard about it in London or New York, the pattern of news from India might sound like a nation on the move. Tales of Indian prowess in everything from answering US phones to buying venerable European industries were fostering a perception of a country whose seemingly infinite size was matched only by its limitless potential. Being 'Bangalored' had become slang for one of the defining processes of the global economy – offshoring, the movement of jobs from the expensive West to the cheap East. Global communications had brought millions of Indian doctors, engineers and IT specialists into the world market. Western retailers were salivating over the idea of a billion new consumers. Put those stories together and the idea of an emerging giant was convincing.

And there is, undoubtedly, a global shift underway. The world's economic heart is moving east. If there is one phenomenon typifying the new interconnected economy, it is offshoring, and China rules in manufacturing, while India is king in IT and back office services. India's overseas outsourcing sector was worth $36 billion in 2005–6, up from $150 million in 1991. The industry is predicted to double again by 2010.[3] Around 90 per cent of that is business transferred from Europe and America. The subcontinent was a cost-cutter's dream. Why employ anyone in the West, so the argument went, when India could supply software engineers, lawyers or financial analysts, diamond cutters, tailors or heart surgeons at a fraction of the price? Instead of a looming Malthusian catastrophe, India's 1.1 billion population was now seen as a gold-plated opportunity. India would become the workforce to the world, plugging the gaps left by falling birth rates in the West. Offshoring was talked about as the panacea that would catapult a land of disease, poverty and stifling bureaucracy out of the Dark Ages. The skinny, barefoot hordes of yore had seemingly been replaced by millions of educated, cheap graduates.

But success was only half the story. Yes, there are new billionaires aplenty in India. In 2007, *Forbes* magazine found thirty-six – more than anywhere else in Asia. But next to 900 million Indians who earn $2 a day or less – a third of all the world's poor – those were thirty-six drops in a very large ocean.[4] Nor was India's boom closing the gap. Contrary to a common supposition in the West, sucking in jobs from around the world had not produced an employment bonanza in India. Offshoring only employs 1.63 million people out of a workforce of 400 million and a population of 1.1 billion.[5] The desperation at the bottom of India's economic ladder can be judged by the 740,000 applications received by Indian Railways when, in 2004, it advertised 22,000 labouring jobs.

There was also little sign of the keenly awaited Indian bourgeoisie. Western bankers and politicians talked confidently about the appearance – as if by magic – of the world's newest and biggest middle class. The two figures I heard most often were 300 million, and 450 million. The truth was that just 58 million Indians earned more than $4,400 a year in 2005–6, according to Delhi's National Institute for Applied Economic Research. In fact, the number of absolute poor in India was actually rising – by millions. Unemployment remained stubbornly high – the lowest official estimates put it at 8 to 10 per cent, or at least 40 million people. And an October 2006 study by India's National Sample Survey Organization found economic growth had almost entirely failed to percolate. During eleven years of 5 to 8 per cent growth since 1993, the proportion of people living below the line of absolute poverty – $1 a day – had fallen by a mere 0.74 per cent to 22.15 per cent. Given a simultaneous increase in India's population, that meant that 40 million more Indians were living in destitution.

The reality is that India continues to be home to more poverty than anywhere on earth – more than all Africa, and more and more each day. It accounts for more than a quarter of the world's extreme poor, according to a 2005 UN report, 380 million people who earn $1 a day or less.[6] At 2.4 million a year, its families cope with more than half of all child deaths in the world.[7] More than 770 million Indians have no sanitation, 170 million drink fetid water[8] and the World Bank says 47 per cent of all children are malnourished. Nutrition, infant mortality and women's health are worse in India than even perennial disaster zones like its neighbour Bangladesh. According to India's 2007 National Family Health Survey, 79.2 per cent of children between six and thirty-five months and 58 per cent of pregnant women are anaemic; 38 per cent of children under three are stunted; 46 per cent are underweight. Even the most optimistic predictions estimate that living standards will take a century to catch the West.

If you took a moment to consider it, India's growth had to be selective. It is a vast nation – more than a sixth of all humanity – whose economy had only been growing significantly faster than its population since the then finance minister Manmohan Singh began dismantling the old socialist command economy in 1991. Business had benefited. But the improvements required to lift all India – programmes to end malnutrition, cracking down on corruption, rebuilding crumbling infrastructure, creating working health and education systems – will take generations. The economy may have doubled in fifteen years, foreign investment may be forty times what it was in 1991 and stocks may have tripled in the three years to May 2006. But multiplications of next to nothing are still not very much. The new wealth was concentrated on a tiny few, and found expression in the explosion of Louis Vuitton and Gucci boutiques in upper-crust areas of Bombay and Delhi that so impressed visiting foreign investors and journalists. If you ventured beyond those smart neighbourhoods you found India proper, and there little had changed in centuries.

Singh, who became prime minister in 2004, was only too aware of this. 'The single most important challenge in today's world is the management of change . . . [and] the problem of growing disparities between rich and poor, which are now becoming acute,' he declared in November 2006. 'I am pained when I see the extent of suffering inflicted on ordinary people.' But his wish to share the wealth was crippled by the limitations of his government. India's national budget is roughly the size of Norway's (population 4 million). In a country the size of India, that rules out a welfare system, meaningful attempts to address inequality or any of the normal state checks on capitalism you expect in the West. The Indian government spent just 0.9 per cent of India's GDP on health in 2002, one of the lowest proportions in the world.[9]. Large parts of the country are still essentially ungoverned. What money the government does hand out is often eaten by corruption or left unused by inept bureaucrats. Add in the restrictions of caste, and you can understand how, whatever the good intentions of its government, India's is a members-only boom. In October 2007, 25,000 low-caste tenant farmers and landless tribal groups marched for a month across the country before arriving in Delhi to demand land reform and inclusion in India's boom. India had swapped its socialist dreams for libertarian ones.[10] But for most of its people, the same nightmarish poverty endured.

That was also a truer picture of globalization than China. Why? Because there's one big problem with China as a place to observe globalization. Watching China tells you a lot about development. But it also tells you a fair bit about big government. Shenzhen is a story of globalization, yes. But it's also a tale of totalitarian advancement (and criminal subversion of the state), rather than organic human development.

India, on the other hand, is free. It is democratic, liberal and entrepreneurial, a place where the currents of globalization are allowed to converge freely and, by and large, play out without hindrance. If most of what goes on in China is to do with government, most of what goes on in India is to do with people.

India's uneven boom, then, is a colossal, chaotic demonstration of globalization. If globalization was born in Shenzhen, today it has made its home in Bombay. (And not Bangalore. The Indian IT capital gets attention for its tech campuses and dotcom billionaires, but you wouldn't confuse Seattle with New York.) Bombay hosts conventions for Japanese bankers and Brazilian anti-globalization protesters. It is where Wall St gets equities analysed, where Kellogg, Brown & Root sources kitchen staff for the US army in Iraq and where your credit card details might be stored, or stolen. It's where a phone operator who calls herself Mary (but is really Meenakshi) tele-sells Texans on two-week holidays that include the Taj Mahal and cut-price heart surgery. It's where club DJs steal back the music of the Punjab – bhangra – from London and New York in the hippest bars between Beirut and Bangkok. And it's where a Canadian, Rohinton Mistry, mixed the sensibilities of Charles Dickens with a little Indian spice to create his Bombay trilogy. To know Bombay is to know modern India. It is the channel for a billion ambitions. And it is globalization made real, a giant cacophonous city where change is pouring in and rippling out around the globe.

India's business capital might be its great hope, but it's also its single greatest problem. Just as New York was America's diseased sewer in the late nineteenth century, so the obstacles hampering India's progress – poor infrastructure, weak government, searing inequality, corruption and crime – converge in Bombay. A 2003 report for the state government by management consultants McKinsey & Co. found that for all its glitz, Bombay was a temple to inefficiency. The city had one bus for every 1,300 people, two public parking spots for every 1,000 cars, seventeen public toilets for every million people and one civic hospital for 7.2 million people in the northern slums. Average rush hour speed was 5 m.p.h. and 90 per cent of the city's garbage rotted in the street. If you judged it on infrastructure, the city was disintegrating. On the railways, passenger groups say the primary cause of 3,500 commuter deaths a year is the city's small and ancient stock of trains, crammed with an average of 4,500 people against a capacity of 1,750, leading to daily tumbles on to the tracks. In housing, city rent controls have kept the price of its swankiest apartments almost unchanged since 1940, encouraging landlords to let them crumble, as they did in the floods. Meanwhile, for newer, unregulated buildings, they charge prices that outstrip New York – brokers say prices rose 40 to 50 per cent in 2005–6. These dizzying costs in turn push 12 million people into slums, where 6 million have no clean drinking water and 2 million no toilet.

The city does have an $8.3 billion, five-year plan to revamp itself. But it's had similar proposals since 1992. In 2005, the Economist Intelligence Unit ranked Bombay 124th out of 130 in its survey of the world's most liveable cities. McKinsey wrote that it was a riddle. Even as it mothered India's boom, it said, Bombay was dying. 'Mumbai is at a critical juncture,' wrote the managing consultants, using Bombay's official name. 'It is in grave danger of collapsing completely.'

Actually, it does – every year. The 2005 floods were the worst for a generation, but each monsoon kills at least ten people in Bombay. And in August 2005, sleeping on the floor of hotel lobbies and sheltering in the slums, stranded businessmen – Indian and foreign – were increasingly questioning what they were seeing. How could this happen? What was wrong with the drains? Where were the police? If there was a disaster management plan, why was it not used? Why did the fire brigade not reach Saki Nagar until the next day? Crucially, for the foreigners: what were they doing here? If this really was the business capital of the next big economy, how come it could crumble in a day of heavy rain? Ramila Sreedhar, a window-blind manufacturer from Madras, fretted about the effect on India's reputation. 'They'll go back home and say, "Forget India. They're fifty years behind".'

Bombay was founded on an empty boast. In 1534, the Portuguese took possession of seven malarial islands off the west Indian coast and called them Good Bay, or 'Bom Baia'. Big talk, however, attracts big crowds, and five centuries of migration has made Bombay the largest commercial centre, by population, between São Paulo and Tokyo. It's still growing. According to the official census, 500 people arrive to live in the city every day.

One result of all the migration is that nobody actually comes from Bombay. Even families who have lived there for generations still refer to a village 1,000 miles away as home. That sense of a city apart is reinforced by geography and architecture. You cross an estuary to reach downtown. And once there, you find a British tropical city of Victorian railway stations, art deco apartment blocks and Edwardian offices. Christabelle Noronha, a publicity director, says the sense of being in a foreign land gives Bombay an uninhibited air. 'If everyone is a stranger, then everyone is free,' she says. It's no accident that the city is home to India's mafia, running an empire of drugs and prostitution that stretches from Phnom Penh to Durban, and, in its dance bars, its only overground sex industry. But crime and sex are merely the raciest examples of a wider phenomenon. Bombay is a city built on a very American kind of hustle. 'Pull anyone out of any part of India and put him in Bombay,' says Sanyah Bhandarkar, managing director of Rothschilds India, 'and he'll acquire that sense of purpose.'

At eighteen, Brij left India's poorest state, Bihar, where average annual income is $105. He hitched and dodged train fares across the country and, arriving penniless in Bombay, found work selling spicy peanuts at traffic lights, and a tin hut for $1 a month. Brij was ecstatic. 'I came to this wonderland, this *Mayanagri*,' he says, using Bombay's Hindi nickname, meaning City of Dreams. 'The beach, the sea, I'd never seen anything so amazing.' Brij was too ambitious to sell nuts all his life. He also realized he couldn't limit himself to legitimate business if he wanted to move up. Opportunity presented itself abruptly. 'One day I was sitting with some friends outside our huts and somebody came and attacked us,' he says. 'They wanted money and they kidnapped one of us. So I got a sword and a chopper and I went to free the guy. I stabbed somebody. He died six months later. After that, I became famous. I became a *bhai* (boss).'

Brij's casual intimacy with murder fascinated me, and he was flattered by the keen attention of a foreigner, and we became acquaintances. He liked to dress in the neat, cheap shirt and slacks of a junior office worker. His appearance was a careful dissimulation. At thirty-two, he owned 30,000 huts in four slums, and made $8,000 a month from rents, bootlegging and gambling dens. By the time I met him, he also had three more murders to his name, and lived on the run, running a gang of 300 men by mobile phone. He loved Bombay. 'I came from nothing,' Brij said. 'Now I have money, phones, cars, houses, a wife and two girlfriends. If you were me, you'd love Bombay too.' A month after the floods, I met Brij in a railway snack house. He was plotting expansion. 'Politics,' he declared when I asked him about his plans for the future. 'It's a natural next step for a gangster.'

I also became friends with Rajeev Samant. Rajeev may have lived in the same city, but he was from a different world. His story was a blueprint for legitimate success in modern India. When he left school twenty years ago, any Indian with ambition and means got out, and Rajeev followed a well-trodden path to Stanford and on to Oracle in Silicon Valley. Then in 1991, Singh began to open up India and Rajeev came home with a mad new plan: to make wine in a country where alcohol was a sin and the closest thing to sophisticated intoxication was illicit hooch. Thirteen years later, Rajeev was managing director of Sula, one of India's largest vintners, producing 1.1 million bottles a year, even exporting to France. And he lived large. He had a chauffeur and a manservant, holidayed in Europe and California and partied every night in Bombay. To recap: Rajeev wasn't married, he made booze and he had chucked in a dream job in the US. Old Mother India would have had a cow. 'This is an incredible time,' said Rajeev one night. 'It's all happening. Right here, right now.'

I began to see Brij and Rajeev as different sides of the same coin. Both were entrepreneurs. Both chose Bombay to realize their dreams. Brij had his backstreet deals and slum bars, and Rajeev had the roof bar at the Intercontinental and the fairways of the Willingdon Club – so exclusive membership has been closed for years. But if the two crossed paths in the street, they did so as equals: two successful Bombay wheeler-dealers. Indeed, Rajeev admitted to bending the rules on occasion. 'If you try to run a business 100 per cent within the law in this town,' he said, 'you're doomed.'

Brij's luck ran out in March 2006. He was arrested on suspicion of attempting another murder and charged under the Maharashtra Prevention of Dangerous Activities Act. When I last heard of him, he was awaiting trail at Yeravada jail in Pune, outside Bombay – and expanding his gang by recruiting among prisoners.

As in Shenzhen, globalization had made Bombay a magnet to poor migrants. The same pattern can be observed around the world. A century ago just 250 million people lived in cities. That figure reached 1 billion in 1960, 2 billion in 1985, 3 billion in 2002 and in 2007 humanity crossed a landmark when it became majority urban. Already in Europe and North America, more than three quarters of the population live in cities. Population growth now occurs only in cities, and by 2030 the UN says two thirds of mankind will be city folk. Many of us will live in mega-cities, urban sprawls with populations of 10 million or more. In 1950 there was one mega-city, New York. By 2000, there were eighteen. The UN expects sixty by 2030. By 2015, the UN World Urbanization Prospects Report expects Bombay to be the world's biggest city, with 22.6 million people; others predict 33 million.

The term mega-city conjures up visions of a technopolis of the type imagined by George Lucas or Ridley Scott. The reality is very different. Most mega-cities are not advanced. They're not even present-day developed. The rich world can count its mega-cities on one hand: New York, Los Angeles, Tokyo and Osaka – and Buenos Aires, if you count Argentina as developed. The developing world has, in descending order of size: Chongqing, São Paulo, Mexico City, Bombay, Shenzhen, Calcutta, Dhaka, Delhi, Shanghai, Jakarta, Beijing, Rio de Janeiro, Karachi and Manila, with Cairo, Istanbul, Lagos and Tianjin poised to join them.

If crime is one of the biggest beneficiaries of globalization, the problem reaches its zenith in a mega-city. Partly because they're so big. Partly because wealth and poverty rub up against each other so closely. In the early 1990s, Bombay's mafia was threatening to spin out of control, with almost daily street shoot-outs between rival gangs. In 1993, multiple bombings by mafia supremo Dawood Ibrahim killed 257 people. The city's police felt they had to take drastic action. So, for a decade and a half, they waged a bloody war on the gangsters, killing 1,200 in and around Bombay. One officer in particular earned himself a name as India's Dirty Harry.

It was late evening in November 2003 when I found Inspector Pradeep Sharma in a roughhouse police station in the north of the city. As we introduced ourselves in his office, a group of officers were punching a pair of men handcuffed to a refrigerator in the room beyond. Sharma initially struck me as having the appearance of a middle-class Bombay commuter – tall, neat, reserved. Then he kicked the door shut on the scene in the adjoining room and growled: 'It's the only language they understand.'

I discovered Sharma had a taste for lethal one-liners. Asked how he policed Bombay's gangland, he slammed a clip into a confiscated Uzi and spat: 'A bullet for a bullet.' Asked why he did what he did, he leant back in his chair, assumed a dead-eyed stare and snarled: 'Criminals are filth.' He thumbed his chest: 'And I'm the cleaner.'

Sharma might have owed much of his tough-guy act to movies. But the violence was real. When I first met him, records showed Sharma had personally gunned down eighty-seven gangsters in the mean streets of India's organized crime capital since 1990. Two years later, we were sitting in the back row of a cinema watching a film dramatizing the 1993 Bombay blasts when I noticed several audience members stopping to shake his hand. 'I made my century,' Sharma whispered when his fans had left. The forty-five-year-old's scorecard made him the country's deadliest cop, ahead of two other Bombay inspectors, Praful Bhosle, fifty-one, who was on eighty-two, and Vijay Salaskar, fifty, on forty. All three were from the elite Criminal Intelligence Unit,[11] which was tasked with taking down the bad guys guns blazing. Few gangsters seemed to go quietly: police shot seventy-one in 'encounters' in 1997, eighty-three in 1999 and ninety-seven in 2001.

The effect on India's crime capital was dramatic. From two a week in the early 1990s, gang shoot-outs were down to two a month by 2003. Once mighty syndicates had crumbled, losing scores of men and millions of dollars in business. Arun Gawli, a former mafia don who became a politician, was a virtual prisoner in his own mansion, living behind a phalanx of armed guards, CCTV and four separate locked gates out of fear of what he calls 'police contract killings'. 'In a democracy, these sorts of killings are unlawful,' he moaned. Gawli, fifty-five, said he had lost a total of sixty associates to encounters. 'OK, there were days a while back when I went astray. But this sort of murder campaign is way beyond acceptable.' It was a view shared by human rights groups. Lawyer Seema Gulati warned that the 'growing trend of police killings' was endangering India's democracy.

The figures, it was true, raised eyebrows. Against the deaths of 1,200 mobsters, only one policeman had died in hundreds of encounters. The police argued they were simply better shots. 'Being a well-trained force, our success rate is high,' said Bombay Deputy Police Commissioner Pradeep Sawant, who had directed 160 encounters between 2000 and 2003. He added no officer had ever been convicted of staging a shoot-out, despite hundreds of complaints filed by the victims' families. 'The allegations of fake encounters are baseless,' said Sawant. 'It's not that we always go to kill. Our idea is to arrest the gangsters. We only retaliate if we're fired upon.'

In private, officers admitted to carrying out executions. But they contended they had no choice, given a judicial system crippled by corruption and a national backlog of 27 million cases. Kanwar Pal Singh Gill, who became India's most famous cop for putting down an insurgency by his fellow Sikhs in the 1980s, was blunt: 'Our legal system doesn't work at all. If there are no legal remedies, there'll be extra-legal ones.'

By and large, this was something the public supported. For a professional enforcer like Sharma, success wasn't just measured in body bags or reduced gang violence, but public praise. He knew the gangsters were unhappy – he called the contest to assassinate him a 'Mafia World Cup'. But when I visited him a second time, he had my article, complete with a picture of him holding an AK-47 and a caption describing him as a 'killer', blown up to double size, hanging on his wall. 'I don't enjoy killing,' said Sharma. 'But after we shoot some mobster, his victims look at me like God. The press love me. That's the best part of the job.'

Some Bombayites like to argue that the weakness of their government gives them an edge over China. They have a point: if Bombay's doing it, it's doing it for itself. Rakesh Jhunjhunwala, a billionaire Bombay stock trader, puts it like this: 'India is like a runner without shoes. But look at that speed.'

That self-reliance crosses over into a city ethos. Newspapers call it the 'Mumbaiker spirit'. Bombay still talks about how when the floods hit, shanty-dwellers sheltered businessmen, slum children rescued film stars and untouchables saved holy men. 'There was a feeling that went through people,' said film producer and director Mahesh Bhatt, who sued the city for its alleged mishandling of the crisis. 'We realized we were going to have to do it ourselves.' The same is true of the economy. 'On the face of it, the city's screwed,' said Rajeev. 'Look at the traffic, the bureaucracy, the sewage, so much poverty next to so much money you'd think the place would erupt.' And yet look at how nimbly the city negotiates these obstacles, he added. Before his arrest, Brij even found ways to make money from the state's inadequacies. He ran a sideline settling business disputes for those who couldn't wait for a judgement from India's unwieldy legal system – for a 20 per cent cut of whatever was at stake. He also made money from the state's poor response to the floods. 'A lot of people needed new slums,' he grinned.

But weak government is mostly a bad thing. As well as dismal infrastructure, it encourages little respect for authority – hence crime, plus city-wide riots in 1992, and Islamist bomb attacks in 1993, 2003 and 2006. Today, with the advent of globalization, even stronger tides of inequality are sweeping across India – and the weak government is unable to tame them. In a city as crowded as Bombay, that means the stratospherically rich live cheek by jowl with the gutter poor. Million-dollar apartments overlook million-population slums. Visitors to the most prestigious offices in the country in south Bombay run the gauntlet of the street sleepers outside. Movie director Shekhar Kapur, who returned to his home city after years in London and Los Angeles, where he won a Golden Globe for *Elizabeth*, says everyone in Bombay confronts the divide daily. 'This must be one of the few places on earth where the rich try to work off a few pounds in the gym, step outside, and are confronted by a barefoot child of skin and bones, begging for something to eat.'

The city's biggest slum is Dharavi, 535 acres of shanty town, open sewers and rat-infested lanes in central Bombay. Once a marsh next to the Mithi River, Dharavi's first residents would catch fish in the creeks and sell them to the Portuguese city to the south. As Bombay grew and industrialized, Dharavi became a 'human dumping ground' for dispossessed cotton mill workers and penniless migrants arriving to seek their fortune in India's commercial capital, according to Dharavi historian and lifetime resident Ram Bhaukorde, sixty-nine. 'Anyone too poor for Bombay proper could find a home and a living here,' says Bhaukorde.

Today, depending on whether Dharavi has a population of 600,000 or a million – the figures are so rough because the area was officially an illegal settlement until 2004 and the authorities have yet to conduct a census there – it is the biggest slum either in Asia or the world.[12] The daily fight for fresh water illustrates the disparity with rich parts of the city. A vast water pipe the size of a man cuts through the maze of rubbish-strewn roofs and filthy alleys heading for the seafront art deco apartments of Colaba, Bombay's flashiest neighbourhood. But in Dharavi, a lost city under the overpasses linking the airport with the steel-and-glass blocks downtown, the only running water is what seeps out of cracks in this pipe. For its entire population, Dharavi has just 150 working toilets. Private suppliers charge 1,500 times the public rate for fresh water. Twenty-five floors up in neighbouring apartment blocks there's water for Jacuzzis. Down below there's barely enough for life.

The picture is worse on the city's outskirts. The favourite motto of even the poorest Bombayite is: 'You don't starve in Bombay.' That isn't true of the surrounding countryside. State government figures show that every year around 8,500 children die of malnutrition in Maharashtra – either directly or succumbing to other illnesses in their weakened state. And yet the authorities deny a crisis. One village they are particularly keen to ignore is Patilpada, a tiny settlement of forty houses a short drive north-east of Bombay.

Scattered reports of mass starvation in the area in late 2004, just on the outskirts of India's booming business capital, seemed exaggerated. I drove out to Patilpada to see for myself. The reports were no hyperbole. Each home revealed a child or two with famine's hideously distended bellies, stick limbs and bulging eyes. Several three-year-olds had no strength to walk and could have been mistaken for infants of six months. Teacher Davidas Bhodore, twenty-seven, said three to four children die in Patilpada ever year, thirty in the small surrounding valley. His figures tallied with those gathered by a survey team from a non-governmental group, Actionaid, who counted fifty-five child deaths in the area in 2004. I found Jaie Bhambruy, thirty-two, slumped in her mud doorway, struggling to pull her one-year-old twins Lalita and Vaishali on to her breasts. The children, one wailing feebly, one limp, were too weak to feed. 'We were admitted to hospital,' she said, 'but they sent us away after a day. The doctors have been told not to make an issue of malnutrition.' In nearby Jawahar Hospital, the admission board added further evidence of catastrophe. By noon, twenty-three children had arrived with grade 3 malnutrition (50 to 60 per cent of normal weight) and fifteen with grade 4 (less than 50 per cent). Dr Marad Randas was reluctant to talk, for fear of repercussions from his government employers. But with disaster swamping his clinic, he was also beyond denial. He talked about parents who produced large families because they expected one or two children to die, and who live 'without education, without clothes, without a sense of time'. Asked if the Bombay skyscrapers on the horizon might as well be another country, he replied: 'Something like that.'

In the face of such stark inequality, it might be wise for the new rich to employ a little modesty to soothe the divide. You'd think it would be particularly unwise to celebrate the new wealth. But that's exactly what's happening.

One night in Bombay in June 2004, India's leading talk-show host, Simi Garewal, threw a party to celebrate the hundredth episode of her show, *Rendezvous*. Simi's party guests had all been on *Rendezvous* and taking the stage in the ballroom at the Taj Land's End hotel, she told them that they were the 'most beautiful, most talented and most powerful' people in the country. It helps to be all those things for Simi to seat you on her couch. But there is another, non-negotiable criterion. You must be rich.

Gathered in the room were a who's who of India –

industrialists, Bollywood stars, politicians, cricketers. To keep out the riff-raff, the guests were given white leather Louis Vuitton wristbands to show to security on the door. They were served champagne, caviar and sushi – in arrangements named after the guests themselves – under a marquee of white chiffon. Garewal gave a short speech. *Rendezvous*, she said, revealed the 'human story' behind glamour. Then she sang her theme song. 'I feel you near me even when we are apart. Just knowing you are in this world can warm my heart. It's been a special rendezvous.' The party continued until 2 a.m. when, as a climax, some of India's richest men looked on as a chorus line of Bollywood actors danced, and superstar Sushmita Sen sang Elton John's 'Sacrifice'. To match the same concentration of wealth and fame in the West, Donald Trump and Richard Branson would be clapping as Angelina Jolie sang, and Brad Pitt, George Clooney and Robert de Niro danced with Cameron Diaz, Julia Roberts and Meryl Streep.

Rendezvous is one of the more extraordinary chat shows in the history of the genre. Broadcast on Sunday on Rupert Murdoch's Star World, it has topped the ratings for English-language programming since its launch in 1997. Its success defies broadcasting convention. *Rendezvous* eschews the acerbic hipness of late-night TV or the coffee-and-couch informality of daytime shows. Simi has no interest in politicians with a point or actors with a new film or even It Girls with a reality show. Instead she celebrates cash, and the ostentation and self-absorption it buys. Simi herself only ever wears white and is so thickly made up and sprayed that it seems to stiffen her movements. She greets her guests on a set modelled on her own sixth-floor terrace in Bombay's exclusive Malabar Hills: white lilies, white walls, white trellises, white cane furniture, and a black marble pond. Describing herself as 'concerned and empathetic', she nudges her guests to stratospheric heights of narcissism. Icing the cake – albeit with a trowel – are soft-focus cameras. It's compelling stuff. On the best shows, the guests cry – at the memory of cruel boyfriends, departed mothers or, once, over the death of a poodle. I phoned Simi to ask for an interview and she invited me to dinner and to her party. At the party, I asked Star World's Indian CEO Peter Mukherjee, who was watching the guests approvingly from the sidelines, whether the show made money. He chuckled. 'In terms of money,' he said, 'Simi is Star World.' What made *Rendezvous* so popular? 'It's the opposite of *Hardtalk*,' he smiled.

It's hard to imagine *Rendezvous* working in any other country. But Simi's genius is to understand that in a nation as traditionally deferential as India, where millions still follow gurus and abide by caste, and where urchins lived alongside maharajahs for centuries, awe still comes easier than analysis. 'It's inspirational,' says Simi. 'Aspirational.' India's newspapers adopt a similarly fawning attitude towards Bollywood bigshots and titans of industry. Hollywood stars would be stunned at how the Indian press cossets its celebrities. In 2005, one tabloid stepped out of line and published a photograph of a leading actress kissing her boyfriend. The next day the actress gave a press conference at which she argued that her good breeding ruled out the kind of lewd behaviour the newspaper was implying, and therefore the picture had to be a fake. That was proof enough for the rest of the Indian media, which duly took her side, and the offending paper promptly issued a grovelling apology.

Such lack of scrutiny encourages India's privileged to ignore the less fortunate. Rich and poor live totally separate lives. The rich live in gated housing colonies and shop for clothes, jewellery and electronic goods in malls, send staff out for food, patronize private schools and hospitals, and relax in gyms and spas. The poor live in slums, send their children to work and can't afford healthcare. There are no melting pot 'scenes' in India's cities. When, over dinner at her apartment under a supersize portrait of herself, I mention my trip to Patilpada, Simi cuts me off, saying: 'I don't want to talk about that other India.'

This rigid divide means the rich never have to account for themselves to the poor. And, with a weak government and corrupt taxmen, hardly to government either. As a result, modern India is seeing the emergence of one of the flashiest elites on earth.

Absent from Simi's party is former guest Vijay Mallya. Which is unusual – Vijay has a reputation for missing as few parties as he can. In two decades, he has transformed his father's business, United Beverages, from a medium-sized concern into the world's second biggest drinks house, making Kingfisher beer a world brand and netting himself a few billion dollars in the process. The publisher of India's only swimsuit calendar, a roly-poly playboy with diamond stud earrings, Bangalore's most famous son wows and scandalizes India in equal measure for being stinking rich, and loving it. In May 2006, Vijay extended his notoriety to France when, to Gallic outrage, he tried to buy the snootiest of brands, Taittinger, before adding insult to injury by blithely declaring the asking price not worth it. 'People call me extravagant,' he said one afternoon as we flew in his 727 ('my Boing' as Vijay pronounces it) from Bombay to a private party for 2,000 he was throwing that night in Bangalore. 'I couldn't give a shit. I sold 38.5 million cases last year and that's a whole bunch of booze.'

Vijay lives in Bangalore on Vittal Mallya Road, named after his father, away from new technology campuses and at the heart of an old British colonial city of elegant Edwardian bungalows and art deco mansions, shaded by bougainvillea and flame trees. But the tastefulness of the setting can't hide Vijay's brass. As you sweep into the portico, you pass Vijay's collection of vintage Ferraris and Rolls Royces. The reception is carpeted with tiger skins. And the walls of Vijay's office are mounted with a zoo of African animal heads, including the whole front half of an elephant, its tusks inches above the floor, its head just squeezing under the ceiling.

Vijay styles himself after the slogan of his beer: the 'King of Good Times'. He bears a striking resemblance to Henry VIII, and over a few in-flight Chardonnays on the 'Boing', he explained that bawdiness is his job. The more he parties, the more the exposure, the bigger the brand. 'Work hard, play hard,' he guffawed. 'Same fucking thing.' The Boing's interior was a testament to a man who takes fun seriously. It had a king-sized bed with purple satin sheets, a bar manned by two tiny Asiatic waitresses and, in the back, a giant plasma television on which Vijay's seventeen-year-old son watched action movies. An aide at the house explained that was just the start. Vijay's appetite for accumulation ran to two helicopters; four jets; six homes in India; penthouses in London, Monaco, New York, Johannesburg and Los Angeles; a Scottish castle; several South African game lodges in Kruger National Park; a stud farm and a stable of 250 thoroughbreds, where he kept the 2004 winner of the Kingfisher Derby in Bangalore, Fantabulous King; a 165-foot yacht called Kalizma, once given to Elizabeth Taylor by Richard Burton (which Vijay later swapped for something 25 foot bigger); and the $100,000 in chains, bracelets, rings and earrings that he wore every day. He was, his bodyguard told me, 'a walking security nightmare'. 'People shake his hands,' said the bodyguard, 'and rip the rings off his fingers.' Towards the end of the flight to Bangalore, even a party animal of Vijay's stature began to show signs of wear and tear. Rolling unsteadily off the plane and bundling into a limousine at the bottom of the steps, he shouted over his shoulder that he would see me at the party at 8 p.m.

His 2,000 guests had been waiting for four hours by the time Vijay showed up just before midnight. He arrived, took a centre table, filled it with friends and Kingfisher cans, and called over the star turn of the night, an MTV India presenter called Sophia, who had just finished a stage show. After chatting for an hour or so – and making no attempt to circulate – Vijay declared he was bored. A motorcade of Mercedes were summoned, and Vijay, Sophia and the others drove to a private go-kart track barely three minutes away. There, fuelled by more cases of Kingfisher, they raced until dawn, whooping, crashing and covering their silk clothes with tyre spray from the wet track.

Vijay's presence loomed over the party even after his departure. Giant screens hanging from the roof played a looped video diary of how he and five Bombay models took the Boing to Thailand to shoot this year's swimsuit calendar. His guests seemed not the least insulted by his leaving. Dhunji Wadia, a forty-three-year-old executive at advertisers J. Walter Thompson, described him as an icon. 'We need more Mallyas. There's been more change in the last five years than the last five decades and he's done that more than anyone.'

*

In some ways, newly minted India is a throwback to an earlier time. For centuries the subcontinent was a land of princes and paupers. After the 1857 Mutiny – or First War of Independence – the British compensated India's kings for the loss of real power by bestowing on them the trappings of power. They elevated rajahs (kings) to maharajahs (great kings), set up the Order of the Star of India and held great parades – or durbars – which were a celebration of pomp and majesty. The Indian royals responded by competing to show themselves most loyal, and most British, by adopting coats of arms, wearing Western clothes, reading and speaking English, and playing billiards and cricket. They took extended shopping trips to London and Paris, patronizing luxury stores such as Cartier, Louis Vuitton, Chanel and Baccarat, single-handedly keeping some of these titans of fashion afloat during the Great Depression.[13]

Then came Mohandas Gandhi. As well as challenging the idea of British rule, the Mahatma fought its substance too. In contrast to imperial pomp and snobbery, Gandhi dressed in homespun rags, walked barefoot and welcomed Brahmins and untouchables alike. His message was one of freedom from oppression by wealth as much as race. Fifty years ago in newly independent India, castes mixed in the street and India aspired to a *pukka* restraint that combined the frugality of Gandhi, Victorian morality and the gentlemanly fair play of cricket. Money was vulgar, credit a sin.

Today most Indians still view the West as tawdry. Millionaire politicians, for example, often feel obliged to wear white homespun *khadi* shirts and conduct meetings on the floor of rooms that are almost Calvinist in their starkness. But for the guardians of Gandhi's legacy, the signs of erosion are everywhere. They point to the garish coffee chains replacing modest *chai* houses, the vogue for blonde highlights and the beery gangs of software engineers in Bangalore's pubs. 'Gandhi may still be an Indian icon,' says newspaper columnist Swapan Dasgupta, 'but Gandhi-ism is dead as a dodo.' A poll rating India's most popular icons for the *Economic Times* in September 2006 found Gandhi scored 30 per cent; Bill Gates was at 37 per cent.

The last of the world's three great state-run economies, India watched the other two open up – China in 1979, Russia in 1985 – before in 1991 it finally loosened the bonds that bound it to a moribund 'Hindu rate' of 2 to 3 per cent economic growth. The economy began expanding by 5 per cent, then 8 per cent, then more. And for the first time in independent India, people other than royalty or foreigners got rich. Very rich, very quickly. Narayan Murthy says when he started Infosys in 1981, India was 'completely inward looking'. 'It took us two or three years and fifty visits to Delhi to get permission to import a computer worth $50,000,' he said. 'It would take ten days to get the foreign exchange I needed to travel abroad. It took two years to get a telephone line.' That sluggishness was reflected in Infosys' revenue, which grew from $130,000 in 1981–2 to just $1.5 million in 1991–2. After 1991, however, Narayan Murthy says Infosys became 'the best example of all the good that came out of the reforms. Between 1991–2 and 2005–6 our revenue went up from $1.5 million to $2.15 billion. That's 1,400 times.' By the time he retired at sixty in August 2006, Murthy was worth $1.3 billion.

According to Merrill Lynch's world wealth report, India is now producing rich people at a world-beating rate. But ballooning bank balances are only half the story. Just as dramatic is the way the new elite can't spend it fast enough.

Management consultants KSA Technopak say the wealthy are leading an urban spending spree that saw consumption grow 12 per cent in 2002 and 16 per cent in 2003. Airline passengers have multiplied sixfold since 1996 to 50 million, and sales of motorcycles and cars have doubled. Consumer credit has tripled in five years and Indian psychiatrists are reporting a new condition among the new rich: obsessive-compulsive shopping. India's rich are spending their way to prosperity. 'Suddenly India's a candy store,' says Simi at her apartment. 'Now it's about wanting to own, to possess, to be in the newspapers, to show off and be recognized.' Adds Gurcharan Das, author of *India Unbound*: 'Money, like sex, is out of the closet. Everybody wants to be rich, and live rich.'[14]

This retail binge finds mass expression in the construction of hundreds of malls. But the truly rich want something more high end. Like private planes, whose makers are reporting record sales in India. Soon after I arrived in Delhi, I was introduced to a man who called himself the 'Flying Sikh'. Dharminder Singh Anand took personal shopping to a whole new, global level. After gathering hundreds of orders from his 1,500 customers at his basement hole store in Delhi, Anand took a weekly flight to London and its department stores. On a typical visit he bought 500 items for 100 people, from $588 of make-up from Harvey Nichols to a pair of $510 Gucci shoes and a Hawaiian shirt from Baby Gap. He charged a dollar for every dollar spent. 'You'd never keep up,' he said when I asked if I could shadow him next time I was in London. 'I'm shopping for a nation.' (The trouble was, in terms of trickle-down theory, he wasn't shopping *in* that nation.)

Such epic consumption produces its own legends. Parmeshwar Godrej, a former air stewardess married to Adi

Godrej, a billionaire industrialist, is famous for dinner parties that rival Hollywood for bling and celebrity, with guests such as Richard Gere, Goldie Hawn and Liz Hurley. A popular legend on the cocktail circuit of Bombay has 'Parmesh' sleeping undisturbed in her London apartment as a burglar pulled a $2.2-million diamond ring off her finger with his teeth. 'These people aren't just rich,' declared Thierry de Longeville, general manager for Louis Vuitton in Asia, another of Simi's guests, 'they're super-rich.'

India has not entirely forgotten its revolutionary past, however. Gandhi is still revered across the country as a demi-god. Many of the most successful Bollywood films today still focus on the heroes of India's independence movement. And the Naxal movement shows that, at least for some, displays of maharajah-like wealth no longer inspire awe, but anger.

Elite India liked to see itself as leading a country towards progress. But was India progressing? In the autumn of 2005, my wife and I drove with our two-year-old daughter through India's most visited state, Rajasthan, famous for desert forts, camels and palaces perched in lake oases. Like thousands of other tourists, we patted elephants, watched puppet shows and scrambled up and down maharajahs' castles in Jaipur. My daughter spent much of the time showing off: posing for shots with Indian tourists, allowing her cheeks to be pecked and pulled and enjoying as much attention as the monuments. And my daughter is a girlie sort of girl. Her dress that day was pink trousers, pink T-shirt with a sparkly pink ice-cream motif, pink shoes with Velcro buckles made to look like pink daisies and a pink sun hat. She was carrying a pair of pink felt rabbits and a large pink plastic baby doll dressed in pink pyjamas. When one young honeymoon couple asked how old my 'son' was, I corrected them apologetically and mused that perhaps her short blonde mop made her a little tomboyish. When an older couple asked the same question, I told myself that to Indian eyes, we Caucasians probably all looked the same. But by the time we arrived at the converted *haveli* where we were spending the night and the urbane receptionist smiled indulgently at the little figure peeping over the desk and asked how old 'he' was, I was becoming a little indignant.

'He's a girl,' I said. 'I mean, she's a girl.'

'I'm a big girl,' corrected my daughter.

'Look at all the pink,' I said.

'Peacock,' said my daughter. 'Bunny. Doggy.'

'Oh,' said the receptionist. 'Sorry.' Then she brightened: 'Maybe a son next time.'

Sociologists and economists agree that how a country treats its women is an acid test of its development. Emancipation is an indicator of progress and also, with the potential to double the workforce, a crucial ingredient for growth. Rajasthan is one of India's poorer states. It is also one of the worst for female infanticide and foeticide. In spring 2002, floods in a Rajasthani village were traced to a drain which, behind a backstreet abortion clinic, had been blocked with a pile of discarded foetuses. (This was not an isolated incident. I read about several more such mass burials of foetuses and in July 2007 the owner and manager of a clinic in Nayagarh, eastern India, were arrested after the remains of thirty-seven newborn girls and foetuses were found stuffed into a disused well.) Meanwhile, newspapers fill their pages daily with tales of fatal and illegal late terminations by doctors making fortunes by breaking a law banning them from telling expectant couples the sex of their babies – and offering discreet abortions if the child is a girl – and the laments of young Indian men about the lack of women. One mainstream newspaper even argued that female infanticide had an upside: with women scarce, the laws of economics meant dowries came down.[15]

In places like Rajasthan, the ratio between women and men is now so skewed that there are only 750 women to every 1,000 men. The nationwide average is 927 to 1,000. In a nation of more than a billion people, that translates to a shortfall of about 40 million women. That's equal to the world HIV/AIDS population. It's like missing Spain. On that trip to Rajasthan, my wife was pregnant again and we'd become accustomed to other mothers praying for a boy on our behalf. Our receptionist and fellow travellers, I now realize, were just being polite.

Why does everyone want boys? First and foremost because of tradition. The son and heir is the focus of an Indian family's pride, and the cost of a dowry for daughters – which in the consumer age can include a house for the newlyweds and cars, holidays and any number of TVs, DVD players and electric rice-cookers for the groom's family – can be ruinous. Also, there's a simple economic imperative: boys earn.

But in new India, you'd expect the situation to be changing. It is – for the worse. Before India began opening up in 1991, the nationwide gender imbalance was 945 to 1,000. The ratio had deteriorated as India had developed. The gender gap is at its widest in the country's richest state (Punjab, where it is as low as 740), the richest communities (Sikhs give birth to 786 girls for every 1,000 boys, Jains 870 to 1,000) and the more prosperous cities (the city average is 903 to 1,000). A study by the Christian Medical Association carried out at government and private hospitals patronized by the affluent in New Delhi found that after giving birth to one girl, 50 per cent of mothers will abort a second female foetus. The figure rises to 70 per cent for families who have two girls. A national study of 1.1 million families by Prabhat Jha of St Michael's Hospital, University of Toronto, and Rajesh Kumar of the Postgraduate Institute of Medical Education and Research, Chandigarh, 'conservatively' estimated that around 500,000 babies are lost every year in India because of abortion determined by gender. In an accompanying article in the medical journal the *Lancet*, Shirish Sheth of Breach Candy Hospital, Bombay, described the practice as the 'female infanticide of the past refined and honed to a fine skill in this modern guise'. Rich families were using technology to suppress women more efficiently. Modernization was meant to emancipate women. In India, it was killing them.

There were some even darker traditions making a comeback in the new India. In the summer of 2002, I read about a rash of ritual killings in northern and eastern India. I travelled to the eastern village of Atapur in Jharkhand. At the police station, the officers showed me the confession they had extracted from Khudu Karmakar.

Karmakar was a Tantric sorcerer. His statement indicated his plan was to paralyse a village girl, Manju Kumari, he had picked out for the purpose with tranquillizers, but not knock her out. For the magic to work, for Karmakar to gain the awesome powers he expected from Manju's death, she had to be a willing victim, or as close as Karmakar could make her. She had to know what was happening, watch him, watch the knife, and not stop it. In the event, Karmakar's concern that she still be conscious led him to underestimate the dose. Manju screamed and struggled, and he had to gag her and hold her down. Then by the light of an oil lamp in his shrine, the thirty-five-year-old former blacksmith wafted incense over the fifteen-year-old virgin and tore off her blue silk skirt and pink T-shirt. He shaved her head and body hair, sprinkled holy water from the Ganges on her and rubbed her with ghee, the Indian cooking fat. As midnight approached, Karmakar began chanting mantras to the goddess Kali and then in ritual order sawed off her hands, her breasts and her left foot. He placed them in front of a photograph of a Kali idol taken at the eastern temple of Tarapith which formed the centre of the shrine. Police investigators say the pools of blood soaked into the ground and spatters across the walls suggest that, after five terrifying hours of captivity, Manju bled to death in two or three merciful minutes.

Karmakar was picked up the day Manju's body was discovered and less than forty-eight hours after her death. He'd made a poor attempt to hide what he'd done. After storing the corpse in his shrine for twenty-four hours – Karmakar deemed the day after the killing, a Saturday, inauspicious for disposing of a body – he dumped her in a field fifteen minutes' walk from his home. A farmer soon found it. Nearby the Jharkhand state police also discovered a tin of vermilion *tikka* forehead marker, incense packets and strands of ritual Hindu thread. The villagers immediately accused Karmakar. Not only had his wife and daughter laughed at Manju's family's frantic efforts to find the girl the day before, Karmakar had been saying for months that his spiritual development demanded a human sacrifice. He had made two previous attempts to kidnap children and rumours had circulated for years about two mutilated, unidentified bodies that had turned up in the area.

The Indian press largely ignored the story, giving it a single paragraph if they carried it at all. But similar brief stories in back issues confirmed the idea that while human sacrifice (*nara bali*) had declined from its heyday 150 years ago, when children were regularly offered to Kali in temples across the country, it was still occurring. That year (2002) alone, a twenty-four-year-old woman named Bhagyamma hacked her three-year-old son to death in the south-eastern state of Andhra Pradesh in January after a Tantric advised her she would be rewarded with incomparable earthly riches. In February, two men identified as Satya and Prem Kumar beheaded a woman in the far eastern state of Tripura saying an unnamed god told them in a dream to sacrifice three women, in return for which he would lead them to hidden treasure. And in May, police dug up the remains of two sisters, aged eighteen and thirteen, in Vasudeopur in Bihar. Their father ran them through with a ceremonial sword before dismembering them and offering their limbs to Kali. In nearby Mahauli village the same week, a forty-year-old man was beaten to death for running into a crowded marketplace with a ritual spear, yelling Kali's name, and stabbing a tea seller in the head, killing him.

It was hard to believe what was happening. The countryside was mired in medieval poverty and superstition was certainly alive and well in India. But this was still the twenty-first century. Villagers no longer needed chicken entrails to predict the weather – they had TV. The eminent Indian sociologist K.S. Singh provided some answers. In the 1960s, Singh had documented practices such as *ogra*, the sacrifice of a child by farmers to 'fertilize' the land with human blood. That was almost unheard of today, he said. But human sacrifice was experiencing a revival. As with the rise in female infanticide, it wasn't in spite of modernization. It was because of it. 'Tantra's back and it's because of the advent of consumerism,' he said. 'People want the good things in life. Unlike other belief systems, Tantra was never abstemious. It sees money, meat, drink, sex and power as tools for advancement. Even businessmen and politicians are thronging Kali's temples. Everybody's using it to try and get ahead.'

Pure Tantra does not call for an orgy of horror and sacrifice. The idea is that by indulging and confronting the five extreme human experiences – meat, fish, alcohol/drugs, aphrodisiacs and sex – the Tantric exhausts his appetites, frees himself of worldly concerns and achieves unity with Kali. The trouble is many Tantrics get stuck on the indulgence. In the 1960s 'God men' gurus discovered that establishing hedonistic ashrams and sprinkling them with a little spirituality was an ideal way to attract moneyed Western hippies.

Today, Tantrics are once again offering a short cut to the good life on earth. Like Singh, other experts agreed that Tantra was on the rise and that its revival was linked to consumerism. If you add in the inequality of India's boom and lack of social mobility, it made macabre sense that people were turning to magic when nothing else would work. Said Ipshita Roy, author and expert on sorcery: 'It's got nothing to do with real mysticism or spiritualism. It comes down to pure and simple greed. It's quick-fix, fast-food spiritualism for the consumer age, and the results are often just as disastrous.' Sociologist Ashis Nandy says he too had noticed that disparity was firing a revival in dark spiritualism. 'You see your neighbour doing well, above his caste and position, and someone tells you to get a child and do a secret ritual and you can catch up. It's a pathological means of making extra money.'

Progress is always messy. During the Industrial Revolution, starvation and forced migration halved Ireland's population.

Russia, pre-Revolution, had the fastest economic growth in Europe, even as peasants starved and a proletariat grew up violent in the cities. But it's difficult to find greater inequality than in India today, where it's possible simultaneously for two men, Lakshmi Mittal and Mukesh Ambani, to become two of the world's five richest men, and for thousands to starve to death.

What normally stops inequality from cleaving emerging nations in two is a middle class. It acts as a buffer between rich and poor and becomes the engine of further progress. In nineteenth-century Europe, the arrival of merchants and businessmen signalled the dawning of a new era: the decline of monarchy and aristocracy, the maturing of democracy and a blossoming of civil society, from newspapers to stock exchanges and universities. Equality of opportunity replaced equality of misery.

So it's a body blow to India's prospects to discover that the country is largely missing a middle class. Not entirely, sure. In the bigger southern cities, there are entrepreneurs and office workers that represent the new India. These are the '5.2 per cent over $4,400' who man the generic drug manufacturers, answer telephones for British power companies or animate *Lord of the Rings*. But in the teeming north or the southern farming belt or the eastern tea estates or the western deserts, in the slums of Bombay or Delhi or the rural wastes of Bihar (pop. 88 million) or Uttar Pradesh (pop. 166 million), you see no middle-class Indians. There are no call centres, no biotech labs, no Internet, no new housing colonies, no McDonald's, not even a good road. Here is where most of India lives. And here the Indian middle class is a myth.

Propping up that myth is another illusion. This is the idea that India has a limitless supply of well-educated English-speaking technology-literate graduates. It's an easy conclusion to draw – there are hundreds of thousands of young Indians who do fit that description. But in terms of a nation the size of India, they are next to insignificant. Government surveys consistently reveal 41 per cent of Indians are illiterate, 96 per cent don't speak English and 98 per cent have never used a computer. Outside the elite schools, Indian primary and secondary education is poor quality, badly funded and sparsely attended: pressured into work by the need to earn, most Indians never complete high school. Higher education is also poor. A 2005 study by McKinsey found only 25 per cent of Indian engineering graduates and 15 per cent of finance and accounting graduates left college with an education sufficient to qualify them to work for multinational companies. Achin Vanaik, professor of International Relations and Global Politics at Delhi University, says many degrees are not worth the paper they are written on. 'We have a significant increase in graduate unemployment – to 5 million today,' he says. 'Most of them are from all kinds of colleges which are not particularly good.' Joe Sigelman, co-founder of Office Tiger, one of India's premier back office firms, confirms Vanaik's assessment. 'For every person we hire,' he says, 'there are thirty-nine we reject. The biggest thing standing between India and greatness is intellectual skill.' Disappointed by the standard of his applicants, Sigelman is now expanding beyond India, to the Philippines and Sri Lanka and up to eight other countries.

The lack of a middle class leaves a situation ripe for unrest. Sanyah Bhandarkar of Rothschild's (India) reckons the country can avoid 'real trouble' only if it continues to grow at 8 per cent or more a year. 'Any less, any shock or depression for a couple of years that means people's expectations are not met, and it would be a disaster,' he says. Vanaik says the experience of Latin America and its history of socialist revolution shows that when those who expect a middle-class life are let down, there's turbulence. 'Then you have explosions,' he says. The editor of the *Asian Age* newspaper, M.J. Akbar, agrees. 'The way to assuage despair is with economic growth with social justice,' he says. 'But economic growth without social justice becomes counter-productive and explosively dangerous. When anger mixes with despair, you get criminality, rebellion and terrorism. India is in social change. And violence always accompanies that in India.'

For hundreds of millions of Indians, prosperity remains a dream. That's where Bombay gets its nickname, *Mayanagri*. Sanskrit scholars will tell you that *Maya* has several meanings. It means hope, yes. But it also means fantasy, illusion. In other words, dreaming is fine. But sooner or later, you wake up.

PART TWO

FIVE FIGHTS

CHAPTER 4

CRIME WARS

In the summer of 2001, in my last few months in Hong Kong, I came across reports of the execution of thirteen Chinese pirates in Shanwei, up the coast from Shenzhen. What caught my attention were the pictures. Taken moments before they went before the firing squad, the pirates were laughing, joking and falling down drunk as they climbed the steps to the execution grounds. In his book, *Blood Brothers: Crime, Business and Politics in Asia*, veteran Asia correspondent Bertil Lintner described how one twenty-five-year-old pirate Yang Jingtao was 'jumping up and down in his rattling chains . . . [and] led the chorus with a boisterous rendition of Ricky Martin's theme song for the 1998 World Cup, ironically called "The Cup of Life": "Go, go, go! Olé, olé, olé . . ." Before Yang and his fellow convicts had time to sober up, they were trucked away to an open field on the outskirts of Shanwei, forced to kneel in a row, and dispatched one by one by an executioner with a Kalashnikov – one bullet through the back of the head, one bullet through the heart . . . Then, in the Chinese tradition, the families were billed for the price of the bullets.'[1]

The newspapers explained piracy worldwide was on the rise. They quoted several trade and security experts expressing fears for the impact on global trade. Policing the oceans was next to impossible, they said. The potential for catastrophe, should the pirates ever hire themselves to terrorists, was real.

The notion of modern-day bands of seafaring brigands seemed a little far-fetched. But the papers were right. The International Maritime Bureau's Piracy Reporting Centre in Kuala Lumpur confirmed that, as they have for centuries, countless groups of privateers operate throughout the vast South East Asian archipelago, raiding ships from Malaysia and the Philippines in the north to the waters off Australia in the south. And as global trade increased, so did the piracy that fed off it. There are more than 200 pirate attacks every year, according to the Bureau.[2] Most are clustered around bottlenecks in global shipping, such as in the waters off Nigeria, teeming with oil tankers, or off Somalia, full of cargo vessels heading to and from the Suez Canal. The thirteen executed pirates had operated off Taiwan, where they hit trade from China. Disguising themselves as Chinese customs officers, they boarded the Hong Kong-owned *Chang Sheng* cargo ship on 9 November 1998, bludgeoned the twenty-three-man crew to death, dumped their bodies at sea and sold the ship for $300,000.

According to the Bureau, the most consistently dangerous waters in the world were off northern Indonesia, the Straits of Singapore.[3] Two in five of all pirate attacks take place here – around one a week – for a simple reason. It is Asia's gateway to the world and the aorta of the global economy: more trade passes through the narrows between Malaysia and Indonesia than any other sea-lane. This was taking the criminality and worker protests I'd seen in Shenzhen to the next level. Not so much demonstrating against the unequal benefits of development and trying to reform it, as simply attacking globalization itself.

The pirates base themselves on an island called Babi, meaning 'pig', on the northern tip of Indonesia. I telephoned *Time*'s stringer in Jakarta, Zamira Loebis, and asked her to help set up a meeting. A week later I was on a plane to Singapore.

Hopping out of a stubby speedboat and strolling down a shaky wooden pier in flip-flops and Hawaiian shorts, the pirate king reels off the history of the other boats tied to the jetty. The boats are all small, weathered and unremarkable but for the monstrous twin engines weighing on their sterns. There's something else they have in common. 'That one's stolen from Melaka,' says the pirate king. 'That's taken from Singapore. That one was picked up from Malaysia.'

We come to a cavernous bungalow on spindly stilts over the black mud shallows. A sign reads *Skydog Karaoke and Lounge*. Next to it is the *Babi Island Billiards Hall*, a dimly lit shack with four new-looking tables. A plump prostitute calls out to the pirate king from a window in the *Skydog*. From the billiards hall, a group of boys watch us pass. 'You going out? You need anybody?' they ask. The pirate king ignores them, pulls out a mobile phone and stabs at it with a finger ringed with a gold and diamond band. We round a corner to find three middle-aged men huddled over beer cans at a battered table, hiding from the midday sun under a corrugated overhang. One looks up and breaks into a gold-plated grin. 'Hey!' he hails the pirate king warmly. 'I thought you were dead!'

Two full plastic bags of cold cans of beer arrive at the pirates' table. All four men are modern-day pirate chiefs and headquarter their crews on Babi. The town is a waterside refuge of stilted shacks, within sight of the Singapore skyline, whose 1,000 or so souls get by almost solely on piracy and prostitution. Such a small place breeds close bonds. The pirates share raids, money and women. Like the pirate king, the men at the table are short, middle-aged and tanned. Their wiry arms speak of physical work, their beer bellies of the bars and nightclubs it pays for. The pirate king checks with a burly buddy at the table to see if he has removed a forearm tattoo. The pair had the same insignia drawn on to their arms with a third friend years ago, when all three were in a gang of teenage muggers. A few weeks before the third man had been shot and killed holding up a truck. The police had announced they were looking for other men with the same tattoo.

As 'Feelings' starts up on the jukebox, the men start trading stories about the old days. Remember the time they boarded a US Navy warship by mistake? Or the Russian tanker that turned out to be full of guns? Or the time when one group boarded a ship to find a hijack by another group already in progress? They drink hard, each man handed a fresh can as he drains his last. One of the four, a grey-haired man, teases the pirate king for leaving one of his crew to guard his speedboat at the jetty. 'What are you so worried about?' he laughs, a gold watch jiggling on his wrist. 'If it gets stolen, we'll just take another one.' Grey hair has an unnerving schizophrenic manner, guffawing uproariously one moment and turning bitter and narrow-eyed the next. You've got to expect a few mood swings, the pirate king explains later, from a guy who lost a testicle sliding down a boarding ladder.

The pirate king claims there used to be times when, on a moonless night, he and his crew would routinely hit fifteen cargo ships before dawn. But he says he has largely given up on hit-and-runs. There is still traffic enough – 300 ships a day pass through the four-kilometre-wide east–west bottleneck of international waters between Singapore and Babi. But these days, because of the pirates' notoriety, fewer and fewer ships carry cash.

More lucrative and safer, says the pirate king, is mercenary work. Nearly all the Babi pirates are *bajing loncat* ('jumping squirrels'), men from Palembang in southern Sumatra who over the centuries developed an unrivalled reputation for hijacking and robbery, on land or sea. Among *bajing loncat*, the Babi pirates represent the elite, specialist raiders hired to steal mammoth 100 metre, 10,000-ton ships and their entire cargo. For as little as $5,000, up to eight masked men will drive a speedboat under a tanker's arched stern and scramble aboard using 20-metre hooked bamboo poles, known as *satang*. After emptying the safe and taking whatever they find – computers, watches, refrigerators ('shopping', the pirate king shrugs) – they hand the ship over to a crew of professional seamen waiting in a second boat. The whole operation can be over inside ten minutes. The men still carry machetes, cutlasses and home-made samurai-style swords like their forefathers before them. 'You don't need guns,' smiles the pirate king. 'Indonesians are very skilful with knives.'

A fellow buccaneer, a captain of one of the seamen crews, explains that he turned to piracy in the late 1970s. He reckons he has taken twenty ships since. He and his crew are from the coastal villages of the Sangir Islands, thousands of kilometres east of Babi near the southern tip of the Philippines. Just as Palembang is famous for *bajing loncat*, Sangir is renowned for producing South East Asia's best sailors. The squat fifty-four-year-old captain has been arrested twice, once in Malaysia when he was busted for smuggling bales of Cambodian marijuana, and once in China. Both times he was released after his bosses intervened and bribed the authorities – though he also suspects his employers arranged both arrests so they could cut his fee. Choosing who to work for is a delicate business, he says. The world of piracy is not noted for its trustworthiness. 'Sometimes we just take the front money and disappear,' he laughs.

As the captain waits for his next sortie, he tells the story of his last outing. A crew member on a Thai palm-oil tanker gave him the layout of the ship and an exact time and place to meet it in the Singapore Straits. The captain contacted the boss of a Hong Kong Triad who agreed to pay the captain and his crew $9,000 up front, and another $50,000 on delivery of the stolen ship. The Triad also hired a crew of *bajing loncat* to accompany the captain and arranged fake papers for the ship under a new name.

On the agreed night, two speedboats raced west out of Babi. After an hour or two, they cut the engines and waited, bobbing in the swell of passing vessels. The captain waited with his men in the second boat. In the first, the boarders assembled their *satang*, lashing together lengths of bamboo with twine. They used more twine to make sword belts and rudimentary handcuffs. In the early hours, the Thai tanker appeared as a collection of bright lights on the horizon. The two teams waited for it to pass. Then they slipped on their balaclavas, fired up the outboards and circled around behind. As they approached, crashing over the bow wave and skidding on the bubbling sea thrown up by the tanker's immense screws, two men from the first team stood and lifted their poles, as though for a medieval joust. As soon as they hooked the side of the ship, they began climbing, the speedboat pilot steadily accelerating to keep the poles steady.

In seven seconds, the first man was over the side and crouching by the rail. Five men followed and headed straight to the bridge. They took the captain and pilot hostage and cut the ship's communications, before assembling the rest of the crew. The sailors' hands were slipped behind their backs into the twine handcuffs, which were then looped around their necks, rigged to tighten if they struggled. The ship's captain's hands were tied in front so he could open the safe. The boarders communicated in rudimentary English to disguise their origins. 'Those guys are the pirate experts,' says the captain. 'We call them the *Kopassus* (the name for Indonesian army commandos). They signal to us that it's OK and we take over.'

At daybreak, with the boarding crew long gone, the captain and his men dropped the former crew with food and water on a deserted island off the east Sumatran coast near Kuala-tungkal. They also left their inside man so as not to identify him. Then they headed north-west, back past Singapore, skirting Melaka and Medan. Over the next seven days, while the captain took care of navigation, the crew of fourteen worked on the boat, repainting the entire ship and plastering a new English name over the Thai lettering on the bow. Off the Maldives, they rendezvoused with another tanker and the Hong Kong crime lord. The palm oil was pumped into the second boat. Then an auction was held at sea for the stolen ship, a Filipino outbidding a Thai buyer with an offer of $100,000. Their work over, the captain and his crew collected their pay-off and caught a ride on the stolen ship to Manila. From there, they flew to Jakarta and split up, laying low for a year before returning to Babi. The captain has no idea where the palm oil was sold, but says shipowners often organize pirate attacks as part of an insurance fraud. Only the Chinese bosses know all the details, he says.

The pirates' open and unpunished presence has led to accusations of complicity with the Indonesian security forces. 'I don't think there is much doubt that they are involved,' says ship security expert Trevor Hollingsbee. Arthur Bowring, director of the Hong Kong Ship-owners Association, has a more worrying analysis. 'Some small-scale military people may be involved. But there is also a theory that the Indonesian government is tolerating or encouraging piracy to get aid for better boats and equipment,' he says. 'Certainly they don't seem to be doing anything to stop it.' He proposes a draconian solution: sanctions against Jakarta. Indonesian patrolmen posit a third culprit, Singapore, for what they say is a lack of cooperation. Despite its squeaky clean reputation, they claim, Singapore's patrols never follow up on their alerts when a pirate they are pursuing slips into Singaporean waters. They add that the city-state, a hub of legal global trade, is also a transit point for smuggled oil, wood and rattan.

So why were there sword-wielding pirates, living in desert island lairs, in the twenty-first century? It was partly about tradition. The pirate king said: 'Our culture is a water culture. There have been pirates here since the twelfth or thirteenth century.' The captain added: 'For us the sea is a huge source. For fish, but also for life. It's the way our people have always lived. My grandfather and great-grandfather before him. And my son, too.'

But the revival of piracy was mainly about survival. The Indonesian economy never matched its Asian neighbours for growth. Economic growth in the Philippines was also concentrated on the cities and the ruling elite. 'The salaries for sailors have gotten lower and lower,' said the captain. 'It's just getting more and more difficult to get legitimate work.' Their choice was a life of subsistence poverty, or a life of crime, ripping off the fat riches that passed daily through the Singapore Straits. They could have begged. Instead, they stole from the global economy that had shut them out.

As I had suspected, this was taking things a step further than Shenzhen. The pirates rejected the idea that they could ever earn a legitimate living. They rejected the place they had been given in the world, and anyone who went along with that consensus. Rather than try to subvert the legitimate economy as criminals, or change it from within as reformers, they had chosen to live outside it, as outlaws.

It's true that piracy is not war. There are few deaths, and while armies sometimes try to hunt down the pirates, pitched battles are rare: pirates tend to cut and run. But the pirates are rebels, rivals to the state. The cat-and-mouse games pirates play with coastguards in Asia and US warships off Africa resemble a guerrilla campaign. And pirates share other traits with revolutionaries. They feel excluded from the mainstream; they target big business; and they'll kill to even the score. Pirates were an assault on the whole idea of society, as Cicero recognized two millennia ago when he defined pirates in Roman law as *hostis humani generis* – 'enemies of the human race'. And globalization, with all the riches it flashed before them, was an opportunity to grow.

Globalization was forging other intersections between criminality and rebellion. In December 2006, I took a new job with *Time*, Africa bureau chief, based in Cape Town. Among foreign correspondents, Cape Town has a reputation as a soft posting – a holiday destination of vineyards and whale watching that was not so much part of Africa as a genteel European outpost tacked discreetly on its southern tip. After five years in India, it was certainly an improvement. The air was clean, the roads were good and there was wine and fresh fish in air-conditioned supermarkets.

But Cape Town also had the worst violent crime in southern Africa. Fifty-two people are murdered every twenty-four hours in South Africa – compared to two in England and Wales, which have a similar population – an annual murder rate of 43.1 per 100,000 people. Added to that each year are 200,000 robberies, 55,000 rapes, and 500,000 cases of assault, serious assault and attempted murder. That violence peaks in the Western Cape, of which Cape Town is the capital, at 60 murders per 100,000 people a year – or 91 per 100,000 in 1999–2000[4] – compared to 5.7 per 100,000 in the US. Many of the deaths are from violent robberies. Others are the result of the gang wars that rage on the Cape Flats.

The Flats is the name given to a sprawling settlement of ramshackle tin huts and ghetto shacks built on the sandy Cape estuary by blacks and coloureds when the apartheid government threw them out of the city. The Flats are home to 2 million people and 280 gangs, whose members number 100,000 people. Scaling up the murder rate to the number of people who lived on the Flats, I worked out that 1,200 people were murdered each year in a place which, with the traffic flowing, it took me ten minutes to cross in a car.

It escapes no one that these same cauldrons of violent crime were once the furnaces of the anti-apartheid revolution. A little more than a decade after the end of apartheid, the new government is sending the same riot police in the same monstrous armoured trucks into the same townships. Hotbeds of insurrection have become hotbeds of crime.

So what had happened to the new South Africa? Answer:

Mandela's dream – the Rainbow Nation – was being starved. The post-apartheid government argued it inherited a grossly iniquitous country, and that was true. But it was also true that the African National Congress (ANC) government of Mandela and his successor, Thabo Mbeki, had proved a disappointment. Unemployment was 40 per cent nationwide[5], 46 per cent in the Flats and 61 per cent for the under thirties who lived there. Townships struggled with refuse collection, medical clinics and toilets, even water and electricity. In November 2007, the South African Institute of Race Relations survey said 4.2 million people were living on $1 a day in 2005, up from 1.9 million in 1996, two years after the end of apartheid. Thabo Mbeki's aides insisted poverty was falling, but conceded inequality had also risen. 'While in real and absolute terms, the income of the poor is improving, this hasn't been at the pace of the richest of the population,' said Joel Netshitenzhe of the Presidential Policy Coordination and Advisory Service in June 2007. 'Inequality has worsened as a result.' Millions of poor black and coloured South Africans could be forgiven for wondering exactly how the end of apartheid changed their lives.

This was partly because the ANC was taking time to acquire the skills that would transform it from guerrilla force into a government. Partly it was because the ANC had embraced globalization and the free market without ensuring the poor shared in the benefits. It staged some market interventions, such as a programme called Black Economic Empowerment, which forced all but the smallest South African companies to hire blacks to senior positions. But without an accompanying drive to spread the wealth, the most obvious effect of that was to make billionaires of a small ANC elite, who set about corralling the most lucrative directorships. Meanwhile, out in the townships, economic apartheid persisted.

That was why the violence also continued. Poverty by itself does not make a man become a criminal. After all, destitution is far worse in India or China than South Africa. But relative poverty – missing out, the burden of unfulfilled expectations – can. 'There isn't as much support for the proposition that poverty causes crime in the international criminological literature as you might expect,' writes South African Antony Altbeker in his 2007 study of his country's crime, *A Country at War with Itself*.[6] 'However, there is a much stronger conviction among academics that inequality causes crime; that the difference between what the rich and poor earn matters more than the depth of poverty.'[7]

South Africa had one of the steepest Gini coefficients in the world. And inequality had worsened since apartheid. By making disparity a global norm, globalization was aggravating that divide. The violence came from the resulting frustration. As any policeman can tell you, a career thief will try to work with the minimum of violence. Violence increases the time spent at the scene, decreases the chances of a clean getaway, encourages the police to try harder to catch the perpetrator and raises the severity of the punishment if he is caught. But young South African muggers and burglars don't just rob for the money. Many also beat, kill and rape. Of the 200,000 robberies every year, more than half – 126,000 – were classed as 'aggravated', meaning the victim was also assaulted. The anger that ignites South Africa's violent crime is the same spark that starts political rebellion. In a society where violence until very recently was part of the grammar of politics, it can still be rationalized as avenging inequality. At the outset of his presidency, if not in his later years, when he retreated in a paranoid denial, Mbeki was haunted by the severity of the problem. 'What happens to a dream deferred?' Mbeki, quoting the poet Langston Hughes, asked South Africa's parliament in a debate on nation-building and reconciliation in 1998. 'It explodes.'[8] South Africa's rampant violence is political crime, revenge on the lucky by the less fortunate.

On 18 October 2007, that point was made with forceful, tragic irony when the international reggae star Lucky Dube, forty-three, was shot and killed in front of his two teenage children in Johannesburg during an attempted car-hijacking. In his eerily prescient 2001 song, 'Crime and Corruption', Dube had demanded the government protect its people from the surging crime wave:

> *'Is it the bodyguards around you?*
> *Is it the high walls where you live?*
> *Or is it the men with the guns around you twenty-four hours a day that make you ignore the crying of the people?*
> *Do you ever worry about your house being broken into?*
> *Do you ever worry about your car being taken away from you in broad daylight down Highway 54?*
> *Do you ever worry about your wife becoming the woman in black?*
> *Do you ever worry about leaving home and coming back in a coffin with a bullet through your head?'*

As well as helping create the circumstances for a crime wave, globalization had a hand in shaping the identity of the gangs on the Flats. They drew their income from the international trade in methamphetamine, a drug known locally as *tik*. And they aped US gang culture, dressing in the same baggy jeans, outsize sports shorts and sneakers, listening to hip hop, pimping their rides and giving their gangs English names, such as 'The Americans' and 'The Hard Livings Kids'. In time, gang bosses became the closest the Flats had to political leaders. At the January 1999 trial of Rashied Staggie, then head of the Hard Livings, the *Mail & Guardian* newspaper reported that women from his local community shouted: 'Viva Staggie . . . He's God's gift. He's the people's hero.'[9] When he was murdered by a vigilante group, a huge mural was painted near his former home that, according to the paper, adopted 'the heroic realist style favored by communists to portray idealized peasants'.

Unlike piracy, this is war. There are frequent skirmishes and shoot-outs with police and the security services. The weaponry is twenty-first century. And the death toll is higher than many out-and-out conflicts. Around 220,000 people were murdered in South Africa in the ten years to 2007, four times greater than the number of Americans killed during the Vietnam War. As Altbeker wrote: 'Pretty much every nation on the planet outside North America spent some portion of the 20th century on its knees, the victim of catastrophic violence directed either by local tyrants or foreign overlords. And yet only a handful has levels of violence that even approach ours.'

One of the most serious eruptions of violence came in 2005 when the Flats broke out in riots. Hundreds of residents battled riot police armed with rubber bullets, tear gas and stun grenades. In Khayelitsha, a Flats neighbourhood that was scene of much of the trouble, Nqabisa Ntete, a protest leader, insisted to a reporter from London's *Daily Telegraph* that the rioters' motivations were political. 'We are not criminals,'

Ntete told the paper. 'But we have no houses, no toilets, no water, and no other way to attract the attention of government.'[10] While excusing his government of blame, President Mbeki recognized the roots of the discontent, and its gravity. 'The riots seek to exploit the class and nationality fault lines we inherited from our past,' Mbeki told parliament. 'If ever they took root, gaining genuine popular support, they would pose a threat to the stability of democratic South Africa.' Altbeker argues that the danger has been exacerbated by the ANC's pursuit of free trade and economic growth at the expense of equality. 'A large body of economic thinking suggests that the widening of inequality is one of the inevitable by-products of rapid economic growth in developing countries,' he writes. 'There is no universal consensus on this, but if inequality really does tend to widen as economies expand, then we had better hope that it is not the principal reason we're so violent. Because it isn't going to get better soon.'

Globalization boosts crime. It eases travel restrictions, lowers borders, and integrates different criminal syndicates. Smuggling, the sex trade, piracy and drugs are thriving. For the professional criminal in the era of globalization, business is good.

But has globalization created new criminals? Is the new global inequality encouraging the poor to break the law to survive?

It's certainly prompting them to travel illegally. As inequality grows and travel becomes easier, illicit economic migration is becoming one of the defining forces of our age. From China, people-smuggling gangs known as 'snake-heads' bring mainland Chinese in containers and cargo trucks to Europe and America, for tens of thousands of dollars each. There are 12 million illegal migrants in the US, mostly Latin American. Africans die in their thousands every year trying to reach Europe's southern tip in overcrowded boats setting sail from Côte d'Ivoire and Senegal: in 2006 alone, 6,000 perished trying to sail to the Spanish Canary Islands. The best guess for the total number of migrants in the world, legal and illegal, is 200 million, or 3 per cent of the world's population.

Migrants, who tend to be young, dynamic and motivated, often thrive. As the *Economist* noted in a series of articles on migration on 5 January 2008: 'Around a third of Americans who won Nobel prizes in physics in the past seven years were born abroad. About 40 per cent of science and engineering PhDs working in America are immigrants. Around a third of Silicon Valley companies were started by Indians and Chinese.'[11] But the new arrivals are generally unwelcome. The authorities don't want the welfare burden. The residents want to protect their jobs. But for many of the new arrivals, going home is not an option. How to pay off the people traffickers? Why pay so much and risk death, only to turn around and go home? So they stay, and break more laws by working in the only jobs open to them, in the underpaid, untaxed grey economy.

The rise of this new illegal underclass has fuelled the rise of a new tide of xenophobia – an example of globalization, paradoxically, fuelling insular nationalism. Though many nationalist political parties have long existed on the fringe, recent years have seen a rise in popularity of groups such as the British National Party, Jean-Marie Le Pen's Front National in France, Pim Fortuyn's eponymous party in the Netherlands (whose popularity forced every Dutch political party to harden their views on immigration and integration after his assassination in 2002) and neo-Nazis in Germany. In October 2007, Switzerland's Swiss People's Party won the largest share of the vote – 29 per cent – and an extra seven seats in parliament in the country's general election after a campaign that featured a poster, described as 'openly racist' by the UN, which depicted three white sheep kicking a black sheep off the red and white Swiss flag. Xenophobia is raising its head even inside the smallest nations. Belgium now seems likely to split in two, into its Flemish and French-speaking Walloon parts. Bigger countries were hardly immune. The US, a nation built on immigration, is now more opposed to immigration than ever in memory. No leading candidate in the 2008 presidential election opposed the plan to fence off Mexico.

Asia and Africa are just as susceptible to this new tide of nationalism. Japan, China and South Korea stage regular diplomatic showdowns, fuelled by chauvinist anger at unrighted wrongs dating back to the Second World War and before. Anti-Chinese prejudice among Africans is becoming ever more prominent as Beijing moves to claim more and more of the continent's minerals, timber and oil.[12] And I'd seen myself how Africans were singled out – generally pulled out of line and interrogated – almost every time I'd seen one try to negotiate an Asian airport.

The 2007 Pew Global Attitudes Survey of 45,000 people found that while the world broadly supported the idea of free global trade, 'they are concerned about inequality, threats to their culture, threats to the environment and the threats posed by immigration . . . and there are signs that enthusiasm for economic globalization is waning in the West.' A majority in every place surveyed except Japan, South Korea and the Palestinian territories agreed immigration should be further restricted and controlled. In the US that figure was 75 per cent. Western Europe was in favour by a two-thirds to three-quarters majority. Most vehemently opposed to immigration was the developing world. Côte d'Ivoire, one of the departure points for Europe, scored highest at 94 per cent. On 89 per cent were Indonesia, Malaysia and South Africa.

Soon after arriving in Cape Town, I flew east along the southern coast to Port Elizabeth. My companion, French photographer Benedicte Kurzen, had found a story that not only undermined the notion of the Rainbow Nation, it made the whole idea of racial harmony through economic integration seem hopelessly optimistic.

It took us less than an hour to find a tiny room at the back of a Somali restaurant by Port Elizabeth's docks, where Abdi Maolin, twenty-six, had spent eleven months lying on a dirty mattress, eating kitchen leftovers and urinating through a tube attached to his bladder. Propping himself up on his elbows, Abdi dug out a police report that described how on 6 June 2006, six men stormed a Somali grocery shop where Abdi and his elder brother Mohammed worked. One shot Mohammed in the forehead, killing him. When Abdi ran, another shot him in the spinal chord, paralysing him from the chest down. Abdi said the killers wanted him to know the reason they had targeted him and his brother. They told him he was stealing South African land, taking South African jobs and money. They called him '*kuwara*' – nigger. 'But they were black,' said Abdi. 'They were African, like me.'

As the richest nation on the world's poorest continent, South Africa is a magnet for migrants. Like Western Europe or the US, the more foreigners arrive, the more xenophobia rises. South Africans commonly blame the millions of Zimbabweans, who fled their country's implosion for a new life in South Africa, for a recent surge in crime. Nigerians escaping violence and corruption in their homeland are viewed as an incoming race of homicidal drug dealers. They, and Congolese, Angolans, Rwandans and Burundians, have all been killed in race attacks in the last few years. Migration is fuelling a murder spree – and occasionally, as on May 2008, during which South Africans burned immigrants alive in the streets, and made refugees of tens of thousands – mass-mob violence.

But it is the Somalis – insular, entrepreneurial and, above all, prosperous – who bear the brunt of South Africa's new black-on-black prejudice. The Somali Association of South Africa says more than 400 Somalis were murdered in the country in the last decade. In three days over Christmas 2004, seven were killed. In 2006, thirty-two were murdered in and around Cape Town alone.[13] Indigenous South Africans have begun purging their neighbourhoods. In August 2005 in Cape Town, a crowd of 200 drove a small group of resident Somalis out of the seaside township of Masiphumele. The hate that cost Abdi his legs culminated in a riot on 12 February 2006 when a Somali shopkeeper fired on a robber and unwittingly killed a passer-by in Port Elizabeth, and a mob of South Africans went on the rampage through Somali parts of the city in retaliation, looting and burning eighty-nine stores.

The wounds of that riot were still fresh. As Abdi talked, a troupe of crippled young Somali men arrived. One had a cast on his left forearm, the bone shattered by a bullet. Another was on crutches, his right leg amputated after a knee-capping. A third had lost his left eye. Abdi's room began to feel like a battlefield ward. It would be a familiar scene in Somalia, by then in its sixteenth year of civil war. But it was to get away from that kind of horror, to forget how militiamen had killed their mother and another brother on their farm outside Baidoa in south central Somalia that Abdi and his brother left in 2004. 'We chose South Africa for a better life,' he says. 'We came here for peace. We got a war worse than Somalia.'

The irony of Abdi's tale was matched by the paradox of black-on-black racism. South Africa was meant to have banished xenophobia when it defeated apartheid in 1994. The country's 1997 constitution reads: 'We, the people of South Africa . . . believe that South Africa belongs to all who live in it, united in our diversity.' But Betri Jama, twenty-one, a Somali whose shop in Port Elizabeth was razed in February, told me those lofty words were empty. 'The same people who know oppression, who know dehumanization, they are the people who are oppressing us now.'

Kate Lefko-Everett is a Cape Town-based researcher for the South African Migration Project and has studied intra-African racism for years. 'It's so ironic,' she said. 'During apartheid, there were so many South African leaders who lived in exile, political refugees who were treated as heroes in foreign countries. Those countries are asking: "And now you treat us like this?" It's the continuation of the apartheid mindset.'

At a police station in Motherwell, the neighbourhood at the centre of anti-Somali violence, Captain André Beetge insisted the protection of Somalis was a priority. But he also reflected what Lefko-Everett described as a widespread official ambivalence towards refugees. 'Immigrants should expect a little difficulty from locals,' Captain Beetge declared. 'And maybe they should weigh up what they are experiencing in their own country with what they are experiencing here. If it really is that bad here, why don't they go back?'

Thirteen years after the end of apartheid, South Africa had learned two lessons from globalization. It didn't bring freedom to the poor; it brought an enduring inequality that fuelled continuing violence. And while apartheid made racist despots out of whites, globalization made bigots out of everybody.

CHAPTER 5

OIL AND WATER

Meeting the Movement for the Emancipation of the Niger Delta was tricky. Travelling into the Delta meant risking arrest by Nigeria's security forces. Even if you managed to evade the army and police, there were the rebels themselves. Since it was founded in 2005, MEND had made a speciality of kidnapping foreigners who worked for oil companies and associated businesses – abducting more than 200 by midway through 2007, and they weren't picky. On 20 October 2007, they took two children along with their French oil-worker parents. I regularly exchanged emails with a man who purported to be the leader of the biggest MEND faction, Jomo Gbomo, who, according to much of the African press, was also known as Henry Okah. Jomo was charming and articulate, and used to joke about the day his 'ugly mug' would appear in the pages of *Time*. But whenever I asked Jomo to help me get into the Delta, as a Briton working for an American magazine, he tried to discourage me. 'For pictures and information, why don't you try . . .' he would say, naming another journalist who had managed to get in and out safely. 'That reduces your risk.' Another time, when I told him an editor had forbidden me to go into the Delta out of concern for my safety, he replied: 'I'm kind of relieved. I was doing that with great reluctance.'

I continued to press him to arrange a trip. But in September 2007, Nigeria detained and accused of spying two German journalists, Florian Alexander Opitz and Andy Lehmann, who were making a documentary about the Niger Delta, and an American aid worker, Judith Asuni, who had assisted them. A few days later, news broke that Henry Okah had been arrested – on gun-running and money-laundering charges in Luanda, Angola. Jomo released a statement soon after denouncing the arrest and, to me, denied he was Henry Okah. He, Jomo, was like 'the elusive Scarlet Pimpernel'. Okah, on the other hand, 'is in a pit with the floor covered with faeces, maggots and urine – a torture chamber of the Angolan state for a crime that he has not yet been charged for.' For proof, he offered his ability to communicate. 'The jails there do not have the luxury of wireless Internet services and a laptop.'

The episode convinced Jomo that the 'Nigerian government is unwilling to justly resolve the crisis in the Niger Delta' and hardened his resolve. MEND was ditching nascent peace talks, he wrote, and returning to full-scale war. 'MEND is committed to the fight for justice and ultimately the emancipation of the people of the Niger Delta. We will not sit back and allow our birthright to be exchanged for a bowl of porridge. With effect from 12 midnight today, we will commence attacks on installations and abduction of expatriates. There will be no forewarning of these attacks.' I wrote to Jomo telling him I'd settle for an email interview after all.

Just as Indonesia's pirates and South Africa's criminals were taking the kind of rebellion I had seen in Shenzhen and investing it with a new, lethal intensity, so MEND was taking that fight a stage further, to an even more significant level.

MEND was a criminal organization. The Delta was lawless – gangs of gunmen roamed the creeks, and occasionally the streets of the regional capital Port Harcourt – and MEND was not above stealing from the government or auctioning oil-company workers for ransom. But since its formation in 2005, MEND had also been an explicitly political organization. It wasn't just stealing to get by, as on Babi or the Flats. It was fighting a war of liberation on behalf of the *Ijaw* tribesmen of the Delta, one of Nigeria's poorest regions. The riches buried under their own ancestral land were being extracted without their permission or consultation – and they weren't seeing a penny. 'Our objective is the complete control of our natural resources,' Jomo wrote.

So MEND had decided to take on the Nigerian government and the oil industry. By the by, that also meant taking aim at globalization. Oil was the ultimate global commodity. It could be extracted anywhere, transported anywhere and sold anywhere – it was, literally, the fuel of the world economy. The world's need for oil had spurred the shamefully iniquitous pattern of development in the Niger Delta. But the rebels could also use the world's thirst for oil to hurt it. In Nigeria, globalization had started a war. And, as though they were throwing a great engine into reverse, globalization was also the mechanism by which the rebels would disrupt the entire world. In April 2008, Jomo emailed to say, 'our sources inside the Shell Petroleum Development Company informed us today that the consequence of our [attacks] is the disruption of ... 500,000bpd (barrels per day) from the combined attacks.' That same week, oil hit an all time high of $120 a barrel.

*

Nigeria is part of a string of countries on the Gulf of Guinea, the shelf in Africa's west coast where the equator splits the meridian, and the new El Dorado for the oil industry. Hundreds of millions of years ago, Africa's movement north, and the resulting outflow of the Niger Delta, created a bank in the Gulf that extends several hundred miles offshore. Marine life and estuary debris was trapped in sand that became rock. Over time those hydrocarbons became oil. Today that means Africa holds a tenth of the world's oil reserves.

That figure belies the importance of West Africa as a source of energy. In 2005, writes Royal Institute of International Affairs associate Nicholas Shaxson in his ground-breaking 2007 book on African oil *Poisoned Wells*, the US imported more oil from Africa than the Middle East, and more from the Gulf of Guinea than Saudi Arabia and Kuwait combined.[1] Nigeria, the giant of the region, supplies 10 to 12 per cent of US oil imports alone. 'There's a huge boom across the region,' said Ernst and Young oil and gas specialist Erik Watremez at his office in Libreville, Gabon. 'Exploration, drilling, rigs, pipes. It's exploding.'

The importance of African oil will only rise. Daniel Yergin, chairman of Cambridge Energy Research Associates, said Africa is 'going to get hotter and hotter. It has the location and the resources; the technology is now there to develop them; and companies from all over the world want to be in on the action.' Increasing demand from India and China and worries over instability in the Middle East have fuelled higher oil prices – breaching $100 a barrel in the first few days of 2008, and nearing $150 a barrel in July of that year. Those high prices have precipitated a new scramble for energy – oil rigs now have to be rented a year in advance.

There are several reasons why the Gulf of Guinea is the focus of this new rush. African oil is high quality – light sweet crude with a low sulphur content that requires little refining to get it to the pump. Its geography is good: close to the US, cutting shipping costs to the world's biggest oil consumer, and mostly out to sea – no need here for tortuous talks in dozens of countries over pipelines that will be vulnerable to political interference. In addition, Africa's are among the last untapped fields in the world that not only accept outside companies, but need them – there are no African drillers. Moreover, the 10 per cent figure is being revised upwards. As John Ghazvinian, author of *Untapped: The Scramble for Africa's Oil*, writes: 'A third of the world's new oil discoveries since 2000 have taken place in Africa . . . There is now an almost contagious feeling in the oil industry that no one really knows just how much oil might be there, since no one's ever really bothered to check. All these factors add up to a convincing value proposition: African oil is cheaper, safer, and more accessible, and there seems to be more of it every day.'[2]

Most importantly, Africa is not the Middle East, Russia, or Venezuela. It may have a history of violence and chronic instability. But even those are easier to handle, particularly from offshore rigs, than Iranian nuclear brinkmanship, Iraqi civil war, or Venezuelan or Russian petro-nationalism – or, the ultimate oilman's crisis, Saudi hijackers attacking New York. Adds a senior American diplomat in the region: 'All that makes West Africa of great interest and great significance.' In 2002, the State Department declared West African oil a US 'strategic national interest', a designation that, under US law, allowed US military intervention to protect it.

Predictions are that the Gulf of Guinea will supply 20 to 25 per cent of total US imports by 2015–20.[3] But Americans are not alone in flocking to West Africa. Angola is now China's top oil supplier. The oil flow to Total's platforms off Gabon moves not just Gabon's financial markets, but France's too. Oilmen from countries as diverse as Russia, Japan and India are showing up in places like Equatorial Guinea, Cameroon, Chad – even perennial war zones like the Democratic Republic of Congo and Somalia. If oil stays above $50 a barrel, calculated Paul Lubeck, Michael Watts and Ronnie Lipshutz of the Centre for International Policy, the Gulf of Guinea will earn $1 trillion from oil between 2007 and 2020.[4] That's roughly double all the aid to Africa since independence.

That should be good news for some of the poorest countries in the world. Britain and Norway used North Sea oil to underwrite their welfare states. Small oil powers like Oman and Brunei used their reserves to catapult themselves out of subsistence living in a generation.

But what if oil fuels corruption rather than development? What if it creates the same noxious mix of great wealth, great poverty, grievance and instability as it has in the Middle East? Academics talk of the Resource Curse, the observable phenomenon that oil-rich countries grow more slowly, more corruptly, less equitably, more violently and with more authoritarian governments than others do. The authors of *Escaping the Resource Curse*, Jeffrey Sachs, Joseph Stiglitz and Macartan Humphreys, write that there is 'a strong association between resource wealth and likelihood of weak democratic development, corruption and civil war.'[5] Western oil workers in the Middle East lived in secure compounds with armed guards long before hijackers hit the Twin Towers. Isn't that same pattern developing in the Niger Delta today, where they live under armed guard for fear of kidnapping by MEND? Would West Africa's oil inevitably make it as unstable a place as the Middle East? 'West Africans have not blown up anything in New York,' admitted Shaxson.[6] Nonetheless, with its ability to affect gas and oil prices around the world, and the militancy it engenders, Shaxson argues West Africa's oil represents 'a threat to liberty, democracy and free markets around the world'.

Shaxson's analysis was predicated on Nigeria, the regional power. A senior American diplomat in the region agreed the country was 'one big problem'. Since independence in 1960, Nigeria has suffered a civil war that killed a million people, thirty years of military rule, four failed coups and six successful ones. The country's anti-corruption watchdog, the Economic and Financial Crimes Commission, says its rulers stole $400 billion between 1960 and 1999. Around 5 to 10 per cent of its oil production is stolen every year through 'illegal bunkering', tapping pipelines and filling plastic jerry cans with crude that are then shipped abroad.[7] The government does little to dispel the impression that it has an inexhaustible appetite for cash. In April 2007, Nigeria announced the sale of new drilling rights to forty-five exploration blocks, worth $500 million. Tony Chukwueke, head of the Department of Petroleum Resources, opened his presentation to bidders by saying: 'If you don't have money, please don't waste our time.'

Most Nigerians have become poorer since oil was first tapped. Two thirds of the country's 130 million people – one in seven of the total African population – live in abject poverty, a third is illiterate and 40 per cent have no safe water supply. They also endure the oil industry's huge environmental cost. More than 1.5 million tons of oil has been spilled in the Delta in fifty years of extraction which, together with the toxic effect of gas flaring, makes it one of the most polluted places on the planet.[8]

Jomo intended the world to feel the Delta's pain. He wanted to fire shocks down the same channels of global commerce that had brought oil companies to Nigeria. So he ordered kidnappings. And he ordered attacks on installations, which cut total Nigerian production by 25 per cent, or 600,000 barrels per day in 2007 and, as he boasted, by 500,000 barrels per day for Shell alone in 2008. That in turn raised prices. Oil hit $50 a barrel for the first time in 2005 when a Nigerian Muslim militant threatened to attack the industry. MEND's activities were continually cited as the oil price reached $100 in early 2008 and kept on rising.

In his email interview, Jomo set out his aims. MEND, he said, was fighting for 'the economic emancipation of the people of the Niger Delta, who have suffered decades of criminal neglect, brazen theft and damage to their environment by the Nigerian state and the oil majors. The problem in Nigeria has a very simple solution. Let the people of the Niger Delta control their resources. Our enemies comprise anyone, state or corporate body, standing in the way of that.' MEND felt forced to use 'attacks on oil facilities and hostage-taking' to draw attention to its plight and because 'the non-violent approach of Ken Saro-Wiwa* did not work. He paid

* Ken Saro-Wiwa was an author, television producer and environmentalist, the son of a chief of the Ogoni tribe, who also live in the Delta. He campaigned against the pollution caused there by multinational oil companies. He was executed by the Nigerian government in 1995.

the ultimate price for a peaceful approach. How do you dialogue with an arrogant people who are deaf at the same time? This time around, we are applying the pen, and the sword.' The state had met violence with violence, and Jomo predicted a long war. 'These soldiers not only raped our women and intimidated harmless civilians, they were involved in extra-judicial killing. They were untouchables. They earned the nickname "Kill and Go".'

I asked him whether he felt this was a war about globalization and whether he felt a sense of solidarity with other rebels worldwide. He replied that globalization helped lay bare what was happening in Nigeria, by revealing it to be part of a global pattern. 'Globalization exposes the divide between poor and rich nations.' He added MEND felt 'a kinship with the G8 protesters'.

Did that extend to groups like al-Qaeda? It did not, said Jomo. 'MEND and al-Qaeda are complete opposites. We are made up of Christians and do not take human lives indiscriminately.' Nevertheless, he agreed there were parallels between the origins of conflict in Nigeria and the Middle East. 'We see a parallel in the Middle East situation with the so called Sultans and Emirs in the northern desert of Nigeria.' Like political Islamists, he also drew on left-wing revolutionary thought. 'We have embraced the guerrilla tactics of the past from the communists in China, [for use] against better equipped armies. Our strategy is to be patient and continue to nibble on the enemy until we reach a point that we cannot be ignored.' Jomo saw no contradiction between this and his Christian faith. In fact, as with Islamist revolutionaries, religion added a righteous veneer to the MEND enterprise. 'Our success lies in God's approval. Believe it or not, we pray before embarking on an attack and thank God when the mission is a success.' Would Nigeria one day experience the kind of turmoil that had plagued the Middle East, as Shaxson had said? It would, predicted Jomo. 'I foresee a degeneration into the Middle East scenario if the situation is not properly handled today.'

MEND's success and the world's reliance on oil raised the possibility that one day Nigeria's rebels might find themselves fighting an international war. The US already has a military presence in the area – warships from the Sixth Fleet, based in Italy, regularly patrol off West Africa. 'I assured both the national security adviser and the defence minister that the US would do what it could to help Nigeria stamp out criminality in the Niger basin,' US Deputy Secretary of State John Negroponte said on a visit to Nigeria in November 2007. And while the American diplomat in the region said 'the notion that we're going to build a base [in West Africa] like Guantánamo or Diego Garcia is unrealistic,' he did admit the US was talking to several countries around the Gulf about a permanent US naval presence to assist with coastal security. (Liberia replied that it was open to hosting a US military command.) 'The question is how do you secure these shipping lanes, these oil platforms, in an area where the Africans themselves acknowledge they are virtually incapable of controlling their own coasts?'

Africa's bad experience of oil wasn't limited to Nigeria. To the south were a string of countries ruined by hydrocarbons. Oil propped up one of the world's most repressive regimes in Equatorial Guinea. In Angola, barely recovered from twenty-seven years of civil war, total oil revenue reached $10.5 billion in 2005 and powered real GDP growth to more than 35 per cent in 2007,[9] but the government elite kept the wealth to itself. The capital was still home to a slum of more than half a million people; 70 per cent of Angolans lived on $1 or less a day.[10] In 2007, the UN Development Programme listed it as 161st out of 171 countries for human development; in its survey of 128 countries for global competitiveness, the World Economic Forum places it flat last.

In Gabon, where the wells are slowly drying up after thirty years of production, oil's legacy was measured by a UNDP ranking of 124th, absolute poverty levels of 27 per cent[11] – and simultaneous thriving Hummer and BMW dealerships. Libreville is said to consume more champagne than Paris. Port Gentil, the tumbledown, potholed, malaria-ridden economic hub on the coast, is one of the world's most expensive cities. In 2007, a box of eggs, imported from France, cost $11. A small bunch of carrots was $10. A bottle of St-Emilion Château Auson 1er Cru Classé 1999, of which there was a rack in every store, was $312. In Libreville, not far from one hypermarket, I came across a community of 10,000 rubbish pickers, living off spoiled fruit and vegetables thrown out by high-end grocery stores. 'It's really two worlds in Gabon,' said Ernst and Young's Watremez. 'Rich. Poor. There's nothing in the middle.' The leader of the opposition, Pierre Mamboundou, said his Union Du Peuple Gabonais (Gabonese People's Union) calculated that 15,000 people in Gabon held 80 per cent of its wealth. Omar Bongo, president for forty years, had appointed fifty cabinet ministers to rule a country of 1.3 million. Even in a country that is 80 per cent rainforest and has coastal waters full of fish, none of them came up with a plan for what might succeed oil when reserves run dry. Entrepreneurial spirit had evaporated. A senior European economist added any sense of right and wrong had also gone. 'The lack of standards shown by Gabon's leadership has generated a complete immorality in the country,' he said. 'That's the real curse of oil.' War hadn't destroyed Gabon. With the inequality and criminality oil encouraged, it hadn't needed one.

There was another type of Resource Curse. It centred on a commodity even more essential to global prosperity than oil. After my trip to Gabon, I flew north to Chad and drove east to the twenty-first century's first war over water.

Darfur, a barren mountainous land just below the Sahara in western Sudan, is one of the world's worst man-made disasters. Four years of fighting has killed 200,000 people and made refugees of 2.5 million more. The immediate cause is well known: the Arab supremacist *Janjaweed* and their backers in the Sudanese government are waging a campaign to exterminate African and Arab settler farmers in Darfur by slaughter, rape and pillage, burning thousands of villages to the ground.

But it was easy to forget that before man added his own catastrophe, life in Darfur was already a gathering natural disaster. To live on the poor and arid soil of the Sahel – the area just south of the Sahara – is an eternal struggle for water, food and shelter. In the past, nomad Arab herders and its settled farmers (Arabs and Africans) worked together: the farmers allowed the herders' livestock on their land in exchange for milk and meat. But as good land became scarcer, the two sides began to fight over it – which they have now been doing for decades. 'You might laugh if I say that the main reason of this issue is a camel,' said Libyan leader Mu'ammer Gaddafi at his failed attempt at Darfur peace talks in October 2007. 'But Africa has thousands of such issues. They are about water, about grass.'

Competition is intensifying. The Sahara is advancing steadily south, smothering soil with sand. The National Centre for Atmospheric Research has recorded a half century of failing rain in the region, further squeezing what fertile fields remain. Added to that – or perhaps explaining it – is global warming. In November 2006 in Nairobi, the United Nations Climate Change Conference heard a warmer earth will put at risk the lives of 65 to 95 million Africans over the next quarter of a century, most of them in and around the Sahara. The UN's predictions prompted the Intergovernmental Panel on Climate Change to declare Africa 'the continent most vulnerable' to global warming.

It's not hard to start a fight in a place like that. As the Sudanese government did, you just find a divide – racial, political, cultural, religious – and promise one side, in this case the *Janjaweed*, as much land as they can steal. But the immediate spark shouldn't be allowed to obscure the war's underlying cause. Says Michael Klare, director of the Peace and World Security Program at Hampshire College: 'In Darfur . . . global warming exacerbates divisions along ethnic lines and produc[es] ethnic wars that are, at root, resource conflicts.'[12]

Even if the cause of Darfur's conflict had as much to do with ecology as ethnicity, what had that got to do with global economics? Plenty. Darfur's problems have little to do with the inequality that results from globalization. But they are intimately connected to the demands of the global economy. Because Sudan may be water-poor, but it is oil-rich. And the global trade in oil blocks resolution to Darfur's war in two ways, both involving China.

China, which has little oil of its own, needs Sudan's to power places like Shenzhen. In return for Khartoum granting it drilling concessions, China stymies diplomatic efforts to censure Sudan for its support of the *Janjaweed*. In addition, the pollution from Shenzhen's factories speeds the growth of the Sahara. The machinery of climate change is notoriously opaque, and we may never plot precisely how burning Sudan's carbon fuels in China increases the size of Sudan's desert. But most scientists now agree on the basics: climate change is happening, its cause is hydrocarbons and China, in late 2007, became the world's worst polluter.[13]

The situation in Darfur was not unique. Many of Africa's conflicts can be explained as dry tinderboxes that had long been waiting for a spark. In northern Kenya, Turkana tribes and armed gangs murder and rob each other in a cycle of violence fuelled by eight years of drought. In Rwanda, there is an increasing consensus that Africa's other recent genocide is at least partly understood as a contest between too many people on too little cultivable land – a dynamic that also explains why the economic revival now underway is raising hopes that Hutus and Tutsis may live in peace again. The UN Development Programme predicted as long ago as November 1999 that one in two Africans would face water shortages by 2025, and said it expected violent flashpoints to erupt along the Nile, Niger, Volta and Zambezi deltas.

Around the world, the UN is eyeing other ecological disasters for their conflict potential. There is the loss of half the Aral Sea to Soviet-era irrigation. The melting of the Himalayan glaciers (which feed rivers from which 500 million people draw water). And Chinese plans to dam the upper Mekong, halving water flow to 65 million South East Asians. Flooding too – along the Mekong, the Brahmaputra in Bangladesh and the Nile in Egypt – is being studied for its potential to spark war. The background to the concern is the

UN Environment Programme's 2003 report which said water shortages already affected 400 million people and predicted that number to multiply tenfold by 2050. At that time, more than a sixth of the world's population, 1.1 billion people, had erratic or no supply of clean water. UNEP chief Klaus Toepfer warned in an accompanying statement that 'the next war could be a war [over] water'. Environmental globalization – climate change – was stirring conflict around the world.

The notion of weather as war-maker attracts influential backers. On 16 April 2007, eleven former US admirals and generals published a report for the Center for Naval Analyses Corporation (a US world military and strategic think tank that had its origins in naval operations in the Second World War) that described climate change as a 'threat multiplier' in volatile parts of the world. 'The chaos that results [from climate change] can be an incubator of civil strife, genocide and the growth of terrorism,' read the report.[14] The next day, the then British Foreign Secretary Margaret Beckett hosted the first-ever debate on climate change and its relation to conflict at the UN Security Council in New York. 'What makes wars start?' asked Beckett. 'Fights over water. Changing patterns of rainfall. Fights over food production, land use. There are few greater potential threats to our economies, too, but also to peace and security itself.' Speaking outside the debate, Philip E. Clapp, president of the New York-based National Environmental Trust, warned: 'Global warming is no longer just an environmental issue. It is a rapidly advancing human crisis threatening millions of people, which could undermine the shaky political stability of countries from Southern Africa to the Middle East and South East Asia. World leaders have a choice: they can fight against global warming today, or fight because of it in the decades ahead.'

As long as globalization increases economic activity, climate change will continue, and the roots of Darfur's conflict will be exacerbated. Around the world, we can expect more violence to erupt over the scarcity of basic necessities. In early 2008, a world food crisis began gathering pace as food prices rose more than 40 per cent in six months from October 2007. Spurred by rising oil prices, greater demand from richer developing nations and a loss of agricultural land to desertification and – ironically – the cultivation of bio-fuels, the price rises sparked unrest and riots from Mexico to India. This was a new environmental slant to the paradox of globalization: the process of getting richer, by wrecking the environment, made many people poorer. Or as the British environmentalist George Monbiot put it in a column for the *Observer* newspaper, which argued for the environmental benefits of recession: 'No country has yet managed to reduce energy use while raising gross domestic product.'[15]

That is why Darfur matters. There is the simple humanitarian imperative – helping refugees – which alone might seem cause enough for action. There is also a moral imperative – if climate change is a root cause of these wars, and the West has caused climate change, then these distant wars become our indirect responsibility. Ugandan President Yoweri Museveni, whose economy depends on hydropower from a reservoir that is now depleted by drought, is explicit in this regard, describing climate change as 'an act of aggression by the rich against the poor'.

But even those who reject these arguments, and insist foreign policy be dictated by self-interest, find themselves swayed by a third argument, the security imperative. If weather starts wars, and wars inculcate terrorists and violent opponents to the West, then it is in the West's self-interest to try to manage the weather. As Anthony Zinni, the retired Marine general and a member of the CNA panel, says: 'We will pay for this one way or the other.'

Darfur is a test case of whether our leaders are able to embrace the kind of broad, long-term view over short-term gains and which, for example, might factor in how globalization contributes to climate change. If they can, they may be able to prevent the pattern repeating. Already, the fighting in western Sudan has spilled into Chad and the Central African Republic. Clapp warns that Darfur, while a catastrophe, is also 'an advance warning' of apocalypses to come. Take predictions of rising sea levels in a warmer planet. Five of Africa's major cities are coastal. Forty per cent of Asia's population of 3.5 billion – 1.5 billion people – lives within forty-five miles of the sea.[16] 'Darfur is small by comparison with what is projected,' says Clapp. 'It may be our last warning before the consequences of climate change become so enormous that they are beyond the capacity of industrialized nations to deal with.'

So can Darfur be saved? We already know what needs to be done. The immediate priority is to end the fighting by brokering a truce and sending in peacekeepers. In the longer term, Darfur needs sensible land use policies and careful water management, while the rest of the world has to cut emissions.

The question then becomes: will Darfur be saved? The response so far suggests: no. On a practical level, a US-brokered peace deal in 2006 was not worth the paper it was written on and UN peacekeepers have been a failure. But even if those obstacles can be overcome, there is a more fundamental problem. At the Security Council, Beckett faced opposition from China, the US and the two main groups representing developing countries, the Non-Aligned Movement and the Group of 77. They complained the forum was inappropriate to discuss climate change. That is, they disputed that climate change leads to war.

Perhaps a visit to north-eastern Chad would change their minds. As I drove out to the area in spring 2007, the first sign we were entering a dead zone was the carcass of a camel, gathering flies and red dust on a stony rise to our right. Camels can go three weeks without water in the Sahara so the heap of fur, hair and bleached bones was an ominous sight. We entered a mud-walled, straw-roofed village. Instead of the usual smiles and waves, the children ducked away. We passed a wild-looking old man, fiddling with a string of worry beads in the wind, and praying to the sky. He didn't appear to see us. The reason for his distraction became evident a few minutes later when we crested a rise in the road and were confronted by nine *Janjaweed* horsemen, rifles over their shoulders, white turbans around their heads. We'd gone before they could react, but we were 100 miles from the Sudanese border inside Chad and their presence on a road in broad daylight showed how invulnerable they felt. Two more hours across scorched mountains and rocky desert and we were in Iriba, north-eastern Chad's logistics base for six refugee camps for families from Darfur. Between showing me how to tune a radio to listen to Sudanese pilots on bombing runs (to discover if your location is a target), aid workers in Iriba told me that as horrific as the suffering was, it was surely going to get worse. 'The water is going. The firewood is gone. The land has lost its ability to regenerate,' said Palouma Ponlibae, an agriculture and natural resources officer for the relief agency CARE. 'The refugees are going to have to move. There's going to be nothing here to sustain life.'

The camps had concentrated populations beyond what the meagre land could support. At another camp, Guereda, staff at an International Medical Corps hospital were increasingly finding themselves mediating conflicts between refugees and local farmers, who complained the influx from Darfur had ruined their land, and occasionally serving as a battlefield clinic, such as on 1 December 2006, when fighting erupted between Chadian rebels and the Chadian army, and three surgeons had to operate on eighty-two people with gunshot wounds in a single day. 'Resources are simply insufficient to meet the overwhelming needs,' warned Serge Malé, UN High Commissioner for Refugees representative in Chad.

At another camp, Touloum, home to 22,400 people, women's welfare officer Mariam Bakhet Ahmed told me that in the previous four months, local villagers raped fifty refugee women who ventured out for firewood. Touloum camp chief Haroon Ibra Diar described how, when his people fled to Chad from the village of Abugamra, Sudan, in April 2004, the *Janjaweed* were already employing their own macabre energy-saving measures. 'They beheaded people and used their heads for firewood,' he said. I asked him what the future held. 'We are farmers,' he replied. 'But how can we farm here? There's not even enough water to drink. It's a land of death. That's all that it offers us.'

While we were talking, a filthy young man in rags approached and started distractedly unpicking the threads of a knitted woollen cap. Diar introduced twenty-two-year-old Abdoolcarim Abdur – 'Adam'. Diar said Adam saw his entire family cut down in front of him in 2004. As had happened to 40 per cent of Darfur's survivors, according to Medécins Sans Frontières, something snapped. Adam became alternately petrified and violent, convinced another *Janjaweed* onslaught was imminent. Afraid of his outbursts, his fellow refugees carried him to Chad tied to a door.

Adam told me he was getting terrible headaches from the *Janjaweed* horsemen in his head. They galloped round and round his skull. He asked brightly if I could give him a lift to Abugamra. It's the time of mangos and guavas, he said. I shook my head and he wandered off. Watching him leave, Diar told me Adam was obsessed by memories of when he was a boy, when the rains were good, the fruit was plentiful and the fighting just an occasional hazard. Sometimes, when the headaches were bad, he disappeared for days. Blinded by visions of plenty, he would run out into the desert and towards the war. Heading home.

CHAPTER 6

THE NEW LEFT REVOLUTION

As the war in Afghanistan entered a lull in spring 2002, I flew north from Delhi to investigate a Maoist rebellion in the Himalayas. Human rights workers and diplomats in Nepal were reporting that a five-year-old revolution against the ruling monarchy had suddenly escalated from ragtag curio to merciless, state-imperilling insurgency, and one whose ambition was to take the fight against globalization to the world. What drew particular attention was the Maoists' new ruthlessness. Three thousand people had been killed in four months. The rebels would saw the heads off fallen comrades rather than leave them to be identified on the battlefield. Indian newspapers reported sacks of severed heads turning up on the banks of the Ganges after being washed out of the mountains to the north.

It didn't take long to confirm that an extraordinary new savagery was sweeping Nepal. I met Ram Mani Jnawali's family on my first day in Kathmandu. They told me that even with knives as sharp as razors, the rebels had taken their time to skin Jnawali. After thirty-five minutes, his flesh was hanging from his shoulders and deep cuts crisscrossed his legs, ribs, arms, hands, ears and chin. His knees and shins were shattered, beaten backwards across the steps of his house until they broke. But he was still breathing. And his teenage tormentors still questioned him. His wife, cowering inside the family home, heard one of the accusers scream: 'Why don't you leave the Congress Party?' Another demanded: 'How much do you earn? Where are your daughters?' But Jnawali, fifty-four, was beyond speech. Eventually his torturers – a crowd of sixty girls and boys in camouflage uniforms and red bandanas – grew tired of the interrogation. Grasping a kukri, one of them stepped forward and, in a single blow, sliced halfway through the back of Jnawali's neck. And that's how his family found him when they dared to venture out in the morning: head partly severed, his body slumped on broken legs. A large dark patch in the dust suggested no one single blow had killed Jnawali. He had bled out.

Jnawali's family lived in the village of Kerunga, a day's drive to the north-east of Kathmandu. After his death on 13 March, his family travelled to the capital to cremate his body on the edge of the holy Bagmati River and, afraid of more attacks, stayed on in a red-brick house in the centre of the city. That's where I found them. I greeted Jnawali's younger brother, Bharat Mani Jnawali, on the steps of his adopted home and, after offering my condolences, expressed surprise that such a horrific murder should fade from the headlines after a day. Bharat explained such cruelty had become routine. 'This is a very common method of killing,' he said. 'It happens to hundreds. They cut different parts of the body off and then only at the end, they chop off your head. Shooting would be easier, of course. But this is more intense. They do it for the fear.'

Going by Bharat's account of his brother's funeral, the rebels' tactics were working. To Bharat, who had seen his brother's wounds, there was something abhorrently dishonest about the sight of him prettified, bound in white cotton and covered in rose petals. So when a handful of Congress leaders arrived, the men for whose party Jnawali died, Bharat swept the orange and purple blooms off the corpse and ripped open his brother's burial cloth. 'I said, "Look at him. Look at what they did to him. Look at how your party suffers." But none of them could look. They were too afraid.'

The then US ambassador in Kathmandu, Mike Malinowski, remarked on the parallels between Nepal in 2002 and the Khmer Rouge in Cambodia in the 1970s and 1980s. 'It's classic Year Zero,' he said. 'Kill or drive away anybody who could possibly be considered an enemy, break down all state and social fabric and replace it with fear. In the end the party is the only thing left.'

But unlike the Khmer Rouge, the Maoists had more than their own people in their sights. My stringer in Nepal, Campbell Spencer, tracked down a former Maoist commander who, disgusted at the rebels' methods, had deserted and was hiding out in Kathmandu. The Maoist revolution had international ambitions, he said. Nepal's war was the first stage in a much larger experiment. The Maoists saw themselves as the vanguard of a new tide of left-wing revolution sweeping the world. Three years before, he said, communist guerrillas from India, Bangladesh and the Philippines had met their Nepalese counterparts in Kathmandu and agreed that the kingdom – poor, feudal and autocratic – was the perfect place in which to restart world communist revolution. Nepal was stage one. Stage two was India. Stage three was the global economy, and America.

This was the boldest opposition to globalization I had yet encountered. Elsewhere, I had seen how globalization could lead to inequality, and how that could lead to war. But those conflicts were confined to the Malacca Straits, the townships of South Africa or the coastal swamps of Nigeria. From their bases and hideouts, pirates, rebels and criminals might have an impact on the global economy. But they were hardly fighting a global war.

The Maoists, on the other hand, were responding to globalization with the promise of global revolution. Theirs was a proposal that Marx was more relevant today than he had ever been and that now, the twenty-first century, was finally the time for a worldwide communist uprising.

It was not a secret agenda. Maoist No. 2 Baburai Bhattaram proclaimed the rebels' aim was to 'hoist the hammer and sickle atop Mount Everest one day', turning 'this beautiful Himalayan country into an invincible Red Fort . . . a bright red base for world proletarian revolution.' In a summer 2005 interview with Charlie Haviland, the BBC's Kathmandu correspondent, Maoist leader Prachanda declared: 'We want there to be a revolution in the USA and even in your UK, and that the working classes should rule. We are a part of a global revolution. America does not work for the improvement of people anywhere. It works only for itself. It works for the benefit of the ruling class, the capitalists.'[1] In proclamations and other interviews, Prachanda would accuse America of being the power behind Nepal's throne. The root of all evil, the Maoists believed, was US-dominated global capitalism. Globalization of Western values had even spawned the scurrilous beauty contests of Miss Nepal and Miss World, said the Maoists, and the rebels made repeated attempts to take broadcasts of the competitions off Nepal's airwaves. 'Bravo. It shows the [Maoists] have their priorities right,' read an exasperated editorial in the *Nepali Times*. 'Of all the problems that beset this country that needed urgent attention, of course it was Miss Nepal . . . that was holding us back . . . from ensuring peace, development and democracy.'[2] The Maoists even apparently believed that capitalism made men gay. In December 2006, Dev Gurung, a second tier Maoist leader, declared: 'Under Soviet rule and when China was still a communist state, there were no homosexuals in the Soviet Union or China . . . Homosexuality is a production of capitalism. Under socialism this kind of problem doesn't exist.'[3]

Gurung's ideas might have been out of step with the modern world. But then so was Nepal. It was a kingdom of legend and fairy tales, where fable often stood in for fact. The peaks are said to hold up the roof of the world, strange man-beasts are believed to roam the valleys and people like to say they live in Shangri La. Until 1950 the country was closed to outsiders, a forbidden kingdom ruled by feudal lords who toured their impoverished estates in Rolls-Royce Silver Shadows.

Outside Kathmandu, Nepal remains a forgotten place of tough people living hard lives. There is little electricity, and few telephones or roads. Average annual income in Nepal has only ever reached a malnutrition-guaranteed $270 per head according to the World Bank, and in 2003 the Asian Development Bank estimated 42 per cent of its 26 million people lived below the poverty line. Even the cities feel like they are from another era. Kathmandu's main tourist drag is called 'Freak Street', a leading national newspaper in the early twenty-first century was the *Space Time Daily* (since departed to another dimension) and the government uses a calendar by whose reckoning 2005 was the year 2062.

In this lost world, democracy, politics and government

En-mei, in traditional Jarawa dress. (Copyright © Denis Giles)

The errant strike at Qala-i-Jangi that scored a direct hit on a Northern Alliance command post, November 2001. We had been standing on this site less than an hour before. (Copyright © Damien Degueldre)

'Harley Davidson'. (Copyright © Damien Degueldre)

The Qala-i-Jangi crew, inside the fort, November 2001. Flanking a friendly Northern Alliance commander. From left: Perry, Oleg Nikishin, Damien Degueldre and Dodge Billinsgley. Oleg won a series of photo prizes for his work at the fort, while Dodge and Damien shared the Rory Peck award. (Courtesy of the author)

Shenzhen. This shot is a good illustration of the smog that blankets southern China. (Copyright © Prashant Panjiar)

Shenzhen at night; the Shenzhen most visitors see. (Copyright © Prashant Panjiar)

Bombay's sea front, with the towers of Colaba in the background. During the 2005 floods, the tide surged straight over these protective walls. (Copyright © Prashant Panjiar)

Vijay Mallya, the King of Good Times, at his Goa villa in 2003.
(Copyright © Prashant Panjiar)

Khayelitsha on the Cape Flats. Reality has changed very little for millions of black South Africans since the end of apartheid. (Copyright © Pers-Anders Pettersson/ Reportage by Getty Images)

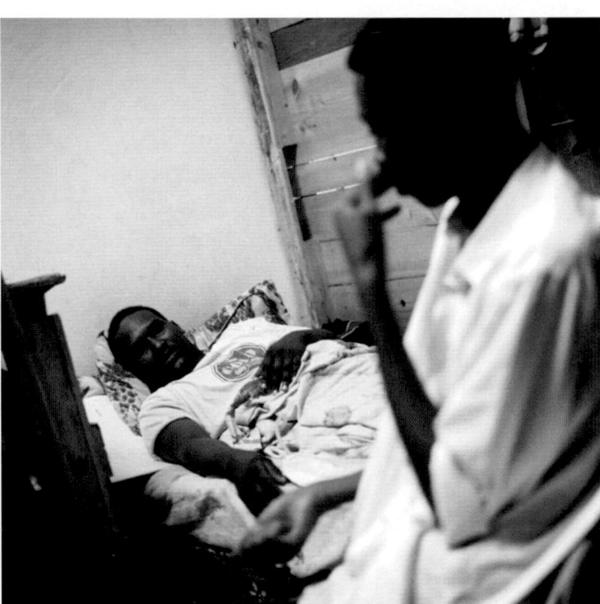

On patrol with Johannesburg's Crime Prevention Unit. As they search his car, police immobilize and humiliate a suspected Zimbabwean thief. (Courtesy of Benedicte Kurzen/EVE)

Abdi, as we found him in a backroom shack in Port Elizabeth. (Courtesy of Benedicte Kurzen/EVE)

Khayelitsha. Poverty doesn't necessarily fuel rebellion or violence. It's more about crushed pride and unmet expectations.
(Copyright © Pers-Anders Pettersson/Reportage by Getty Images)

The logo for the Movement for the Emancipation of the Niger Delta (MEND). (Courtesy of the author)

This black and white shot, taken outside Oure Cassoni relief camp in eastern Chad on the border with Darfur in 2006, dramatically illustrates the exhaustion of food and water in the area. (Copyright © Pers-Anders Pettersson/Reportage by Getty Images)

Tomas and I on the trek to Thabang, centre of the Nepalese Maoist revolution in the Himalayas, February 2005. Tomas had blistered his feet badly and had to hire a pony. (Copyright © Tomas van Houtryve)

Maoists on parade at Gairegaon, February 2005. (Copyright © Tomas van Houtryve)

A Maoist soldier plants the hammer and sickle in a tree on the trek to Thabang, February 2005. More than almost any other, Tomas' picture captures the global ambitions of the rising tide of revolution happening in some of the world's most remote corners. (Copyright © Tomas van Houtryve)

Samandi, summer 2002. The ceasefire that allowed me access to the Tamil Tigers has crumbled now. (Copyright © Dominic Sansoni)

Outside a mosque in central Bombay. Despite being the second largest Muslim population in the world, India's Muslims largely live on the margins of the far bigger Hindu population. (Copyright © Prashant Panjiar)

Two Somali women walk past the ruins of the old cathedral in the blown-out centre of downtown Mogadishu, June 2007. Like any work of painstaking craftmanship, downtown Mogadishu is stunning. (Copyright © Sven Torfinn)

The remains of an Islamist convoy hit in the 23 January airstrike on the Somali-Kenya border, June 2007. (Copyright © Sven Torfinn)

The moment of invasion. I took this photo as US forces crossed the border from Kuwait into Iraq at dawn on 20 March, 2003. (Courtesy of the author)

British journalist arrested for operating without licence

ALEXANDER John Perry

Chronicle Reporter

A BRITISH journalist working for the United Kingdom edition of *Time Magazine* was arrested in Matabeleland South after sneaking into Zimbabwe and clandestinely working without accreditation from the Media and Information Commission, police confirmed yesterday.

Alexander John Perry (37), the South African correspondent of *Time* — a mass circulating United States publication with European and Asian syndication — was arrested in West Nicholson on Friday after a small-scale miner tipped off police about the presence of the scribe.

Time Magazine is a subsidiary of the *Time Warner* media empire which incorporates the Cable News Network (CNN) and other media outlets.

Provincial police spokesman Inspector Tafanana Dzirutwe said Perry was arrested for breaching Chapter 10:27 of the Access to Information and Protection of Privacy Act (AIPPA).

It could not be established how long the Cape Town-based reporter had been working illegally in the country but Insp Dzirutwe said Perry was compiling information on Operation Isitsheketsha Sesiphelile/ Chikorokoza Chapera when he was nabbed by the police in West Nicholson.

He was transferred to Gwanda police station where he spent the weekend in the cells before appearing in court yesterday.

Gwanda Provincial magistrate, Mr Enerst Chidawanyika, convicted Perry for contravening Section 79 (1) as read with Section 80 (1) (d) of AIPPA after the reporter had pleaded guilty to the offence.

Perry, who was represented by Mr Simbarashe Chivaura, was fined $100.

The prosecutor Mr Admire Zvongouya told the court that Perry approached Mr Tranos Nkomo, a small-scale miner at West Nicholson and started interviewing him about Operation Chikorokoza Chapera and its effects.

Nkomo called the police and alerted them about the presence of the scribe who was asked to produce proof of accreditation to work as a journalist in Zimbabwe.

When he failed to produce the required accreditation, he was arrested.

Lately, there has been an influx of foreign journalists who sneak into the country disguised as tourists to illegally work in Zimbabwe. Their renewed interest in Zimbabwe is linked to the latest developments on the political front.

There has been a spate of bombings and acts of terror around the country allegedly carried out by the opposition MDC, with the support of the West, to effect regime change.

Arrested in Zimbabwe, April 2007. This is a clipping from the regime mouthpiece, *The Herald*. The paper stole the picture from a documentary in which I appeared, called, ironically, *Press Pass to the World.* (Courtesy of the author)

King Gyanendra Bir Bikram Shah Dev at the height of his powers in 2005. (Copyright © Tomas van Houtryve)

The spring 2006 riots in Kathmandu that were to lead to Gyanendra's downfall. (Copyright © Tomas van Houtryve)

The houseboats of Dal Lake, Kashmir, perhaps one of the most beautiful war zones of them all. (Copyright © Prashant Panjiar)

The Mirwaiz, Kashmir's young spiritual leader. (Copyright © Prashant Panjiar)

were a new experience. Political parties only became legal in 1990. Whole swathes of the country existed in an ungoverned vacuum. Nepal's civil war added a little fairy dust of its own. On one side was a prince, King Gyanendra, who reigned as a Hindu living God from a palace hung with chandeliers and tiger skins, where servants were forbidden even to look upon his face. On the other was a pauper, Prachanda, leader to a band of urchin rebels who hid in the hills by day and fell on the king's army at night, slaughtering and looting, before melting away with the frost at dawn. One Western diplomat agreed the war sounded 'truly bizarre' in the twenty-first century. But he cautioned: 'If the situation feels historic, remember much of the country is still in the Middle Ages.'

But Nepal's backwardness had echoes across the developing world. Its reaction when confronted by globalization was also symptomatic of the upheaval that was being felt across the poorer parts of the globe. And the blood was no fairy tale.[4] At ten killings a day before a ceasefire in spring 2006, Nepal's was the deadliest conflict in Asia. At times – such as when 1,023 died in a single month in May 2002 – this kingdom of yaks, yetis and year-out backpackers briefly became the single most dangerous place on earth. In 2005, the UN was warning that Nepal was being pushed 'towards the abyss of a humanitarian crisis', while the Hong Kong-based Asian Human Rights Commission described it as 'drowning in a madness of barbarity'.[5] The International Crisis Group accused Gyanendra of running 'a no-party state that has decimated democracy and kills people at will',[6] while Human Rights Watch said his 85,000-strong army were responsible for a world record number of 'disappearances'.[7] Amnesty International charged the rebels with kidnapping, torture and murder, and a particular penchant for clubbing people to death. An

October 2003 report by relief group Mercy Corps spoke of crowds of Maoists watching their leaders break every bone in a 'class enemy's body, skinning them, cutting off tongues, ears, lips and noses, gouging out eyes and hammering in teeth and finally sawing them in half or burning them'. The study concluded the 'almost identical pattern' of atrocities suggested 'a policy coordinated at senior command levels'.[8]

None of this dented the appeal of the kingdom's communist parties, the most popular in the country with the combined backing of 44 per cent of voters, according to a survey in June 2003.[9] And the support began to make sense. If Nepal subsisted in nineteenth-century destitution and inequality, then it was easy to understand why the nineteenth-century theories of Marx and Mao might seem to promise progression and modernity. Prachanda's father Muktiram Dahal told me that before he adopted his nom de guerre, which means 'the fierce one', Pushpa Kamal Dahal was a 'kind-hearted boy' spurred by injustice. 'He really cared for the poor people in the village,' said the seventy-six-year-old. 'He used to share his food with them and tell us we shouldn't exploit them.' Prachanda himself later told me in an email interview: 'I am from a poor peasant family [and] from my childhood I knew the meaning of poverty and inhuman exploitation. In high school, I came across communist ideology, then I was involved in student politics, and by the time I graduated, I was already communist.' Back then, said Prachanda, his aim was straightforward: 'a democratic new Nepal, free from feudalism, working towards economic and cultural prosperity'. An American diplomat in Kathmandu commented: 'I don't think any reasonable person would disagree with what he was trying to do.'

Most Nepalis shared Prachanda's desire for a better future,

and his disappointment with what democracy had achieved. Like him, they watched as left-wing revolution swept the world after the Second World War, from China to Cuba, but missed Nepal. Then, after Gyanendra's brother King Birendra ceded autocratic power to an elected government in 1990, they looked on as their shiny new democracy quickly collapsed amid in-fighting, corruption and venal ambition. By the summer of 2004, the country had had fourteen prime ministers in fourteen years. The political parties had split so many times that Prachanda's Communist Party of Nepal (Maoist) was one of forty left-wing groups, including ten separate Communist Parties of Nepal. Meanwhile the only evidence that democracy brought prosperity was the rows of new ministerial residences and chauffeur-driven cars.

By February 1996, Prachanda had had enough. He took to the hills with a band of guerrillas, taking with him two dog-eared texts: Mao Tse-tung's *Basic Tactics* (1936) and *On Guerrilla Warfare* (1937). At first, the rebellion was a bad joke. Prachanda had only a few hundred men armed with axes, hoes and a handful of antique Second World War .303 Lee-Enfield rifles. Casualties were light – 1,500 by mid 2001 – and the Maoists themselves accounted for two-thirds of them. The world noted the existence of these ahistorical rebels on China's southern border, but paid scant attention. Even Beijing restricted itself to occasionally castigating the rebels for taking the Chairman's name in vain.

All that changed on the night of 23 November 2001. The Maoists, whose strength was now at 500 commandos, 8,000 regular troops and 20,000 to 40,000 militiamen, abruptly broke off peace talks with the government and launched forty-eight simultaneous attacks on police and army posts across the country. A whirlwind of atrocities ensued. The guerrillas singled out teachers, civil servants and members of the ruling Congress Party for execution, wiped out all trace of previous authority by blowing up government buildings and infrastructure, and orchestrated massed strikes by thousands of their fighters on isolated security force posts that left no survivors. In return, Nepal's army and police began arresting and 'disappearing' hundreds of suspected guerrillas.

Thousands died. According to the UN High Commissioner for Refugees, 350,000 to 400,000 civilians fled to the cities. Many went further, the rich buying new homes in Delhi and London, the poor fleeing to brothels in Bombay, sweatshops in South East Asia and servants' quarters in the Gulf. (Not all found a happier life. In September 2004, Iraqi insurgents shot dead twelve Nepali porters and cooks en route to US bases in the west of the country.) Thomas Marks, author of *Insurgency in Nepal*, says Maoists destroyed 1,321 out of 3,913 village administration buildings and 440 post offices, while police abandoned 895 out of 1,682 stations and teachers abandoned 700 schools.[10]

But in their Himalayan hideouts, the Maoists were nurturing ambitions beyond Nepal. They viewed the disparity prevalent in Nepal as part of a pattern around the world, and something that was becoming more pronounced with globalization. They saw America as the dominant, ruling controller of all of this – and expressed kinship with all of America's enemies. In April 2003, in a move that appeared calculated to raise US hackles, the Maoists released a manifesto expressly welcoming 'citizens of any foreign nation who were compelled to leave due to their involvement in revolutionary activities.'[11] Washington took the bait, adding the Maoists to its list of proscribed terrorists alongside al-Qaeda. It also began supplying training and equipment to the Royal Nepal Army.

In early 2005, I returned to Nepal with photographer Tomas van Houtryve, a Belgian who had made Nepal's rebellion his speciality. We wanted to find the Maoist heartland and see for ourselves the kind of society the rebels wanted to build. The only way to reach it was to walk into the Himalayas.

A distant clattering bounced off the snowy hills as twenty guerrillas approached a mountain pass deep in Nepal's rebel territory. There was something in the rhythm – spaced, deliberate – that suggested man and machine. But the sound was too faint to fix as gunfire, and the Maoists pressed on up the goat track. Then came the explosions.

One, two ... Unmistakable.

Three, four ... And close.

The rebels halted and, panting in the thin air, squinted up at the forest ridge a few hundred metres above, which now marked the edge of the newest battlefield in their war.

Five ... 'Mortars,' said a political officer.

Six ... '81 mm,' added a stocky, Tibetan-looking girl who had led our four-hour ascent from the valley floor. 'And a chopper.'

Minutes later, a helicopter marked with the scarlet emblem of the Royal Nepal Army (RNA) skimmed the pass. The rebels scattered into the trees, crouching and peering up as it passed overhead. A radio operator raised command. 'Anniversary attack,' he relayed.

The Maoists later claimed the RNA pilot killed scores of unarmed villagers when he came across a festival marking the rebellion's ninth birthday in Kharikot, a day away. The RNA insisted the strike was legitimate, boasting it surprised a group of 800 armed fighters and killed 25. Both sides agreed on one detail – with no guns mounted on his aircraft, the pilot dropped mortar shells by hand from his cockpit window.

The helicopter didn't spot us, the fighters hurried up the pass and by dusk we had descended 2,000 metres to the village of Gairegaon to join 400 other soldiers of First Brigade, People's Liberation Army Mid Division. Despite the attack, spirits were high, almost giddy. A closer examination of the rebels revealed why. One female fighter wore a Britney Spears T-shirt under her ammunition belt. Another had a Jurassic Park top. As the cold crept in, several wrapped themselves in towels sporting images of Spiderman, Winnie the Pooh and Australian road signs warning of wombats for 15 kilometres. The 'men' joked and play-fought, the 'women' giggled and hugged. Everyone played volleyball and swapped Bollywood tapes. For the truth about the People's Liberation Army was this: it might more accurately have been named the Little People's Liberation Army. The New York-based rights group Watchlist reports 30 per cent of PLA recruits are under eighteen.[12] In Gairegaon, where their rucksacks, woolly hats and sleeping bags evoked a high-school camping trip with guns, that felt like an underestimate. First Brigade's vice political commissar, Atal, admitted that recruiting children was the norm. 'According to Lenin, once they are fifteen, they can join up,' he said.

As well as reflecting poorly on human rights, the guerrillas' youth raised doubts over their effectiveness. While the Khmer Rouge proved children could be suicidally obedient and imaginatively cruel, young fighters generally lack training or experience. Atal confirmed that while 'according to Maoist theory, they learn in battle', almost none had seen combat.

Few even seemed to have working knowledge of their weapons. Some carried them slung backwards over their shoulder, safety catch off, barrel pointed at their comrades' waists. Others stuffed the muzzle with cloth and mud to keep out the damp. Ammunition was also a problem. Only a handful of fighters had a spare clip. And keeping loaded such a variety of weapons – American M-16s, Indian rifles and Belgian 5.56 calibre Minimis captured from the RNA; shotguns and AK-47s bought from gun smugglers; and ancient .303s and home-made grenade launchers – would be a challenge for a Texas gun store, let alone a child's army a week's walk from the nearest town. But the guerrillas did have one world-class weapon, the Himalayas. Their territory, a maze of giant ravines so remote that many maps of Nepal feature large tracts of blank, unexplored space, made Tora Bora seem like Central Park.

A day's walk from Gairegaon was the Maoist capital Thabang. Here, in a steep valley just under the snow line, Prachanda had built his brave new world. His hierarchy was traditional Leninist, running from himself as party chairman and commander-in-chief, to Party Central Committee, politburo and army command, district and sub-district committees, and village heads. Prachanda also constructed several 'model' villages nearby, which embodied his vision of a Maoist Nepal and displayed a sternly monolithic theme. Thabang was the foremost of these. In the town, a crowd of red and gold hammer and sickle flags flew from the roofs. A vast hammer and sickle rock garden adjoined the school. And a mural in the main street depicted Prachanda alongside Marx, Engels, Lenin, Stalin and Mao and listed Thabang's twenty-nine 'martyrs' alongside a third, vast hammer and sickle.

I had hoped to meet Prachanda. In every village we passed, we were told he was one village ahead. The junior rebels we met sent foot messengers over the hills conveying our request. At one point, we were told we had just walked through a village in which Prachanda was also sheltering with a phalanx of bodyguards. But after waiting ten days, the answer came back that only an email interview was possible. I scribbled down a list of questions in red biro and was told to expect an answer by email in several weeks.

The interview, the first Prachanda had ever done,[13] duly arrived in my inbox two weeks later. He declared that the 'earth-shaking struggle of the masses' had 'entered its last stage' and accused 'the remnant of medieval feudal autocracy, the infamous fratricidal and regicidal King Gyanendra' of 'desperately resorting to a last reign of terror [to suppress] the democratic aspirations of the Nepalese people'. He admitted Nepal's Maoists were playing catch-up with other socialists around the world – 'so many countries have already finished this task over the last centuries' – but added that in today's world, Nepal's rebels were now spearheading a much larger struggle. Modern communists, he wrote, had a bigger, global enemy in their sights – 'the evil of the imperialist world [and] the hypocrisy of so-called democracy that a superpower like the US represents.' To a question about whether he really believed Nepal's revolution would spread, he suggested it already had, citing a growing kinship with anti-globalization protesters. 'The imperialist world order makes a handful of rich richer and the vast majority inhumanly poorer. Developing [the] sharp differences between the haves and the have nots [will] generate the basis for world revolution. Anybody can observe [how there is] growing global unrest in this world order. We deeply believe that what we are starting in Nepal is part of worldwide 21st century revolution.'

We moved on to human rights. 'In war, it is inevitable some people will die,' wrote Prachanda. 'But they will never be able to crush the growing resistance of the masses.' The question asked about abuses on both sides. 'We are fighting for the liberation of the masses, whereas the RNA is fighting against the masses,' he replied. '[The two] cannot be compared. Because we are at war, I can't rule out mistakes.' But he insisted: 'We strictly do not allow those below the age of 18 to join. One thing [that confuses] commentators is the thousands of orphans of our martyrs. Our party naturally undertakes the responsibility to feed, educate and train them so as to be good successors to their parents. We never use them in fighting, but we educate and discipline them as a children's organization. When we are taking care of poor children, how can one draw parallels with things like the Khmer Rouge?'

Some of my questions focused on Prachanda's personal motivation, and whether he regretted the life he chose. His reply was emphatic. 'This war helped me to understand the enormous energy and the depth of feeling that the masses carry in their souls. I am proud of this understanding. I have never dreamt and will never dream of a life dissociated from the masses. No! I never have doubts about dedicating oneself to the noble cause of liberating the masses. I never worry about personal success or failure, but I have absolute confidence in the victory of the masses. I have no time, nor interests outside the party, the campaign and the masses. To sacrifice myself to change the world for the betterment of humanity, [to fight] against the evil system of exploitation of men by men, this is my first and last dream.'

At the end of his email, Prachanda apologized that 'due to some serious technical difficulties, I couldn't meet you face to face. I hope in the near future I will.' He was, he added, 'not so hidden from my people'. He signed the email 'With best regards, Your Prachanda. (Chairman, Central Committee, CPN (Maoist). February 25, 2005.)'

With Prachanda unavailable in person, I met the Maoist mayor of Thabang, Raktim. He sketched out the sort of society the rebels hoped to build. Religion was discouraged and would eventually be 'eliminated', he said. A new Marxist curriculum for the schools would teach Maoist Party history to children from the age of five. Raktim and his subordinates collected tax, dragooned recruits for the PLA, refused or approved marriages and handed out new revolutionary names – 'Raktim' means Red – to formalize their new recruits' entry into their communist family. The rebels had press-ganged 1,000 villagers to build a road east from Thabang, said Raktim, but that was the extent of their development work. Pointing out a 100-metre-square patch of razed buildings in Thabang's centre, one of his subordinates, political officer Gulab ('Rose'), explained: 'If we build clinics or irrigation channels, the army just comes in here and destroys it. We do the same to them. There's no point in building things.'

There was a basic justice system, 'people's courts' whose primary work was punishing traitors to the revolution. 'If his offence is serious, we give him hard labour,' said Raktim. 'But if he doesn't change, we shoot him. Or use a kukri if we don't have the bullets.' Raktim admitted to overseeing 'two or three' executions personally. Human rights groups have documented hundreds.

The suffering wasn't only measured in dead. In another

village, a thirty-three-year-old teacher approached us, curious about the two foreigners walking past his door. When he discovered we were journalists, he urged us to hear his story of living under Maoist rule. As a teacher, he said he had endured years of intimidation and indoctrination. 'They take people to the hills for days, weeks, even months. They call it "camping".' They tell you everyone must be proletariat, that we are too materialistic, too middle class, that it doesn't matter how people think, only how the Party thinks, that nothing can happen without their permission. They want our heads empty, and our eyes sightless so that we follow them blindly. That's why they like children.' He added that the rebels banned him from holding university entry exams 'because they don't want people getting their own ideas'.

Raktim had admitted the Party mainly took teenagers to its instruction camps – the Kathmandu charity Child Workers in Nepal said a total of 6,600 minors had been abducted in this way – but he insisted the sessions were educational rather than coercive. 'We feel if people understand us, they'll support us.' The programming seemed to work. In the village of Pipal, Jhima Rana Magar, a girl guerrilla who looked fifteen, told us: 'I am ready to give my life for the Prachanda Path', referring to the Chairman's own Little Red Book. 'If we follow the Prachanda Path, the people will get their rights.' Asked how she squared this with taking food and shelter from villagers who barely had enough for themselves, she was adamant: 'We are fighting for the people. So we eat in their houses. How can people say we are doing bad things?' Her certainty had no limit. 'Not only will we be in Kathmandu in months,' she said, 'we'll spread all over the world.'

The teacher reckoned this self-assurance was misplaced. The rebels assumed support rather than earned it, he says.

The truth was, 'people hate them. They're stupid and vicious, and they take and give nothing back. They think power and the gun are everything. And they have a point. What can we do if they've got the guns?'

In a village in the frontline district of Dang, a few days' walk to the south, the rebels were less secure, more suspicious and more ruthless. Postmen, health workers, moneylenders, landowners and teachers had all been targets for public flogging or executions. Bands of rebels regularly descended on villages and forced a child from each family to join their ranks or, in the case of young girls, to become sex slaves for the male soldiers. State infrastructure – power substations, telephone exchanges, village administration offices, bridges, clinics, dams, irrigation and drinking-water projects – and the homes of those deemed 'people's enemies' had been levelled. Here the Maoists openly admitted to pursuing their own version of Year Zero. 'At first, we just wanted to destroy all the government institutions in the village,' said Ghopal Phandari, who, at twenty-three, was Maoist leader of the village of Junge Kuna. 'But then we decided to block any access to the villages by blowing up bridges – one time we hit forty-eight in one day. Inside our territory, we also attack the water projects or cut the drinking water or hit the electricity supplies because it is symbolic. We have to make these sacrifices to protect the people.'

Asked about executions, Phandari explained the procedure with the ease of a man unburdened by conscience. First, he said, a villager will lodge a complaint about another person with the People's Militia, a group of seven to twelve cadres that patrol the village. 'We do not execute them immediately,' said Phandari. 'The militia gives notice to the person that they must reform. We can give three ultimatums. But if they do not change, then we execute them. Sometimes, we use torture – it depends on the interests of the people.' Normally the militia made up a report, which was then passed up to the district party leadership to rule on a suitable punishment and who should administer it. 'We use the kukri, the bullet, or beat them to death with a wooden stick,' said Phandari. 'It's the party leaders who decide.'

In the nearby village of Pancha Kule, a Maoist leader known as Commander Hikbat dismissed innocent deaths as the unavoidable price of revolution. 'Sometimes what you plan, your intentions, don't always work out in the field,' he said. 'One time, we went to attack the police in the village of Panchakatia and found they were hiding in a house owned by some local people. We warned the police to surrender but they did not. So we had to burn the house down and four innocent people were killed. We take responsibility for that. It just happens that way sometimes.' Phandari, on the other hand, had convinced himself that he never made mistakes, not with the two people he executed nor the fifteen he tortured. 'They were all spies,' he insisted, 'enemies of the people.'

In many ways, Nepal was following a script written in nineteenth-century Europe. And if history was repeating itself, there were some certainties in Nepal's future. Foremost was this: once again, thousands would die in the name of global communist revolution. As Prachanda wrote in his email: 'Sacrifice is inevitable.' In Gairegaon, political commissar Atal even suggested death was part of the plan. Regarding his teenage soldiers, he said: 'Many had family killed by the army. It changed their thoughts. It gave them great thoughts. They're ready to die.' No doubt many did.

*

The conviction that the US must be confronted militarily is not confined to Nepal. It resonates across the Middle East, Asia, Russia – and Latin America. Here is not the place to recount the long history of left-wing insurrection in South America and the Caribbean. It is enough to note that Latin America gave the world its biggest left-wing revolutionary icon, Che Guevara, its most enduring symbol of communist autocracy, Fidel Castro, and two of its most feared communist guerrilla armies, Peru's Shining Path and the Revolutionary Armed Forces of Colombia (FARC).

What nurtures this appetite for rebellion? The same inequality that fosters it elsewhere. Latin America has defined the divide between rich and poor in the developing world for decades. 'Inequality is as Latin American as good dance music and magical-realist fiction,' proclaimed the *Economist* in 2003.[14] The same year, the World Bank released an extensive study into why the schism had endured, and grown, in Latin America for so long. It found the 'richest 1/10th of the population ... earn 48 per cent of total income, while the poorest 1/10th earn only 1.6 per cent.' That compared to 29.1 per cent and 2.5 per cent in industrialized nations. 'Latin America and the Caribbean is one of the regions of the world with the greatest inequality,' said David de Ferranti, World Bank vice president for the region. 'Latin America is highly unequal with respect to incomes, and also exhibits unequal access to education, health, water and electricity, as well as huge disparities in voice, assets and opportunities. This inequality slows the pace of poverty reduction, and undermines the development process itself.'[15]

Today, there are signs that some of the most egregious disparities may be narrowing.[16] But leftist, anti-US populism lives on in the governments of Argentina, Bolivia, Brazil,

Chile, Cuba, Nicaragua, Uruguay and Venezuela – and FARC. There are two types. There are presidents like Brazil's Luiz Inácio Lula da Silva, Chile's President Michelle Bachelet and Uruguay's Tabaré Vázquez. This centre-left brigade will take on the US, but rarely take matters to the brink. As Jorge Castañada noted in *Newsweek*, Chile opposed Washington on Iraq in the Security Council, but simultaneously signed a free-trade agreement with the US; Brazil rejects US trade policy, but Lula welcomed President George W. Bush into his home in Brasilia; and Uruguay renewed diplomatic relations with Havana while also negotiating an investment protection agreement with the US.[17]

The other left is more radical. It is led by Chávez in Venezuela, Bolivia's Evo Morales, Argentina's Kirchner family and Cuba's Castro family. It adopts a far more strident opposition to globalization and US domination. Its most colourful figure is Chávez, who delights in insulting Bush[18] and selling discounted oil to other left-wing politicians, such as former London mayor Ken Livingstone in London. Nicolás Maduro, Venezuelan foreign minister, has described the oil sales as designed to help create 'a multipolar world based on solidarity'.

The boldest manifestation of Chávez's opposition to the US is his formation of a 2-million-strong army of reservists, created to foil what Chávez warns is an imminent US invasion of South America. Many see Chávez's army as proof that the Venezuelan president is a wasteful and grandiose fantasist. That may be. But the significance of his militia is less in the motives of its creator than its acceptance by many Latin Americans. It's not whether Chávez is right that South America needs an army to protect it from US aggression, but whether South America thinks he is.

Nevertheless, even if he ever deploys it, Chávez seems likely to use his new army purely for defence. Likewise, Nepal's Maoists, while they are deadly serious in their intent and even won a general election in April 2008, lack the capacity to attack New York and can expect to have little effect on the US from the Himalayas. But what if the revolution was to spread somewhere more significant?

A year after my walk in the Himalayas, in February 2006, I covered a tour of India by George W. Bush. As his hundreds of burly Secret Service agents made clear, the president didn't expect to be universally adored. But even Bush's bodyguards might have been unaware that by visiting Afghanistan, Pakistan and India, he was risking not two war zones, but three. In Kabul, security was so tight that accompanying White House correspondents were kept ignorant of their destination until Air Force One began its descent. In Pakistan, a Karachi suicide bomber greeted Bush's arrival by obliterating a US diplomat at the gates of the city consulate. By comparison, the tour of India – full of grand talk about a new India and intricate negotiations on nuclear energy – was worthy, but dull. So when Bush flew to the southern Indian city of Hyderabad to see how an ancient hill fort had turned itself into a technology centre, most of the White House press corps took the day off to go carpet-shopping in Delhi.

They missed a story in Hyderabad. The city is home to the Indian offices of Dell, Oracle, Motorola, Ericsson, Google and a Microsoft campus, and is an example of everything that's right about India. But outside its broad stone walls is a barren, poverty-stricken land that embodies everything still wrong with it. Andhra Pradesh state is part of a vast pebble-dust farm belt that stretches across central India where rains fail more often than they arrive. More than 150,000 farmers committed suicide here in the nine years to 2005, sucked under by a vortex of poverty and debt.[19]

For some, despair had turned to rage. And in the four years that I had been covering Nepal's Maoists, I had watched that revolution bleed south into India. These forsaken fields were now home to India's own army of Maoists, the Naxals, a force of 10,000 who were waging war on India's security forces.[20] Their aim? To level the shiny new shrines to globalization like Hyderabad that had sprung up on the horizon and, ultimately, to take that fight to their Enemy No. 1: America.

Two days before Bush arrived in India, the rebels killed fifty-five men, women and children in a landmine attack in the village of Darmagura, a few hours north of Hyderabad. The victims were returning from a pro-government rally when their two crowded open-top trucks ran over a carpet of explosives carefully concealed in the road. After the blast, the guerrillas worked through the carnage, slitting the throats of survivors with scythes.[21]

Even if they noticed the Darmagura attack, it prompted no comment from the US government or mention in the US press. But an August press release signed by a rebel spokesman who called himself Azad ('Freedom') made clear the guerrillas intended the US as the real target. Their war was with the Indian government and Washington, they said, and they regarded the people they had killed as agents of both. They went on to accuse the US of 'more and more openly intervening . . . in the suppression of countries in the region.' Shadowy 'US diplomats' and 'US officers' were 'entering every sphere of society' in South Asia. Just as in that summer of 2006 the 'America-backed Israeli regime' had launched a 'brutal attack' and 'mass massacre' on the 'guerrilla resistance' in Lebanon, so they alleged the Americans were undertaking a similarly sinister effort against poor, left-wing rebels in India. America wanted to meddle in South Asia, and to 'suppress the Maoists' in particular. The area of Darmagura was particularly contentious – the rebels accused US officials of touring an Indian army 'jungle warfare camp' in the area, part of a US effort to wipe them out.

This positioning of the US as the puppeteer of the Indian government and Indian villagers might have been absurd. But it was also a widely accepted argument, and had been a central tenet of the Naxal doctrine for years. In July 2003, a communiqué from the 'Fifth South Asia Regional Conference of the Parties and Organizations of the Revolutionary Internationalist Movement' held in rebel-held eastern India, denounced the 'US-led imperialists' for 'waging an aggressive, military, political and hegemonistic [sic] offensive against the people of the world'. It congratulated 'the emerging new wave of world proletarian revolution' that was spearheading 'stiff resistance from the people throughout the world, [even] in the very citadels of imperialism' and in 'Nepal, Peru, India, the Philippines and Turkey'. The rebels' message was plain. From their point of view, their assaults were not offensive, but part of a defensive resistance against outside – specifically American – aggressors.

India's revolution began gathering steam around five years after Nepal. It was in July 2001 that the People's Guerrilla Army was formed as the military wing of the People's War Group. And in September 2004, the PWG joined forces with another Marxist rebel group, the Maoist Communist Centre, to form the Communist Party of India-Maoist. Though they are known as Naxals after a short-lived rebellion over land reform in the town of Naxalbari in West Bengal in 1967, today's revolutionaries are spurred by modern grievances. They oppose globalization and free markets. They despise Western consumerism, Western technology and Western morality. They have creed in common with anti-globalization activists the world over, with whom they share a violent hatred of international capitalism and multinational conglomerates, and Islamic radicals, with whom they share a visceral dislike of America and Israel. Their ideas draw directly on Marx and Engels and the old Communist International. The world is in chains. For world revolution, just join the blots.

There was plenty to keep them busy in India. In 2005, Michael Carter, then World Bank country director for India, spoke of a country that occupied 'two worlds simultaneously', one developing, one deteriorating. 'In the first, economic reform and social changes have begun to take hold and growth has had an impact on people's lives. In the other, citizens appear almost completely left behind by public services, employment opportunities and brighter prospects. Bridging the gap between these two Indias is perhaps the greatest challenge facing the country today.'[22]

When they formed their united Naxal force in 2004 – then a combined forced of 7,000 armed men and women and a further 40,000 party cadres – the joint leaders, Kishan and Ganapathi, declared themselves the enemies of India's urban boom.[23] They said they would 'complete the revolution ... through armed agrarian revolutionary war ... encircling the cities from the countryside and finally capturing them.' The two leaders were explicit about drawing their strength from rural resentment. 'The countryside will remain as the "centre of gravity" of the party's work,' they said.[24] A month later, a massed band of rebels ambushed a convoy of police in Uttar Pradesh, killing twenty. The leader of that attack, Kamewar Baitha, announced: 'The poor have retaliated against a repressive government. Our battle will continue. Our fight is against the exploitative forces in the government. The poor are now waking up.'

To take the fight international, the Coordination Committee of Maoist Parties and Organizations of South Asia (CCOMPOSA) was formed in June 2001 as an alliance of revolutionary communists. Its aim was to create a rebel heartland combining Nepal, eastern India and parts of Bangladesh. Spokesman Sagar said left-wing rebels in India, Nepal and beyond 'have every reason to come closer together. We have to link up all the people's revolutions and our aim is a Compact Revolutionary Zone slicing through the Indian heartland.' In another proclamation, CCOMPOSA declared: 'Hold high the red banner of Marxism-Leninism-Maoism! Spread the flames of revolution from the high Himalayas to the seas! Develop South Asia as the storm centre of world revolution and as a base area for marching towards world communism!'[25]

The Naxals are optimistic about spreading their revolution precisely because of the resentment and violence that globalization provokes around the world. Ajay Sahni, executive director of the Delhi-based Institute for Conflict Management, says the rebel movement 'has systematically expanded its scope and influence' as a result of Indian governments who 'ignore the fundamentals of governance and fail to provide large populations with the basics of security, welfare, education, health, opportunities for gainful employment and the essentials of human dignity. This is how nations are weakened and this, eventually, is how they disintegrate.'

Meeting the Naxal leadership proved unnervingly easy. A friend in the capital of the impoverished eastern state of Bihar, Patna, managed to make contact with one of the members of the Naxal Politburo, Aravind Shravan. I was given an address to meet him, and took a taxi, expecting to be driven to some far-off jungle hideout. Instead, I was dropped outside the city jail. I began to think there must have been some mistake. Expecting to be accused of breaking *into* jail at any moment, I pushed open a door at the side of the main gates, met a guard, blanched, and asked nervously for Shravan. The man saluted, and walked me into a jail of perhaps 1,000 inmates in a few hundred cells. None of the cell doors were closed. The guard then took me into the prison office. At least, I thought it was the office until a short man in a clean *kurta* leant across a stack of paper on a desk, introduced himself as Shravan and apologized for the untidiness of his cell. At which point the guard saluted again and left.

For the next hour, much of what Shravan said was Marxist rote. But his insight into the Naxal strategy was deep. The fifty-three-year-old reflected CCOMPOSA's confidence. The Naxals were going to 'fight capitalism and imperialist forces and liberate people across the world'. He reacted angrily to mention of Chandrababu Naidu, chief minister of Andhra Pradesh who had survived two Naxal assassination attempts. 'He's a fascist. He only looks after the interests of a particular class. He's done nothing for the common man.' As I had heard several times before by now, Shravan also claimed links to other communist groups in Peru, Turkey and the Philippines.

After an hour, Shravan indicated the interview was over. As I made ready to go, I mentioned the jail. Why stay, I asked, when it seems like you could walk out any time you wanted? 'Being in jail works better for me at this time,' he smiled. 'I can control my security. I am safer here.' I left the prison by the main gates, by now wide open. Behind me, around twenty inmates followed. I watched as they mounted scooters parked outside and rode off into town. 'Night out,' sniffed my driver.

A senior north-eastern Indian intelligence officer I met later said he was not surprised by Shravan's open display of power. 'There is no doubt that all the militant groups in this area are better organized, better funded, better armed and better trained than they were a few years ago.' The world was also beginning to notice. The US has proscribed the Naxals, like Nepal's Maoists, as terrorists. And in June 2006, the World Bank warned the rebellion put India's entire future at risk. 'If inequality between regions rises above a certain threshold, [the] violent conflict [that results] can lead to decades of reduced growth,' wrote the bank.

Shravan too had been confident his revolution was gathering strength, and there seemed little reason to doubt him. Yogendra Singh, emeritus professor of sociology and development at Jawaharlal Nehru University in New Delhi, warned: 'The sudden emergence of a small urban middle class and the stultification of the poor and the lower middle class have ignited an alienation, a resentment in the rural population and urban poor.' Lower castes, the rural poor and urban slum dwellers were discovering the inequality of India's boom had reinforced their exclusion. The Naxal revolution was a symptom.[26]

Shravan, of course, was heartened by all of this. From his prison cell, he described a rebellion that was moving from embryonic to adolescent. The Naxals, he said, were creating an alternative and separate communist state, deep inside central India. He described a rudimentary justice and education system – called the People's Courts and People's Schools. He claimed the Naxals had built some basic infrastructure, such as irrigation channels. And whereas India's inequality might have been unsettling to some, Shravan saw it as an opportunity. 'The future's very good for us,' he says. 'The economic gulf is uniting the masses. They're realizing that their aspirations have not been fulfilled and that this system of development should be destroyed.'

CHAPTER 7

TRIBES, AND THE CULT OF THE MARTYR

High up in the mountains of the northern Rift Valley is the village of Kiambaa, a place of maize farms and mud huts where the air is so light and pure, it is said to hold the secret of Kenya's long-distance runners, who train in the surrounding hills. On New Year's Day 2008, a mob of several hundred armed with machetes, clubs and bows and arrows surrounded Kiambaa's tiny tin-roofed church where up to 200 men, women and children were huddled, freed those who gave up mobile phones or money, raped the women, then closed the doors on the rest, heaped mattresses and dry maize leaves against the entrances and set them alight. The Kenyan Red Cross says it pulled seventeen bodies from the ruins. Survivors say thirty-five died and behind the neat row of blackened bicycles parked by what was once the front porch, there was evidence for that. White fragments of incinerated bones – a pelvis here, a child's finger there – indicated bodies too badly burned to collect. Much of the ash, said villagers, was human. At least one more body, that of a young man called James, lay in a nearby field, where the boy collapsed after running out of the church with his hair and face on fire. Daniel Mwangi Nganga, thirty-seven, whose disabled brother was hacked to death in the family home as the crowd approached the church, said he recognized the killers as friends and neighbours. 'We went to school together,' he said. 'They used to come to our homes. We prayed together.' He searched for an explanation. 'We just don't know what happened.'

During the first few days of 2008 when a tide of tribal violence swept Kenya, killing 1,000 and making refugees of hundreds of thousands, talk of an African renaissance might have seemed misplaced. But Africa is back. After three decades beset by genocide, famine, AIDS and wars as obscure as they were endless, and in which it actually grew poorer, there is a new international scramble for Africa. Soaring global demand for oil, timber and minerals – especially from China – has pushed economic growth for sub-Saharan Africa to more than 5 per cent for four years and is inching towards 7 per cent, according to the IMF.[1] Peace reigns in the old war zones of Angola, Côte d'Ivoire, Liberia, Mozambique, Rwanda, Sierra Leone and, albeit fitfully, Burundi, Ethiopia and Eritrea, and the Democratic Republic of Congo. Since the collapse of the Soviet Union, almost all African countries have held multi-party elections.

Kenya is one of the stars of this renewal. Ranked a medium on the UN's Human Development Index and growing by 6.4 per cent in 2007, according to the IMF, it has elections every five years and, until this New Year, was considered the stable hub of East Africa. So why did it erupt?

The precise psychology of the ferocious bloodletting which overtook Kenya will probably always remain a mystery. Other questions were easier to answer. The immediate cause? A civilian coup by President Mwai Kibaki, whose paramilitary police stormed the Kenyatta International Conference Centre on live television on 30 December, where the votes from an election on 27 December were being counted. Six minutes later, the head of the Election Commission of Kenya declared Kibaki the winner on state television. The underlying problem? Simmering resentment among Kenya's forty-one other tribes, particularly the then opposition leader Raila Odinga's Luos and the Kalenjin of the Rift Valley, at how Kibaki's Kikuyus – Kenya's largest clan with 22 per cent of the population of 37 million – dominate government and business. The historic culprits? Britain, whose farmers sold their farms to the highest bidder at independence in 1963, allowing wealthy Kikuyus to encroach on the ancestral land of Luos, Kalenjins and others in the Rift Valley; and father of the nation Jomo Kenyatta, a Kikuyu who laid the foundations of the ruling Kikuyu cabal.

Rage at this inequality explained the speed with which Kenya fell apart. 'This is a war about rich people and poor people,' said Evans Luseno, thirty-seven, as he faced off against riot police at the entrance to Africa's largest slum, Kibera, in Nairobi. 'One tribe is rich. We have no jobs, and no food for our children. So we will fight to the end, until there are no more Kikuyu.' Despite its overall economic growth, 55 per cent of Kenyans live on less than $2 a day. Richard Dowden, director of the Royal African Society, told my colleague Laura Blue in London: 'There's a Kenya that tourists and visitors see. But Kibera has been rotting for decades. The word "stability" is inappropriate to say the least. There's always been this explosive dispossessed.'

Tribes were the key to understanding how Kenya's growth and democracy had proved hollow for the majority of its 37 million people. Tribes, and corruption. Kenya came eighth last in anti-corruption watchdog Transparency International's

2007 rating of Africa's fifty-two countries.[2] And if government is reduced to a trough, democracy degenerates into a fight to feed. The mandate of the victorious politician is not to steer the nation towards progress, but to steer its assets towards his tribe. The advent of the age of globalization had only raised the size of the potential rewards. The regime of former President Daniel arap Moi, a Kalenjin, stole more than $1 billion in twenty-four years, according to a leaked report by investigators Kroll.[3] The biggest scandal under Kibaki's regime was the Anglo-leasing affair, in which Kenyan officials and ministers defrauded the government of $777 million in bogus arms deals in three years.

The competition to plunder the state explains the tribal nature of politics in Kenya, and how elections can so easily plunge the country into chaos. Everything hinges on winning. 'Elections are a fight to the death,' said Mwalimu Mati, director of the Nairobi-based anti-corruption lobby group Media Analysis and Research Services (MARS). The inequality also helped to explain the violence that has accompanied almost every election in Kenyan history. The price of a loss to a ruling elite was severe, so presidents and ministers would fight tooth and nail to hang on to their livelihood. On the other hand, the disadvantaged and out-of-office had nothing to lose. As Titus Odiambo, a Luo fish trader and opposition supporter, said during one protest in Nairobi: 'If there's civil war, it's the Kikuyus who will lose. It's their buildings that will burn. We don't have anything at stake.'

As in South Africa, inequality also contributed to the rampant violent crime that had given Nairobi the nickname 'Nairobbery'. Many of the jobless looters and rioters I spoke to said they had to steal to feed their families. The corruption of the government also freed them from any guilt. If the nation's leaders were thieving, why not the slum dwellers? Just as in Gabon, corruption had corroded ethics and respect for authority. At a roadblock at Kamosong, south of Eldoret, Thomas, a Kalenjin tribesman armed with a hockey stick, was checking passing cars, dragging any Kikuyus he found out for a beating, or worse. Anyone who wasn't a Kikuyu in Kenya was living under 'our own Kenyan apartheid', he declared.

Corruption and tribalism also eat at state institutions. During the New Year violence, a Nairobi policeman called Datsun, on patrol in the slum of Mathare, told me that the Kenyan police were splitting along tribal lines. Kikuyu cops were manning the road blocks, but Luo officers were entering the townships and urging their tribesmen to fight against their oppressors. The strong Kalenjin presence in the Eldoret police's rank-and-file most likely also explained why, five days after the massacre, not a single officer had visited Kiambaa, a Kikuyu village.

Electorates are to some extent complicit in this tribal dynamic. Often they swap one corrupt leader for another, hoping he will be more generous with his ill-gotten gains. Since independence, power and wealth had been reserved for Kikuyus under Kenyatta, then Kalenjins for twenty-four years of Moi's rule, then Kikuyus again under Kibaki. The contest between Kibaki and Odinga, both centrists, was a straightforward power struggle. 'Kibaki has ruled for five years,' said Evans Luseno. 'Now it is our turn.'

As in Kenya, so it is across Africa. Disparity, corruption and tribalism remain rife. The 2005 UN Human Development Report found that while Latin America had the most enduring inequality, the gap between rich and poor in Africa was the widest on earth.[4] A 2005 UN Department of Economic and Social Affairs study found the number of poor (defined as those on $2 or less a day) in Africa had risen from 288 million in 1981 to 516 million in 2001.[5] Africa is also the world's most corrupt continent, according to Transparency International, with thirty-six out of fifty-two countries afflicted by 'rampant' graft.[6]

Africa's other economic powers displayed divisions and tensions strikingly similar to Kenya. Nigeria had record-breaking corruption, raging violent crime, its 2007 presidential election was rigged, and, in MEND, it had a full-scale tribal *Ijaw* rebellion. Barely a week passes in South Africa without a new corruption scandal among the political and business elite. In the last few days of 2007, for example, the ruling African National Congress chose as its new leader Jacob Zuma, who a week later was indicted on one charge of racketeering, one of money-laundering, two of corruption and twelve charges of fraud in connection with bribes paid by a French arms company. This did nothing to deter the fervour of his supporters, who signalled their tribal allegiance (and desire for change after two Xhosa presidents, Nelson Mandela and Thabo Mbeki) with the slogan '100 per cent Zulu boy'.

The international community shares some blame for the fragility of Africa. Concerned primarily by access to Africa's resources, the West largely contents itself with the appearance of democracy, not the reality, and gives billions of dollars in aid to corrupt governments. The World Bank and the IMF periodically suspend their operations over concerns about corruption, but just as quickly resume them. The East also plays a part. In the past few years, China has approved billions in aid to corrupt governments in Angola and the Democratic Republic of Congo.

Taken to extremes, African tribalism produces the kind of clan chaos of Somalia, now entering its eighteenth year of civil war in 2009. Acute corruption and vote-rigging also often escalates to outright repression. That's been the recipe for the emergence of a long line of African Big Men, such as Zaïre's Mobutu Sese Seko, Uganda's Idi Amin, Liberia's Charles Taylor, Zimbabwe's Robert Mugabe, Uganda's Yoweri Museveni, Angola's José Eduardo Dos Santos and Equatorial Guinea's Teodoro Obiang Nguema. 'Democracy in Africa is not what is understood in the West,' said Catholic Bishop Cornelius Korir, fifty-seven, surveying 9,000 Kikuyu refugees camping in the grounds of his Sacred Heart of Jesus Cathedral in Eldoret, north of Kiambaa. 'Since their wealth depends on power, our leaders are never ready to admit defeat.' Kibaki, Mugabe, Museveni, and former Presidents Olusegun Obasanjo (Nigeria), Gnassingbe Eyadema (Togo) and Sam Nujoma (Namibia) are among those who tried to alter their nations' constitutions – some successfully – to cling to power. At the roadblock at Kamosong, Thomas declared: 'The source of violence on this whole continent is these leaders. Our rights are being raped.' For hundreds of millions of Africans, the new African dream was turning out to be empty. In that case, Kenya was a warning for a whole continent.

A common refrain in the slums of Nairobi, and on the roadblocks across Kenya, was that people weren't afraid to die for their rights. The rioters' chant was 'No Odinga, no peace!' Time and again when I spoke to the looters and murderers, they expressed a willingness to sacrifice themselves. 'We'll fight to the end,' said Evans Luseno in Kibera. 'People will sink and people will swim. I can't swim. I can't swim when the army is fighting us. But I'll keep fighting for my children.' And fighting, and dying, they were. Hundreds of the bodies were piling up in mortuaries across the country, adding up to an eventual toll of 1,500.

That do-or-die commitment reminded me of a teenage girl called Eraj Samandi that I had met in northern Sri Lanka in June 2002. Apart from a burning desire to die before she got old, Samandi was about as far removed from traditional teenage preoccupations as an eighteen-year-old could get. She didn't care about clothes, music or parties. She couldn't remember the last time she had to swot for a test. As for boys, she dismissed all the men in Sri Lanka with a fierce frown and sharp shake of the head. But asked when she hoped to achieve her dream of being a suicide bomber, she grinned, squirmed and buried her face in her arms. 'She's already written her application,' said her commander, Lieutenant Colonel Dewarsara Banu, smiling at her charge's shyness. 'But there's still no reply.' 'Why hasn't there been a reply?' whined Samandi, looking up with the one eye, her left, that survived a shot to the head and fiddling with the capsule of cyanide powder around her neck. 'I want this. I want to be a Black Tiger. I want to blast myself for freedom.'

Samandi's chances of a normal life were shaky from the day she was born in the narrow strip of Tamil Tiger territory in northern Sri Lanka. The area was once a paradise of red-tiled bungalows, purple bougainvillea and powdery white shores, where Tamil boatmen lived by shrimp-fishing and smuggling coconut whisky to India, a day's sail away. But when civil war erupted in 1983 between the Buddhist Sinhalese-dominated government to the south and the Liberation Tamil Tigers of Eelam (LTTE) demanding a homeland in the north and east for their Hindu and ethnic Tamil people, it found itself on the frontline of one of Asia's bloodiest conflicts. Around 70,000 people have since died.

With so much tragedy concentrated on such a small area – even at its widest point and using narrow, single lane roads, you can drive across Tamil territory in just over two hours – most Tiger fighters could offer their own individual calamities as reasons for joining up. For Samandi, it was the death of 125 friends and neighbours in the government's carpet-bombing of her village. 'I saw all that, all that blood and all those bodies and I thought, "Tomorrow, I will die like this too. So I will join the LTTE and die for a reason."' Samandi was not alone. Banu said every time there is a call for suicide mission volunteers – called Black Tigers – more than fifty young guerrillas apply. So many, in fact, that the Tamil Tiger's autocratic leader, Vellupillai Prabhakaran, has created a martyrs' lottery. 'They put everyone's name in a tombola,' said Banu. 'They swirl them around. Then the leader pulls out two names, reads them out and the forty-eight who aren't chosen are all crying. But the two who are chosen, they are very happy and the people around them raise them on their shoulders and are all clapping and celebrating.'

Fighting for a separate state for 3.2 million people in the north of a small Indian Ocean island was, on a world scale, an obscure cause. But years before the world had heard of al-Qaeda, the Tigers were sketching out the blueprint for modern terror. The first Tiger killed himself attacking the Sri Lankan army in 1987. Hundreds followed. When they signed a ceasefire with the Sri Lankan government in February 2002, the Tigers accounted for around a third of all suicide attacks in the world.

The Tigers did not invent suicide attacks. Japanese kamikaze pilots spread terror through Allied navies in the Second World War, and the first suicide bomb of modern times was against the US embassy in Beirut in 1983. But the Tigers turned suicide bombing into a science. Their technical expertise was ingenious. They adapted explosives so that they could be used on land, sea and – with the purchase of what Sri Lankan intelligence services say are two microlight aircraft – air. Bombs were disguised to fit around, and even inside, the body. Among Tiger victims: a president, the head of the Sri Lankan air force, a minister of national security, a foreign minister, an opposition leader and a former prime minister of India, Rajiv Gandhi. In July 2001, they blew up half the fleet of the national airline.

The Tigers also displayed considerable art. Their true genius – and what so many terrorist groups later copied – was realizing the power and attraction of suicide bombing as the ultimate weapon of the oppressed. This was victimhood distilled into martyrdom. Since independence, Sri Lanka's majority Sinhalese had discriminated against Tamils, much as Kikuyus had discriminated against Kenya's other tribes. They reserved government and state industry jobs for Sinhalese and banned the Tamil language in schools. It was revenge for the way their British colonial masters had favoured the Tamils under their divide and rule policy. This was the ethnic resentment that Prabhakaran tapped into when he launched his rebellion in the early 1970s.

But Prabhakaran fashioned it into something else entirely. By the mid 1980s, he had transformed righteous Tamil grievance into an appetite for noble sacrifice and death. Martyrdom had become the central totem of Tamil identity. To die for the cause was the ultimate glory. This was rage refined, and a powerful testament to undefeated will. Killing yourself, and using your death to kill your enemies, said: I am not beaten. I can still choose my death. I can still kill you. With my death, I free myself and crush you. It was an exact forerunner of jihadi terrorism.

Prabhakaran's commercial operations ensured his ideas and methods spread. Money was scarce in the dirt-poor salt marshes of northern Sri Lanka, and from the late 1980s the LTTE hired out trainers on a commercial basis to other insurgent and terror groups in Africa, the Middle East and Asia, who showed these other rebels how it was done. They also assembled a fleet of boats to smuggle weapons across the Indian Ocean and beyond – again, for other rebels groups as well as themselves – which Sri Lankan intelligence estimates at twenty-two ships. 'They are an integral part of the international terror network,' said a Western diplomat in Colombo. 'They are consultants, freight forwarders, money-launderers and instructors. And they are extraordinarily well funded.' Asked how they rated on an international scale of insurgents, the diplomat replied: 'They are the most successful terrorist organization in the world.'

Above all, the Tigers were disciplined. Samandi rose at 4 a.m. from her bed on the earth floor of a house she shared with fifty other women for a quick breakfast before an hour and a half of studying revolutionary thought. Then there was an hour to tidy the base and wash up before 6.30 a.m., when every Tiger cadre takes their daily oath of allegiance to the LTTE. Then the women of her squad set out for surrounding villages, going from door to door hearing grievances and settling disputes. At 4 p.m., they returned for two hours of sports, volleyball, cricket or *taraball*, Prabhakaran's own variation on soccer in which the players squat like ducks and pass the ball by hand. Then it was more study, this time of Tiger rules and regulations, first aid and perhaps an English class, before lights out at 10 p.m. Her duties didn't end there, however. At some point during the night, Samandi had to take a forty-five-minute guard shift.

Almost nothing in Samandi's life was left to personal choice. The only jewellery the Tiger women were allowed to wear were three dog tags, around the wrist, neck and waist that ensure identification of even the most dismembered of bodies. The Tigers enforced a hairstyle for women of two plaits tied in loops across the back of the head to avoid long hair snagging on thorn bushes during an attack. Music was limited to revolutionary songs. The photos that plastered Samandi's bedroom walls were not of pop stars, but dead suicide bombers. And movies in Tiger territory were a strict diet of action flicks, both home-made efforts using real war footage and Hollywood shoot-'em-ups. For the unmarried Samandi, sex or even holding hands, like cigarettes and alcohol, was banned. The Tiger leadership also reserved the right to prevent any marriage it deemed unsuitable – that is, outside LTTE ranks – and sometimes arranged unions between guerrillas. Even Tiger fashion had a military origin. Lieutenant Colonel Banu explained that the pleated baggy slacks once fashionable among Western pop groups in the 1980s were still de rigueur among Tiger men because they were great for hiding weapons.

A quarter-century at war, cut off from the world, will do strange things to a place. The normal stuff of living – shops, towns, communication – existed only in a marginal sense in Tiger territory. At one stage, 800,000 refugees lived by scavenging leaves and grass from the jungle and using sticky palmyra palm fruit for soap. When the fighting raged, there was no post, no telephones and no power. News of September

11 and the death of Diana, Princess of Wales had made it to Tiger newspapers. But most Tamils I spoke to when the 2002 ceasefire allowed contact with the outside world were astonished to learn of China's opening to capitalism or the existence of the euro.

In isolation, the Tigers loomed ever larger over their people. They set up a civil service, health clinics, a welfare system, and even created a separate time zone. They ran the police and courts, which judge according to Tiger law. (In one quirk, witnesses were required to look directly into the judge's eyes as they give their oath of truth. The judge then ruled on their credibility.) Naturally, the Tigers demanded absolute loyalty – residents of the 'capital' Killinochchi say suspected spies were regularly hanged from lamp posts, a wooden board around their necks detailing their crimes. As for religion, suicide bombers became saints, many with their own days of remembrance. Prabhakaran himself was God. Daya Somasundaram, a psychiatrist in the northern city of Jaffna, said thousands make pilgrimages to Prabhakaran's ancestral village on the north coast and fill little boxes of soil 'like a holy ritual, as though they are collecting water from the Ganges'. He added: 'Many of my patients regard Prabhakaran as higher than their own god. They lost their faith because of what happened to them. They've replaced God with Prabhakaran.'

Families became redundant too. Education administrator Thanarajah, fifty-six, said he gave up on the idea of being a father to his three children. 'When we heard the whirring sound of mortars, my children would run into our room and throw their arms round us. They were looking to us, their parents, for protection. And yet all we could do was say "It's all right. It's all right." We couldn't protect them.' Thousands of children found a substitute family in the Tigers. 'That's a feeling no parent should experience,' said Thanarajah.

It's stories like that which persuade many in Sri Lanka that two decades of ferocious conflict may have brutalized the island beyond repair. Paikiasothy Saravanamuttu of the Centre for Policy Alternatives, a Colombo think tank, said: 'There is a cumulative damage. We are becoming increasingly dysfunctional.' Dayan Jayatilleka, visiting scholar in South Asia Studies at Johns Hopkins University and later Sri Lanka's ambassador to the UN, said he was amazed in the days after the December 2004 tsunami to see soldiers donate blood for Tamils. 'I thought, "My God. There is hope. Underneath all this hate and suspicion, there is a humanity to us."' But then, to his disappointment, hostilities restarted within days. 'It was a magical moment,' said Jayatilleka. 'Then it was gone.'

For Samandi, peace would surely be too late. She had made up her mind to kill and to die, and her distress at taking part in just one battle, and surviving, was palpable. 'Five of my friends died in that attack,' said Samandi. 'I was very sad for them. But then I thought, "After we die, we all have freedom." And I want that freedom too.' War erupted again in Sri Lanka in 2006. Maybe Samandi got her wish.

When I heard the bombs were left in first-class compartments, I was sure it was Omar. Between 6 p.m. and 7 p.m. on 11 July 2006, explosions ripped through seven rush-hour trains on Bombay's Western commuter line, killing 186 people and injuring hundreds more. The targets were picked for maximum effect. The Western starts from Bombay's busiest station, Churchgate, through which a million people pass every day. A typical commuter train carries around 4,500 people – three times its official capacity. At rush hour, that figure would have been even higher, each carriage stuffed, with passengers hanging four-thick outside the doors and sitting on the roofs.

Given the similarity to bombings in Madrid and London, television pundits immediately concluded 'al-Qaeda' was to blame. That made little sense to anyone who followed Islamic militancy. Britain had already said the London attacks were as much a result of Muslim alienation in northern England as of Osama bin Laden. Madrid was just as rooted in local grievances as global terror. Sure enough, when the Indian police arrested and charged four men with the attacks a few days later, none were al-Qaeda. They had links instead to a group called the Student Islamic Movement of India (SIMI). And I knew their boss.

Maoists are not the only people trying to destroy the new India. In June 2003, I flew to Bombay to investigate who was behind a nascent bombing campaign in the city. By then, there had been four small attacks on buses and trains since late 2002, which had killed fifteen and injured hundreds. My friend Hussain Zaidi was a veteran Bombay crime reporter who had written a book about the Muslim underworld's 1993 bombings, which killed 257 people.[7] He told me that this time SIMI, or more accurately a loose group of Islamic radicals some of whom had connections to SIMI, was the most likely culprit. Hussain said the bombers would be in hiding. I asked him to try to arrange a meeting anyway.

Three weeks later, we were given instructions to drive to a mosque in the northern backstreets of the city. We assumed we were going for a preliminary meeting to see if we passed muster. As our taxi passed the mosque at a crawl behind cycle rickshaws and wandering cows, Hussain and I looked around for anyone who seemed to be waiting. Then Hussain's mobile phone rang. 'Yes? . . . yes . . . the Sheraton . . . yes . . . right.' He told the driver to return to my hotel. 'Good news,' he said. 'They've been checking us out since we arrived, and we pass. They'll meet us at your hotel tomorrow.' 'They've been watching us?' I asked, peering out of the cab. 'They *are* watching us,' corrected Hussain.

Neatly bearded and smartly dressed in a suit, Omar came to my hotel door alone a day later. He claimed he had positioned armed men all over the hotel should there be any trouble. When I asked him whether he was behind the bombings, by way of an answer he took a seat by the window, surveyed the sunset over Bombay's southern coastline and began a long reflection on a life spent entirely outside the Indian mainstream.

At forty-four, Omar held the senior rank of *ansar*, or guide, in India's loose-knit Muslim militant movement and was now near the top of India's most wanted list. A member of the ultra-orthodox Ahl-e-Hadith Sunni sect, he joined SIMI as a teenager soon after its formation as an extremist militant group in the late 1970s. Since then, he had spent his life on the run working inside India's radical Islamic movement, changing his appearance, identity and address every few months. For most of his three decades as a jihadi, Omar had been content to act as a facilitator for foreign Islamic guerrillas from Pakistan, Afghanistan and even western China, providing them with safe houses, weapons and identities as they transited India on their way to missions inside the country and beyond.

But since late 2002, he had become a frontline bomber, planning and carrying out the blasts in Bombay. Why the change? Omar said the answer lay in India's opening up to the world. As a Muslim in a country dominated by Hindus, he had always been an outsider, he said. But the situation had become worse over time, as India integrated ever more closely with the outside world and adopted Western mores and the rules of global commerce. Muslims in India were increasingly shunned as backward, a tribe that belonged to the past. On occasion, prejudice turned to hate. 'Sometimes it seems the Hindu way of protecting India is killing Muslims,' said Omar. Even well-to-do Muslims were oppressed, he said. 'Middle-class Muslims are being sidelined, so they join our organization. They are even angrier than me because they are top-level people and still they do not get a job.'[8] Hindus, Jews and others had historical complaints against Muslims, he said. But Muslims like him wanted 'revenge for the present'. Nevertheless, he said violence had been a last option. 'We started peacefully, and we were attacked. So now we attack others. We have no choice.' And since he had taken up arms, Omar had been carefully calibrating the violence in an attempt to broadcast his message. 'We are trying to draw attention to our problems, and show the world we are being oppressed.'

I wanted to know whether he and SIMI were part of the international Islamic militant brotherhood, the rumoured 'network of networks' around the world. Omar replied he had connections with militants in Afghanistan, Saudi Arabia, Kashmir, in the Palestinian territories and, 'in the past', al-Qaeda. Had he protected fugitive Taliban fighters? 'We have done this,' he said. 'These people have come to India and we have been protecting them. There are hundreds of them. Some of them have been killed, some of them are roaming here and there.'[9]

But Omar stressed he was an Indian Muslim at heart, and that his was a local fight. Indeed, he'd agreed to meet only because he wanted me to understand his very personal, very Indian reasons for doing what he did. 'Nobody is born a terrorist,' he said.

No injustice or cause could excuse Omar's actions. And the toll resulting from his actions was mounting. Three weeks after our meeting, his men detonated two car bombs in central Bombay, one in a market, the other next to a crowd of tourists at the Gateway to India, killing a total of sixty people. In October 2005, three blasts in Delhi, two in markets, one on a bus, killed another sixty. In March 2006, three more outside a Hindu temple in the holy city of Varanasi killed twenty. Then in June 2006, Omar's men hit the trains.

But Omar had at least attempted an explanation. There are those who don't want to hear about a bomber's reasons. Understanding them, they feel, means accepting them. A line must be drawn. The bomber must know he has put himself beyond civilization and will be treated as he behaved – as a barbarian.

Still others would say Omar was merely the Indian manifestation of a global tide of Islamic anger – shorthanded by 'al-Qaeda' – that takes in the Koranic literalists of Deoband in northern India, the Wahhabis of Saudi Arabia, the international jihadi camps of Afghanistan, Algeria and Somalia, the backstreets of Western Europe, Palestinians, Iraq, Chechnya, Kashmir and Bosnia. By this view, the bombers are extremists – madmen – and almost impossible to understand, so why bother?

And it was true that Omar exhibited a terrifying nihilist streak. 'We are against politicians, we are against the system,' he said. 'We even kill Muslim politicians who take part in the system. We kill Hindu children. It's good – you stop the *kafir* there, at the beginning.' He predicted a future of relentless violence, something he almost seemed to be looking forward to. 'I see a dark future, a violent future. It will get worse and worse. It's going to increase.' Omar was reflecting a mindset common among militants from the camps of Afghanistan, who succeeded the first wave of modern political Islamists in the mid to late 1990s. They renounced the debate and politics of their predecessors in favour of absolutism, mysticism and death.[10] Theirs was not a fight of this earth, but a millenarian, cosmic struggle. What was new about those who attacked New York, London and Madrid was not that they railed against oppression and exclusion, but rather that almost none were direct victims of injustice themselves. Theirs was not a cause. It was a hate. There was to be no talking these people down, no deal to be done, no compromise to be reached. The violence was the point and it was limitless. Omar had a touch of that. 'We enjoy this work,' he said of the bombings. 'We live for this work. We regret nothing.'

But I'd also heard Omar's account of how he became who he was. And I knew he was not 'al-Qaeda' or even Pakistani[11] but a modern Indian with real, local grievances. At times, his complaints were almost pedestrian. 'This country doesn't work for us,' he said. 'You can't get a proper education, you can't get a job.' He was talking about alienation in modern, globalized India.

That made Omar a cousin to the left-wing insurgents killing and attacking across India and the world. The Maoists, the Naxals, MEND, Kenya's Luos, Sri Lanka's Tamils – even Indonesia's pirates – all had taken up arms out of a sense of exclusion. Omar shared their frustration. Communists and Islamists have the same angry roots. They share many of the same grievances – and use the same language of revolution. Prachanda and Prabhakaran spoke of 'martyrs' to describe fallen comrades. Omar, the Islamist, used communist terms like 'bourgeois' and said his sense of alienation rose as India became more consumerist and Western.

Omar reflected a reality underpinning many Islamist insurgencies. They have their origins in real, local complaints. When you examine the Palestinian militancy, or the Chechens, or the Kashmiris, these are conflicts that all began as quarrels over land. The political Islamist movements of the 1980s and 1990s were populist, anti-establishment national movements, concerned with social justice. Their efforts to reach out to the oppressed and condemn the elite borrowed much from the Western labour movement, just as the Naxals or the Maoists did. The Jamaat-i-Islami, the conservative Islamic political party founded in Pakistan and with branches across the world, was set up in 1941 by Maulana Abu Ala Maududi as an instrument to foment Islamic revolution using Leninist methods. Hamas and Hezbollah were mass social movements, grounded in the anger of a broad community. In the southern Philippines, a communist rebellion led by the Moro National Liberation Front split in 1978 when an Islamic faction broke away to become the Moro Islamic Liberation Front – and the two armies have fought the government side by side to this day.

Like all rebels, political Islamists reject the prevailing orthodoxy and fulminate in angry estrangement. They also rail against tangible injustices and lack of opportunity – real transgressions that had concrete solutions. Even al-Qaeda tries to present itself as a champion of the oppressed. In September 2007, when that year's credit crunch and subprime mortgage crisis hit, bin Laden startled many when he reached out in a video message to the 'people of America'. He expressed sympathy for 'those reeling under the burden of interest-related debt, insane taxes and real estate mortgages' and urged them to do away with the democratic system that 'serves the interest of the major corporations' and leads to 'global warming and its woes'. He called on people who have 'previously liberated yourselves before from the slavery of monks, kings, and feudalism' to liberate themselves from 'the deception, shackles and attrition of the capitalist system' which 'seeks to turn the entire world into a fiefdom of the major corporations under the label of "globalization".' As the South Asia Analysis Group noted, the statement read more like the text of a disgruntled American than that of an Arab sheikh, with 'more allusions to contemporary American history than to ancient Islam'. Nor was bin Laden's message al-Qaeda's first attempt to appeal to the poor. His deputy Ayman al Zawahiri said earlier in 2007 that al-Qaeda was fighting on behalf of 'all the weak and oppressed in North America and South America, in Africa and Asia, and all over the world'.

While his methods displayed a horrifyingly cavalier regard for life, Omar was motivated by the same issues that once spurred the Black Panthers or the IRA or even left-wing student protesters in France. The reason first-class compartments had made me think of Omar was that a terrorist who hated everyone – like the freedom-hating al-Qaeda of popular legend – would be happy to kill anyone. But a man like Omar, brimming with personal injustice, would prefer to target. He'd want to kill the people he blamed for his situation, the success stories who were keeping the Indian boom to themselves. The kind of people, in fact, who travelled first class across India's business capital.

*

In the eyes of many Hindus, no Muslim can ever truly belong in India. The origins of this antagonism are centuries old. Hard-line Hindus regard as a national humiliation the Islamic influence that pervades India's history, starting with the Mughal renaissance in the sixteenth century, continuing with the birth of Islamic fundamentalism at Deoband in northern India in the 1860s and enduring even today in India's national symbol, the Mughal mausoleum of the Taj Mahal. This distrust of Islam has only increased since independence in 1947. Modern India was founded in the Muslim and Hindu bloodletting of Partition, in which a million people died, and since then three wars against Islamic Pakistan have killed more than a million more. That tension has been further stoked by India's rule over Muslim-dominated Kashmir in the face of strident Pakistani opposition, and the growth of Islamic fundamentalism in Bangladesh. Washington's invasions of Afghanistan and Iraq and the 1998 election of a Hindu nationalist BJP government lent further legitimacy to India's lurking anti-Muslim prejudice. 'Muslims are a despised minority, disliked by a large section of the majority,' wrote Muslim commentator Firoz Bakht Ahmed in the *Hindu* newspaper.

India's 150 million Muslims do have their high achievers: former President Abdul Kalam; Wipro chairman and offshoring billionaire Azim Premji; and a host of Bollywood stars (Shah Rukh Khan, Aamir Khan, Salman Khan, Saif Ali Khan). But for every Muslim entrepreneur or movie actor, there are 1,000 others with tales of discrimination in the workplace or the education system, harassment by police officers or segregation into ghettos by Hindu landlords. Just as it does in other parts of the world, orthodox Islam also restricts Muslim education and discourages participation in globalization and India's Western-style, credit-fuelled boom. As a result, Indian Muslims are less educated, poorer and live shorter, less secure and less healthy lives than their Hindu counterparts. Censuses paint a bleak picture. In rural India, 29 per cent of Muslims earn less than $6 a month, compared with 26 per cent of Hindus. In the cities (where a third of all Muslims live) the gap rises rise to 40 per cent versus 22 per cent, while 30 per cent of urban Muslims are illiterate, versus 19 per cent of Hindus. Only 27 per cent of Muslims have a salaried job compared with 43 per cent of Hindus. Some 13 per cent of India's population is Muslim, yet Muslims account for just 3 per cent of government employees, and an even smaller percentage are employed by private Hindu businesses.[12] This prejudice can turn violent – against Muslims. In all the riots since independence, official records reveal three quarters of the casualties in terms of lives lost or property destroyed were Muslims. University of Washington political scientist Paul Brass has written that over time, Hindu 'institutionalized riot systems' have become part of Indian life.[13] 'There is often a tendency in India to treat Muslims as them rather than us,' says K.C. Tyagi, former leader of the moderate Hindu Samajwadi Party. 'And this tendency does have terrible manifestations. Even today, by and large, Muslims have not been admitted to what we call the Indian mainstream.'

The history of Muslim alienation in India is crucial to understanding the creed now espoused by radical Islamists across the world. Muslim humiliation begins with the Indian mutiny of 1857 or, as it is called in India, the First War of Independence. The revolt was sparked by the hanging of Mangal Pandey, a soldier in the East India Company's native regiment at Barrackpore, near Calcutta, who had attacked his

British lieutenant on 29 March. When he was executed a week later, native soldiers across India revolted. Though Pandey was a Hindu, the target of British revenge was India's Mughal rulers, the Muslim dynasties who had dominated the subcontinent for 500 years. The Mughal empire was dismantled and Bahadur Shah, the last emperor, exiled to Burma.

As my *Time* colleague Aryn Baker wrote in an article tracing the history of Islam in South Asia: 'Following the 1857 war, Muslim society in India collapsed. The British imposed English as the official language for both education and communication. The impact was cataclysmic. Muslims went from near 100 per cent literacy in Urdu to 20 per cent within half a century ... Between 1858 and 1878, only 57 out of the 3,100 graduates of Calcutta University – then the centre of South Asian education – were Muslim ... It was as if the whole of Muslim society had retreated to lick its collective wounds. From this period of introspection two rival Islamic movements emerged to foster an Islamic ascendancy.'[14] One, based at Aligarh outside Delhi, embraced the modern world and adopted a secular approach, promoting Muslim culture, philosophy and language, but leaving religion to the mullahs. The other, founded a few hundred miles away at Deoband in 1866, advocated a return to Islam's fundamental origins, an outright rejection of the West and demanded adherents live strictly according to the teachings of the Koran and the example set by the life of the Prophet Mohammed.

Both schools thrived. But it is the Deobandis, and their brothers from the like-minded Wahhabi sect in Saudi Arabia, that make headlines today. The 9,000 Deobandi institutions around the world include Islamabad's Red Mosque, scene of a full-scale Pakistani military attack in July 2007, and Dara-ul-Uloom Haqaniya Akora Khattak, near Peshawar, where

Mullah Omar and the Taliban were educated. It was the students at the Deobandi madrassahs that the CIA encouraged to fight its proxy war against the Soviet Union in Afghanistan. Soldiers in this jihad were known as mujahideen. The trouble was, as Aryn noted: 'Jihad, as it is described in the Koran, does not end merely with political gain. It ends in a perfect Islamic state. The West's cynical resurrection of something so profoundly powerful and complex unleashed a force whose roots can be found in al-Qaeda's rage, the Taliban's dream of an Islamic utopia in Afghanistan, and in the dozens of radical Islamic groups rapidly replicating themselves around the world today.'[15]

This, then, is modern terror. It's about wounded pride, and a determination to rectify humiliations stretching back a century and a half to the first, colonial era of Western imperialism – by targeting the instruments of modern-day imperialism. Today Muslims are on the less well-armed side of fights in the Palestinian territories, Chechnya, Afghanistan, Iraq, Somalia, Algeria, Bosnia and even western China. Islamic terrorism finds its immediate cause in the bodies of dead Muslims that result from these conflicts. It finds its broad support in the hundreds of thousands of Muslims who share the perception that they are victims in this world, a scattered tribe excluded and marginalized by globalization. Those few willing to give their lives – the martyr terrorists – are, to many Muslims, courageous proof that, though they are down, they are not beaten.

CHAPTER 8

FIRE-STARTERS

The wars we have covered so far are rebellions, instances of the weak attacking the strong. But what happens when the strong attack the weak?

On 8 January 2007, news broke of a US air strike in East Africa. On 9 January, Pentagon spokesman Bryan Whitman confirmed a US AC-130 propeller gunship had targeted 'what we believe to be principal al-Qaeda leadership'. He did not specify a location, nor confirm reports of other US attacks. Asked about another AC-130 strike on 23 January, Whitman said simply: 'We're going to go after al-Qaeda and the global war on terror, wherever it takes us. I don't have anything for you on Somalia.'

Most people don't have anything on Somalia. It is a hot, poor swathe of desert and swamp in the Horn of Africa, sparsely populated by camel herders, mango farmers and fishermen. It's not Iraq or Afghanistan; it doesn't even attract the attention Darfur gets. The hundreds of cargo ships that skirt its coast en route to Europe or Asia each day are a reminder of how the world passes Somalia by.

But East Africa looms large on the map for Islamic militants. The oldest al-Qaeda training camp in Africa, Ras Kamboni, is perched on Somalia's south-eastern tip, surrounded by swamps and jungle that make it as inaccessible as the hill caves of Tora Bora. Radical groups such as al-Itihaad al-Islamiya (Islamic Union), set up and built into a 1,000-fighter organization by Osama bin Laden, have existed in Somalia as long as the Taliban in Afghanistan. Bin Laden and al Zawahiri hail Somalia as a key battleground. The same bin Laden T-shirts that fill Pakistan's dusty bazaars are sold in the markets along Kenya's Indian Ocean coast.

Since the outbreak of civil war in 1991, Somalia has also suffered from the kind of chaos that provides good cover for militants, as the US knows well. On 3 October 1993, eighteen US soldiers protecting a UN mission died fighting militiamen in the capital Mogadishu – a battle portrayed in the book and film *Black Hawk Down*.

Five years after that battle came the first shots in what became known as the war on terror. At 10.45 a.m. on 7 August 1998, car bombs detonated simultaneously next to the US embassies in Nairobi, Kenya, and Dar es Salaam, Tanzania. In Nairobi, 213 people were killed and 4,000 injured. In Dar es Salaam, 11 and 85. Just 12 Americans died – most casualties were Kenyan and Tanzanian passers-by. The FBI named three Somalia-based suspects: Fazul Abdullah Mohammed, originally from the Comoros Islands off Mozambique; Kenyan Saleh Ali Saleh Nabhan; and Sudanese bomb-maker Abu Talha al-Sudani. The FBI described them as members of the 'Osama bin Laden network' and offered $5 million for Fazul's arrest or death.

The US response prefigured much of what was later to come after 9/11. Thirteen days after the bombings, President Bill Clinton ordered cruise missile strikes on a factory in Sudan and a camp in Afghanistan, both thought to be operated by bin Laden. The operation was code-named 'Infinite Reach'. Hitting targets in two new countries in retaliation for attacks in two others showed the US considered it was dealing with a global terror network, and would attack that network wherever it could. The Clinton administration set another precedent. When Saddam Hussein's son, Uday, praised bin Laden as an Arab and Islamic 'hero', Richard A. Clarke, national coordinator for security for both Clinton and George W. Bush, made the first direct connection between al-Qaeda and Iraq, suggesting Baghdad had offered bin Laden asylum.

Fazul's group appeared to be encouraged rather than deterred by the US response. It struck again on 28 November 2002, killing thirteen people when gunmen attacked the Israeli-owned Paradise Hotel outside Mombasa, Kenya, and fired two missiles at an Israeli airliner in Kenyan airspace the same night, which missed. In 2003, staff at the US embassy in Nairobi evacuated for a week over reports that Fazul wanted to level the new building. In 2006, al Sudani was implicated in a plan to attack the US base in Djibouti. And on 28 September 2007, the US warned that Somalia-based militants were planning to kidnap Western tourists from Kenya's beaches.

The Pentagon made priorities of Afghanistan and Iraq after 9/11. But Africa is an increasing worry. 'If we're successful in denying al-Qaeda sanctuary in Waziristan and the North West Frontier Province [in Pakistan], where are they going to go?' asks a retired senior Special Operations commander. 'Africa.' To counter this perceived threat, in 2002 the US opened a base in Djibouti – the Joint Task Force Horn of Africa (JTFHOA) – and staffed it with 700 Marines and air force personnel, and 800 Special Operations soldiers. In the last few years, says Daniel Volman, director of the Washington-based African Security Research Project, the US has quietly opened bare-bones bases – often an airfield and a warehouse – in Algeria, Gabon, Kenya, Mali, Morocco, Senegal, Tunisia and Uganda. In 2003, Washington allocated $100 million to the East Africa Counter-Terrorism Initiative, an inter-agency task force focused on the continent. In 2004, it expanded its programme of training and intelligence sharing to a Trans-Sahara Counter-Terrorism Initiative with nine African countries close to the equator. The Sixth Fleet, based in Gaeta, Italy, now spends much of its time patrolling the coasts of Africa. In 2007, using another $100 million allocated to Africa under the Global Peace Operations Initiative, US soldiers trained and equipped units in Benin, Botswana, Ethiopia, Gabon, Ghana, Kenya, Malawi, Mali, Mozambique, Nigeria, Senegal, South Africa and Zambia, and possibly Angola and Namibia. US Special Forces are also training African forces in Chad, Mali, Mauritania and Niger. And the US army has held joint exercises in Côte d'Ivoire, Guinea and Uganda, and trained thousands of officers from forty-four African countries at its military academies in the US. Much of this is done discreetly 'in recognition of Africa's colonial past and likely popular resistance to anything resembling a permanent military garrison,' writes Volman. But the pattern of a growing US military presence in Africa is unmistakable. It culminated on 1 October 2007, when the Pentagon opened a new 200-officer command dedicated to operations in Africa – Africom – initially based at Stuttgart, Germany. Priorities include rebels in Nigeria's oil fields and an al-Qaeda branch in Algeria. But the focus is the Horn – Somalia, Ethiopia, Kenya and Eritrea.

Opportunity for US action came at the end of 2006 when

Ethiopia invaded Somalia to topple the Union of Islamic Courts (UIC). The UIC took power in Mogadishu that summer, bringing the first semblance of law and order to the capital in fifteen years of civil war. But they rang alarm bells in Addis Ababa and Washington, particularly when its leader, Sheikh Hassan Dahir Aweys, declared a jihad on Ethiopian troops in October 2006. 'That was unacceptable,' Ethiopian Prime Minister Meles Zenawi said in interview at his offices in Addis Ababa. Washington initially advised against an invasion, according to witnesses on both sides of a meeting in Addis in November 2006 between Meles and the then head of US Central Command, General John Abizaid. Abizaid told Meles he was 'not allowed' to invade Somalia, adding Somalia would become 'Ethiopia's Iraq'. Meles was adamant. And when Ethiopia invaded, Meles says small groups of US Special Operations personnel went along with them.

The advance was a stunning, bloody success. 'They came at us in wave after wave after wave,' says an Ethiopian minister involved in the operation. 'We just cut them down.' With thousands of UIC dead in days, Ethiopia took Mogadishu and installed the government-in-exile, the Transitional Federal Government (TFG). On 5 January, Zawahiri released a message telling Somalis to 'consume' the 'crusader' Ethiopians 'as the lions eat their prey'. He was too late. Thousands of UIC fighters and refugees were already streaming south from Mogadishu towards Ras Kamboni and Kenya, convoys of beaten-up trucks crawling across potholed dirt roads. There was every chance the embassy bombers were among them. As Whitman said, after years of shadow games, al-Qaeda's African leaders were out in the open and presenting themselves as 'targets of opportunity'. Said Meles: 'The American military involvement started after the Islamic Courts were defeated. In the southern part of Somalia . . . some US air assets were used for bombing operations on two occasions.'

Months later, the US was still keeping a tight lid on its actions in Somalia. In June 2007, I flew with photographer Sven Torfinn and security adviser David Snelson to Mogadishu, and caught a UN flight to Kismayo. There we hired twenty gunmen and two pickups, picked up a local journalist to act as guide, and drove for thirty-six hours, off-road, through the jungle. It was the rainy season and the cars grounded in the mud every few miles. Around midday on the second day, our driver hit a tree and flipped our car. But although the pickup, which had already lost much of its paint to the thorn thickets, took a beating and one of our gunmen cracked a couple of ribs, we were able to right it and drive for another ten hours, stopping for the night when another of our gunmen signalled his fatigue by the arresting tactic of jumping off the back and firing his AK-47 in the air. The following morning, we reached one of the two US strike sites, just south of where the equator intersects Kenya's border with Somalia.

An area the size of three soccer pitches was littered with shell casings and live rounds, punctured by the regularly spaced apple-sized holes of aerial cannon fire. The trucks and cars remained in camp formation. Six 10-ton trucks were destroyed, several flipped on their backs. The three-metre barrel of an anti-aircraft gun had been blown thirty metres from its mount.

Our trip revealed some surprises. Nine bomb craters, twice as deep as a man and four times across, in a grouping tight enough, agreed the US Special Operations commander, to suggest precision-guided munitions from US warplanes. Discarded plastic covers from American-made mortar rounds also spoke of the presence of infantry: the convoy was hit from the air, then again from the ground. In addition, while the nearest human habitation was the Somali village of Waldena, GPS receivers revealed the strike site was not in lawless Somalia, but 500 yards inside Kenya.

We were still walking in the area when 'al-Qaeda' showed up. Three men in a blacked-out SUV and carrying AK-47s pulled up on the track. Our militia surrounded them and demanded they dismount. The men said they worked for Hassan al Turki, a Somali insurgent commander notorious for declaring that all Somalis were terrorists and demanding George W. Bush invade. The SUV was full of tea and sugar. The men said they were taking it to a new training camp in the area. Our militia urged us to let them kill the fighters. 'Al-Qaeda,' they said and, by way of further encouragement: 'Nice car.' We demurred and instructed them to let the militants pass. 'We could have had three cars,' our militia commander complained as he watched the SUV drive into the distance.

Meeting al-Qaeda was not good. And as our fighters kept pointing out, we hadn't killed them when we had the chance. We left the site quickly in the other direction. When we stopped at the nearby town of Hosingo to talk to some witnesses to the bombardment, word reached us that the same SUV had followed us into town. We departed, drove ten hours to Kismayo, finished our interviews and caught a UN flight out two days later. I spent the next few months trying to reconstruct what happened, talking to government ministers, soldiers, diplomats, analysts and spooks in Nairobi, Addis Ababa and across the US. What I discovered was this:

On the night of 7–8 January 2007, a lone herdsman walked

out of the grasslands and thorn trees towards a circle of trucks, cars and pickups mounted with heavy machine guns in Southern Somalia, not far from the Kenyan border. According to an Ethiopian army officer who was watching, he skirted the camp, avoided a group of guards carrying AK-47s and, unobserved by the Islamists, dropped a small electronic beacon.

A US Special Operations AC-130 propeller gunship was already taking off from a dirt strip in eastern Ethiopia. A squad of thirty US Special Operations soldiers had accompanied the Ethiopian army when it invaded Somalia fifteen days before and, the Special Operations commander told me, had tantalizing intelligence on one of the fleeing Somali convoys. Travelling with it was Aden Hashi Ayro, an Afghanistan-trained guerrilla accused by the US of being behind the assassination of four aid workers in Somaliland and a string of other killings. Also said to be there was Fazul. With the Ethiopians pressing from the north, and the Kenyan army and US Marines blocking to the south, the AC-130's mission was to obliterate the trapped convoy. The plane was fit for purpose. Down one side it had a 120-rounds-per-minute 40 mm cannon, a 105 mm Howitzer and a 20 mm Gatling. Operating with cockpit black-out, it was to circle lazy, left and low over its target, pouring fire on whatever was beneath.

A Western analyst in the region describes what happened next, as related by a man who survived it. 'The guy said the strike came out of nowhere. The ground exploded. They were hit once, and scattered. Then they were hit again – that one really got them.'

Bryan Whitman issued no death tolls. On 17 January, US Deputy Assistant of Defense for African Affairs Theresa Whelan told a Washington press conference the raid killed 8. A Western diplomat in the region says 20 to 30. The Ethiopian officer says 100 to 200. 'We will never get the exact figure,' says a Nairobi-based observer. 'It depends which side is giving you the information.'

Ayro was wounded. Initial reports said Fazul was dead, but the US now believes he was not there and went into hiding in Kenya. Whelan denied there were civilian casualties. The Western diplomat qualified that, saying there were 'no substantial civilian casualties, per se'. The Special Operations officer said his men made every effort to 'mitigate risk to non-combatants' but replied 'I really don't know' when asked if civilians died. Meles said they did perish – in US and Ethiopian strikes – but added the distinction between fighter and accompanying sympathizer was trivial. The Waldena convoy was made up of 'hardcore refugees', he said. 'There may have been some family members of these radical Islamists with them, but this was not by any imagination a civilian or mixed convoy.'

What I had seen were the results of the second strike, two weeks later. Precisely who was targeted, or how many were killed, remained unknown. The biggest success of the operation resulted from an accident, or what the Special Operations commander describes as Ethiopia's 'different view of collateral damage'. Ethiopia has a poor reputation for human rights and its troops are known as trigger happy. At the time, said the Western diplomat, by cooperating with the US on terrorism, Ethiopia had 'bought itself a free pass on human rights'.

That may have been why Somali witnesses described free-firing Ethiopian helicopters and MiGs attacking vehicles up and down the border in January. The member of parliament for Kismayo, Abdirashid Mohamed Hiddig, drove a 50-kilometre stretch soon afterwards and estimates he saw forty to fifty destroyed cars and trucks. Al-Sudani, the third member of Fazul's group and an explosives expert trained by Hezbollah in Lebanon, was killed as he tried to cross the border in a truck. But the Ethiopians didn't realize for months. His death was only known to a handful of UIC fighters who returned to bury him. Eventually, the news filtered up to the Somali government, and to Ethiopia and the US.

There was more evidence that the Ethiopians were shooting wild. At the border village of Kulbio, witnesses said the dead included a woman and child. Aisha Whitehead, twenty-one, was sure the woman was an American friend from Mogadishu. I met Whitehead when we caught the same UN flight out of Kismayo. Squeezing down the narrow passageway on the prop plane, I bumped into a woman in a full-length black burka.

'Sorry,' I said in English.

'No worries,' came the reply in a broad Australian accent.

Aisha was from Melbourne. After years as a drug user, she found Islam, graduated to Wahhabism, and married an Australian Somali, Ali Ahmed. They had a daughter, Hafsa, and with spectacularly poor timing moved to Mogadishu in December 2006 to live under Sharia law. In the few weeks before Ethiopia invaded, Aisha became friends with a fellow émigrée, an American. The woman called herself Um Mohammed – which means 'wife of Mohammed' – and had three children of nine, four and six months. When Ethiopia invaded, Ahmed and Um Mohammed's husband were killed. Ahmed's mother later told the *Australian* newspaper that her son had joined al-Qaeda,[1] but Aisha insists her husband was killed filming the battles in the first few days of the Ethiopian invasion, and was not fighting. The two widows and their children joined a convoy fleeing Mogadishu. But Aisha was nine months pregnant and the rough roads triggered her labour. Um Mohammed left her at Kismayo to give birth and continued to the border. 'She died in the car,' said Aisha. 'They killed one of her kids too.'

If the US kept al Sudani's death to itself, it also hushed up the size of the US operation. In October, the US Navy moved the aircraft carrier USS *Eisenhower*, carrying 3,500 men and 72 warplanes, to join 4 other US warships off the Somali coast. Several vessels from the 15-ship international Combined Task Force 150 joined them. The deployment was announced. Not disclosed were patrols over Somalia by US F-15e fighter-bombers, Predator drones and the deployment of US boots on the ground.

Kismayo airport became an Ethiopia–US base. Fuel manager Hukun Abdi Koreyo, twenty-eight, says that for a month transport planes, one marked with the US flag, the others from Kenya's air force, brought in thirty to forty US soldiers at a time from Nairobi and a secret US strip at Manda Bay, Kenya. They weren't just there to kill. In early January, the Kismayo MP Hiddig says the Ethiopians asked him to fly to Kulbio. In a former UIC base, two US plain-clothes personnel – who he took to be CIA – and a handful of US soldiers this time brought in by helicopter from the *Eisenhower*, were sifting prisoners, looking for al-Qaeda. 'They corralled hundreds,' he says. Hiddig was asked to identify locals. He says the sorting produced up to twenty 'white people' whom he took to be Europeans from the nationalities printed on their confiscated passports.

It was the start of a long process. Human Rights Watch says Ethiopian and Kenyan security forces detained hundreds more suspects, including women and children. In April, Ethiopia acknowledged forty-one people were in jail in Addis

Ababa, including four Britons and an American from Brooklyn, Amir Meshal. But, according to manifests shown to my *Time* colleague Christopher Thompson by Human Rights Watch, at least eighty-five more people were also deported from Kenya to Somalia on three flights by African Express Airways and Blue Bird Aviation, on 20 and 27 January and 10 February. Human Rights Watch claims 300 people were held without charge in the two countries and accuses the US of complicity in 'Africa's Guantánamo'. Most suspects were released in May.

The operation amounted to a short, secret US war in East Africa, alongside its ally Ethiopia. Involving thousands of US servicemen on land, sea and air, its scope was unprecedented for a clandestine operation since 9/11. It showed how the US military was expanding into Africa. And why. US generals had long described the region as a looming 'third front in the war on terror' after Afghanistan and Iraq. This was its grand opening. The increasing focus by the US military on Africa also suggested Somalia was not an isolated attack, but the shape of things to come. Sure enough, on 1 June that same year, a US warship off the coast of northern Somalia unleashed an artillery barrage on an area known as Puntland, killing eight jihadis, including Europeans and an American. On 2 March 2008, US missiles hit a house in the village of Dobley, on the border with Kenya and close to Waldena, killing between six and fourteen people, many of them believed to be civilians. And on 1 May, another attack on the northern town of Dusamareb killed around a dozen more, including Ayro.

The US had every justification to pursue those who bombed its embassies. The threat from al-Qaeda was real before US intervention. But the presence of the American military was also provocative. Somalia shared the same pronounced feeling of disadvantage felt across the Muslim world, a mixture of humiliation at Muslim backwardness and rage at perceived American oppression. You could find this anger anywhere on the long list of places that were focuses for the Muslim sense of injustice. Al-Qaeda regularly cited distant conflicts such as Kashmir and Somalia as evidence that Muslims were under attack worldwide in a US-led world war. This made events in any one of those conflicts a potential fire-starter for the others, hard-wired into the circuits of every radical Muslim group on the planet.

By the end of 2007, as a direct result of the Ethiopia–US operation, Somalia was shaping up to be a new focus of Muslim grievance. The country was in the grip of a humanitarian disaster. More than 600,000 refugees had fled Mogadishu to live in hovels of twigs and plastic bags in the bush. Because of poor security, aid deliveries were few, and regularly interrupted. The UN's Central Emergency Response Fund said 1 million Somalis were in need of assistance and protection. The UN Office for the Coordination of Humanitarian Affairs (OCHA) said the figure was more like 1.8 million – and that in a country of just 9 million, where both drought and floods are annual events and where 71 per cent of the people are classed as undernourished. 'Somalia is into its worst humanitarian crisis in nearly fifteen or sixteen years,' said OCHA in the summer of 2007. 'Of [those] who fled to Mogadishu due to heavy fighting, only 60,000 can be reached by the humanitarian community.' On a visit to Mogadishu in May 2007, the UN Undersecretary General for Humanitarian Affairs and Emergency Relief Coordinator, John Holmes, concluded: 'I do not think you can say this is a recovering city. It is a fairly depressing prospect.' By November, UN envoy to Somalia Ahmedou Ould-Abdallah was describing the humanitarian crisis as the worst in Africa. Even Pope Benedict XVI expressed concern at the 'fragility of the humanitarian situation in Somalia'.

The operation had other bad results. The newly installed transitional federal government proved a crashing disappointment, falling back on narrow clan loyalties, excluding much of its opposition from the reconciliation process and, in November, splitting when President Yusuf Abdullah fired Prime Minister Ali Mohamed Gedi. Along the coast, piracy was at record levels, further deterring business and aid.

Moreover, as soon as the Ethiopians pulled out of southern Somalia in February, the jihadis were back in control of Ras Kamboni and the swamps of the south-east. 'Government control here is zero,' said Hiddig in June. 'The militants are just waiting for the chance to take over the country again.' By the end of the year, gun battles were a daily event in Mogadishu. Ayro, at that stage recovered from his wounds, was back at the head of the UIC militia, the *Shabab*. In November, he issued a proclamation, hailing bin Laden and calling on Somalis to target peacekeepers and to pursue the Ethiopians to Addis Ababa, where he said they should behead their women and children. Some of the battles in Mogadishu were the worst the city had ever seen. In April, 1,000 Ethiopians, TFG troops and Somali insurgents died in just four days.

An additional looming concern was Eritrea. Somali nationalist rebels, remnants of the UIC and separatist rebels from the Ogaden National Liberation Front in eastern Ethiopia formed an alliance and based themselves in the Eritrean capital Asmara. In July, the Nairobi-based UN Monitoring Group on Somalia said Eritrea was supplying Somali insurgents with 'huge' amounts of arms. Ethiopia alleged Eritrea was doing the same for the ONLF. That had observers speculating that the US-backed Ethiopian invasion might unwittingly be making real the nightmare that has long haunted the Horn of Africa – a regional war that drags in Ethiopia, Eritrea, Somalia and perhaps even Kenya. In June, Meles told the Ethiopian parliament he was strengthening the army with a view to countering the threat from Eritrea.[2] 'These three crises (Somalia, Ogaden and the Eritrea–Ethiopia enmity) are fusing into one,' said the Western analyst.

A centripetal force in the centre of this crisis was the presence of US forces. They emboldened their allies with superpower backup. They galvanized their enemies by giving them a superpower to shoot at. If al-Qaeda had taken a local war and made it global in Afghanistan, the Pentagon was doing the same in Somalia. The Western analyst said that by summer 2006, Mogadishu was teeming with 'hundreds' of newly arrived foreign jihadis, keen to fight the US. Mogadishu *Shabab* commander Mohammed Mahmood Ali told me the US presence had invigorated the resistance. 'America's aggression helped us a lot,' he said. 'We got a lot of support from that.' The Western analyst concluded that, if it was hyperbolic before, the US military's view of Somalia was becoming correct. 'It now *is* the opening up of a third front in the war on terror.'

The potential for a wider conflict had long existed in Somalia. Now that was becoming reality. As in Afghanistan, the Islamists had wanted to take one country's crisis and turn it into part of a global war. The US was obliging them. In the short term, US forces damaged al-Qaeda's operations there. In the long term, they spurred a wider anti-Americanism and helped accelerate a regional crisis. The jihadis' plan was playing out like an old schoolboy trick. You set a paper bag of dog excrement on fire in the street outside the housemaster's door and ring the doorbell. What happens? The hapless victim stamps on the flames, and gets covered in turd.

In a January 2003 afterword to *Globalization and Its Discontents* that discussed the Bush administration's unilateralism, Joseph Stiglitz wrote: 'Our system of global governance without global government can only work if there is an acceptance of multi-lateralism.'[3] American boots on the ground in Africa was an example of unilateralism. For the extremists, it was also proof they were right. Here was America in the flesh, raining death on Somalis and muscling in on Africa as though it were part of a grand White House scheme to preserve the US's place at the top of an unfair world order. The *Shabab* commander Ali asked me: 'What is their motive? What is their cause here? How far away is America from here? Can we disturb America from here?' Ali concluded the sole reason for US soldiers to travel to Somalia was hatred of Islam. 'With this war on terror, they are trying to eliminate Muslims from the globe.' That meant Muslims like him were fighting for survival. They saw themselves as victims fighting the evil America, with all the everlasting and righteous fury that bestowed on them.

By the end of 2007, there were clear parallels between Somalia and Iraq. Ethiopia was stuck in a quagmire, unable to withdraw and suffering daily losses, much as Abizaid had predicted. And like Iraq, the Somali war was attracting jihadis from across the world.

The difference between the two wars was that Iraq had no international terrorist presence before the US invaded, except for a rebel group in the far north. Instead, invading Iraq had made the delusion of that country's links to al-Qaeda a self-fulfilling prophecy. Bin Laden took his war international with 9/11. The US invasion of Iraq, by sucking in jihadis from around the world and armies from Europe and Asia, had made it truly global. It was the biggest fire-starter of them all.

What stood out in the years of horrors that followed that March invasion was the chaos of it all. As in all war, any noble intentions that may have existed in the minds of commanders at the outset evaporated the moment the first shot was fired. The Bush administration may have had plans to bring democracy to Iraq and the Middle East, and eventually spread their creed around the globe, and so starve terrorism of the frustration that was its oxygen. But war was a maelstrom. The special urgencies of kill or be killed left little room for high politics. I'd seen that happen at Qala-i-Jangi. I saw it again at Karbala.

Squinting at the golden dome on the horizon in the days before the battle in April 2003, older soldiers would suck their teeth and declare Karbala was going to be brutal. In AD 680, Mohammed's grandson Hussein and seventy-two men fought to the death in Karbala over the right to lead the Muslim faith. Hussein died with a sword in one hand and a Koran in the other, and his last words, 'Better to die with dignity than live with humiliation', became the defiant founding stone of the Shia faith. Thirteen centuries later, as Karbala remembered Hussein's death with black flags flying from every rooftop, a small band of Iraqi militiamen were showing every intention of matching Hussein's suicidal courage.

The Shia holy city was a crucial objective for coalition forces: left unhindered, its Iraqi garrison of a few thousand could place a stranglehold on the US supply route to the frontline troops further north around Baghdad. US and British warplanes had bombed the surrounding areas for weeks and American intelligence reports indicated two nearby Iraqi tank divisions and a light infantry division were at as little as half strength. In Karbala itself, most Iraqi soldiers had fled when the 3rd Infantry Division's big guns blasted the narrow gap between Razzazah Lake and the city at the start of the final US advance to the Iraqi capital. But US Special Forces probing Karbala's outskirts had reported that 500–700 Fedeyeen volunteer militias had dug in for a fight. Every night just after dusk, small squads of Iraqis would venture out from the city into the surrounding onion fields and test the alertness of the American M1-A1 Abrams tanks and Bradley Fighting Vehicles around the city. It had been a car driven from Karbala that had detonated at a checkpoint killing four US servicemen in late March. An attack on an American tank a week later on 2 April appeared to confirm that the Fedeyeen had settled on a pattern of suicidal attacks. Then, as evening settled over Karbala, an Abrams crew spotted a lone figure running towards them and the tank's gunner fired a 50-calibre warning shot. The figure kept running. At about 100 yards out, the gunner lowered his aim and fired again. The man exploded. 'I guess he was wired up and ready to blow,' said one lieutenant colonel at the time. 'One thing's for sure: these people aren't giving up.'

Just after 11 a.m. on Saturday 5 April as the last 3rd Infantry tank rolled north towards Baghdad, three waves of Black Hawk helicopters and two Chinook set down beside the highway to Karbala's west. Ten lines of men from the 3rd Battalion 502 Brigade, 101st Infantry Division – 'The Widow-Makers' – ran down the ramps and out into the dust, advancing east across the desert. The 502's 1st and 2nd battalions did the same from the south and east. 3rd Battalion's Charlie Company – 'Hardcore' – crossed the northern part of a vast landfill site, aiming for a school building on Karbala's eastern side. A mile to the south, Charlie's 2nd platoon linked up with eight Bradleys from the 141st Infantry Division from Fort Riley, Kansas, each a nine-man team of a driver, commander, gunner and six infantrymen squeezed in the back. In between, the hundred men of Bravo Company, the 'Bulldogs', joined four more Bradleys from the 141st and headed for a water treatment plant on the city's south-eastern edge. Fifty foot overhead flew pairs of two-man Kiawa OH-58 attack helicopters – 'Little Birds' – watching for the enemy.

Bravo was still two blocks south from the city, the men struggling in the 98°F heat under 70 pounds of Kevlar, weapons and ammunition, when the Kiawas began taking a fire. Bravo made it to an alleyway leading into Karbala and immediately, said 1st Platoon Staff Sergeant Jose de la Garza, twenty-ight, 'an RPG cut through our line and bullets started kicking up dust around our feet. We were two minutes in, fire was coming down the alley and we were in full contact.'

The infantrymen inched their way around to the water plant and took cover. Gunfire was constant. One ricocheting round struck an air force radio man in the chest armour and lodged, still hot, under his collar. Sheltering by his 'Red Four' Bradley outside, Sergeant David Brown, thirty, radioed Sergeant Patrick Jarchow in Red Three. 'We're taking fire from left and right,' he said. 'The Little Bird too. We've got to do something to quieten those guns.' Starting at noon and at the end of one alley, the two six-man squads kicked down the door of a mud-brick house, ran in and ordered the family inside out into the driveway. Jarchow's men climbed on to the roof while Brown's squad ran through the house into a narrow alley behind. The two squads moved steadily northeast through the city. As Jarchow's men jumped from roof to roof, Brown's matched them on the ground, clearing houses, identifying targets, killing them. Lieutenant Colonel Chris Holden, in command of US forces at Karbala, would later estimate enemy forces in the area at 150. 'We had a sniper and Sergeant Osbourne saw to that,' says Brown, 'and we moved on down, firing, taking fire, and clearing. I popped one guy with an AK. Every time the Little Birds went over, the fire would start up and we'd zero in on that.' When the squads reached an intersection, both now on the ground, Brown pivoted left and saw a man holding two RPGs. 'I popped two rounds at him and I see the impact in his chest and gut. He reaches down, grabbed one RPG, and it goes off and blows his foot off, ricochets off the ground and comes straight at us. I take cover and Sergeant Jarchow pops the dude again. We cross over the intersection and that's when I see Specialist Brown get hit.'

Behind Sergeant Brown, Specialist Larry Brown reached the junction to be met with a short burst of fire waist-high and from dead ahead. 'He fell against the wall on his left,' says Sergeant Brown. 'I yelled: "Get Brown to cover! He's hit!" And Specialist Michael Carter kicks in a door, pulls him in and starts his procedure while Sergeant Christiansen pops the dude that shot Brown. Meanwhile, the guy with the RPG is up again.'

Jarchow and Brown took turns firing at the RPG gunner now crawling across the road. Sergeant Brown called for an evacuation by Bradley and then threw smoke grenades into the road for cover. Through the smoke, Brown and Jarchow could see two figures, perhaps a father and a daughter, approaching the fallen RPG gunner. 'The father looks like he's trying to go for the RPG or help the guy on the ground,' says Brown. 'So I say, "Sergeant J., pop the father!" and Sergeant J. says "All right!" and dropped him. The girl helps him up and they're walking away and I popped him again, twice, one in each leg and he's down. He moves again and I empty my magazine into him.' As the rest of the squad helped the wounded Brown into the back of a Bradley, Brown was amazed to discover the original RPG gunner still moving and trying to get to his weapon. As Brown approached him, he opened his eyes and began talking. 'So I shot him again in the head,' says Brown. 'I walk away, he starts up again. So I call up the 240 Bravo (heavy machine gun) to put him out of his misery. We emptied fifty rounds into him, and then we shot him with a 7.62 on the Bradley.' Brown pauses. 'He's still talking when we leave.'

All four Bradleys pulled back to the city outskirts where a Black Hawk helicopter was waiting to evacuate the injured Specialist Brown. 'Just then, the 101st guys are moving out,' said Staff Sergeant Mathew Werner, twenty-eight, in Red One. In the 101st, Bravo 3rd Platoon leader First Lieutenant Jason Davis described how Brown's bloody body was the first thing his men saw as they prepared to enter the battle. 'Everybody was just stepping up into the city,' he said. 'Then we had to part ranks and let the casualties through. That was a scary fucking moment.' While medics shot morphine into Brown, 101st Bravo Captain James McGahey, twenty-nine, called in artillery to prep the few city blocks just ahead. Three hundred rounds landed in ten minutes. When crowds of panicking women and children began fleeing out of the city past his troops, McGahey called a ceasefire. The moment the barrage lifted, the Bradley crews mounted up again and headed back into the gunfight, this time followed by Bravo's 1st and 3rd Platoon. It was 2 p.m.

A few hundred yards to the south-east, Pathfinder, and Charlie's 2nd Platoon, were also meeting heavy resistance from a further 150 Fedeyeen. They had been in a close-quarters gun battle on the outskirts of the city for two hours. One of the first casualties was Private First Class Lucas Utterbach, a dismount infantryman from one of the 141st's Bradleys, who took some shrapnel in his leg from an RPG even before he entered the town. 'The Bradleys could go in further,' said Sergeant Joseph Gashi, 'so we took our positions in the nearer building. We were under real heavy fire.' Describing deception tactics that were to be repeated throughout the day, he adds, 'The enemy was using white flags and buildings with white flags on them. They would shoot from a building, climb down and cross the street waving a white flag, and then climb up another building, pick up another weapon and start firing again.' The platoon was pinned down and the battle was at a virtual stalemate. Gashi decided they needed a big gun on the other side of the street and Private First Class Edward Elliott said he'd take his 240 Bravo to the other side of the road. 'He got halfway across and got caught in a hail of fire and was hit in the leg,' says Gashi. 'But he got up again and kept running with that heavy gun. It was extraordinary.' The round had passed through Elliott's right calf just below the knee, shattering the bone. First Lieutenant Kevin Newell, twenty-seven, of New Jersey, whose Bradley had been peppered with machine-gun fire and who had been two inches from death when a bullet shattered his hand microphone next to his face, was called back to evacuate the twenty-one-year-old. As he lowered the back ramp and his gunner reached out to grab Elliott, AK-47 rounds again bounced on the metal, sending splinters of metal into the gunner's forearm. But by 2:20 p.m. Elliott was back at the water plant alongside Brown and also being administered morphine.

Back with 101st's Bravo, the Bradleys pushed north-east into the city. The 1st and 3rd Platoons took an alley each. 'The Bradleys threw in some prep and waved them through. But as soon as we moved in, we were taking sniper rounds,' said 3rd Platoon's First Lieutenant Jason Davis. 'Two blocks in, we kicked in a door to try to identify a crow's nest three blocks further up.' Steadily, Davis's platoon advanced through the city, destroying fire positions and walking over the bodies of their enemies. After an hour, they reached a three-storey building, broke in, and ran up to the roof to lay down a deadly blanket of fire around them as the Fedeyeen converged on their position. To their west, 1st Platoon was making slower progress, spending forty-five minutes just 100 yards into the city pinned down behind the carcass of a dead horse. But eventually they brought forward a shoulder-launch anti-tank missile, blasting their way forward, and at 4 p.m., they joined the 3rd Platoon on their rooftop position. Bravo's 2nd Platoon, which had been guarding the water plant, followed at 5:30 p.m. First Lieutenant Davis estimated his men were on the roof for four hours. 'The Fedeyeen started out in uniform, but once we identified their positions, they would drop down as civilians into the streets and pop up again in other positions,' says Davis. 'We got to know their clothes, you know? "There goes the guy in the checked shirt," "There goes the guy in the green."'

The corpses were piling up below. With them were the bodies of two boys, perhaps seven or eight years old. 3rd Platoon had been on the roof for twenty-five minutes when two small figures came spinning out into a courtyard below, almost as if they had been pushed, and began inching towards an unused RPG round. 'They'd been testing us, getting closer to us and walking away,' says 3rd Platoon squad leader Staff Sergeant James Dyer. 'All the guys are saying, "Don't pick it up, don't touch that." You can hear all the guys, talking to themselves, then shouting, maybe twenty or thirty guys: "Don't do it, don't do it."' A warning shot kicked up a puff of dust at the leading boy's feet. He stopped and looked up at the M-4s, M-16s and heavier mounted SAWs and Bravo 240s above him, levelled at him from three storeys up. Then, fixing the Americans with his clear, brown child's eyes, he walked forward, slowly and deliberately, and picked up the round. 'The moment he touched it, you could see a wall of lead slam into those kids,' says Dyer, thirty-two. 'It dropped the first kid immediately. The second one was hit a second later – you could see him tumble as he was running.'

At the same time to the east, two of the Bradleys – Red One and Red Two – found themselves in a dead end at the end of a labyrinth of ever narrower alleys. 'We were engaging guys on the right,' says Staff Sergeant Werner. 'There were bodies all over the ground and we were taking a lot of fire from guys down in foxholes. Then this RPG comes out of nowhere from the left, passes over Red Two and slams into us.' A precision shot, the round struck the Bradley at its only weak point, where the turret swivel meets the main body. 'I yelled "RPG!" and all the lights went out,' says Werner. 'The flames burst out through the turret. I had my hands over my face. First Lieutenant [Stephen] Thorpe looked at me and said my face and my hair was all burned. Then he asked, "Am I hit?" and I saw blood on his leg.'

Inside the Bradley, the six-man dismount squad took the

full force of the explosion, but survived with a few burns and burst eardrums. With the vehicle crippled, driver Specialist John Ator, twenty, jumped out of his hatch, ran around to the back, and manually lowered the rear ramp. The crew spilled out, climbed on top of the burning Bradley and pulled Werner and Thorpe free. 'And right then, we were taking fire,' says Corporal Abraham Acton, the twenty-one-year-old radio operator. Werner adds: 'All nine of us were taking cover around the back, all nine unloading into wherever the fire was coming from.' In Red Two, Sergeant 'Crusty' Crage drove alongside the stricken and burning Bradley to provide cover. Crage also dropped the ramp on his Bradley to allow his squad of six to join the fight. Ator was thrown into Crage's track and Werner, disoriented and temporarily blinded, was hurled into the vehicle. He said: 'The doc yelled "Get in the fucking track, let me see your eyes!" and I jumped in. But then the ramp was going up and there was no one else in there but Ator and I said, "Fuck that!" and jumped off.' With Crage covering their rear, the fourteen men joined up with Red Three and Red Four and began retracing the path of destruction they had blasted through the city. 'We're shooting people, people are shooting at us,' says Werner. 'AKs, RPGs, tracers, people on the rooftops, people in the streets. It was Black Hawk Down times ten. We were just dropping magazines on the ground as we ran and reloading. Anywhere where we started taking fire from, we just lit them up.' Adds Acton: 'Anything that moved, we shot it. It was us or them. If they were innocent, shit, they shouldn't have been there.' Two heavy SAW gunners took the lead. Covering their rear was Private Morales with a third SAW. 'Morales was a badass,' says Werner. 'The guy was just tearing shit up. That's all you could hear.' Says Acton: 'It was fucking fucked, man. It was fucked up. We were taking fire from all around – you didn't know where you were gonna get shot from. I shot four guys, then two guys, then others running down the alleys. The Bradleys were giving people crimson vests – close range 50-cal shots in the chest. All you see is a cloud of blood.'

Eventually after an hour of unrelenting fighting and running, the squad made it to the water plant. They suffered no further injuries. Thorpe and Ator were evacuated to the Black Hawk waiting nearby with Elliott and Brown still onboard. The Black Hawk took off around 6 p.m., a full four hours after Brown had been shot. A few hours later, the 141st heard that Specialist Larry Brown had died of his wounds.

Back in the city, the fight around Bravo began to die around 5:30 p.m. Lieutenant Colonel Holden said the remaining Fedeyeen to the south made a last suicidal charge on the American positions. 'That was really getting like Somalia for ten minutes or so, the way they came at us,' he said. 'We just cut them down.' A brief firefight also erupted at Karbala's Baath Party headquarters, but was quickly silenced by a barrage of high explosive rounds fired by Alpha and Delta companies that Holden had held in reserve. And as Bravo and Pathfinder received their first drinking water for five hours and moved into a former Feyedeen barracks to the north, the mortar teams kept up their barrage into the evening. The Little Birds too were still flying, spotting and engaging anything moving on the ground. Finally, at 8 p.m., with guards posted, the guns began to fall silent and the men snatched some sleep.

Dawn brought confirmation of the slaughter. US forces had one killed in action (Brown), four serious casualties and thirteen light ones. Scores of civilians had died. Holden said his men had killed 279 Fedeyeen. 'We didn't take a single prisoner of war,' he grinned.

But as an old man on a donkey cart made his way through the blackened fire zone to collect the dead, the new day brought some surprises. In addition to the Iraqi corpses, said Holden, he was astonished to discover the bodies of Syrians, Sudanese, Pakistanis, Yemenis and Lebanese. And as the day went on, the American sense of triumph turned to relief, then foreboding. Working their way across the city, US forces discovered hidden in schools and government buildings an indoor firing range, sophisticated explosives, training manuals and thousands of uniforms, as well as seventeen large armed caches yielding a hundred thousand 7.62 mm rounds and tens of thousands of mortars and RPGs – more than nine trucks could carry.

When they invaded, the soldiers were told the Iraqis would welcome them with open arms. More than one US commander had predicted that the advance to Baghdad would be like Italy in 1944 – crowds throwing flowers at soldiers, children riding on the tanks, women kissing infantrymen. Even three weeks into the war, they were still using the word 'liberation'.

Karbala changed all that. As they sifted the debris, men like Holden were discovering how Iraq was really going to be. This wasn't liberation. They were fighting Iraqi nationalists, and what seemed to be a global resistance alliance of mujahideen. It was like the Alamo had been switched around. It was the Americans who were the invading Mexicans; it was the Iraqis who were fighting to the last man to defend their homes. And then there was the sheer viciousness of the fighting. How could the US hope to hold on to the moral high ground in a war like this? 'We shot and killed children,' said Holden. 'That's the kind of fight it was.'

The White House's short-term plan for Iraq was to end the rule of an old Middle Eastern foe. Its long-term hope was to plant the seed of democracy and watch it grow through the region, choking autocrats and drying up the well of frustration that nurtured Islamist terror. It was a bold and ambitious plan. It was a plan with freedom at its heart, a proposal to export democracy and bringing a reformed Middle East into the global fold once and for all.

The plan's big practical flaw was that war was war. How was a soldier meant to dispense liberation through the sights of his gun? There was a theoretical flaw too. In Iraq, US diplomats and soldiers would argue that while the Arab world may have disagreed with US foreign policy, ordinary Arabs had a voracious appetite for jeans, burgers and MTV. Arabs, and Afghans, Africans and Asians, all coveted the American lifestyle. The implication was that the world desired and believed in the 'American way' and the human race was actually American at heart. America represented the pinnacle of mankind's achievements, and the rightful destination for every human being. Iraq and other oppressed parts of the globe just needed to be liberated.

This was the old theory of inevitable progress towards a single civilization. Get with the programme, and the world would be flat and history would end. But envy isn't always a good thing. It can motivate people to improve their own lives. Incentives, after all, are the foundation of the free market. But it also breeds resentment. The view that dominates much of the Middle East – and Asia, Africa and Latin America – is that, in the era of globalization, the US uses its military and political power to take a disproportionate part of the world's wealth for itself. Iraq wasn't about democracy, according to this view. It was about oil and contracts for Halliburton. Whatever the accuracy of those allegations, that was the overwhelming perception. What escaped the advocates of an-American-lifestyle-for-all is this: the fact that many non-Americans aspired to an American way of life did not preclude them from simultaneously resenting the inequality the US represented. For the disenchanted, there were two ways to even the score. Campaign for the US to give more to the world in trade, aid and debt relief. Or bring the US down to your level.

In that sense, Iraq was a bloody, intractable variation on a theme. Globalization starts wars. The difference between the war in Iraq and conflicts in Nigeria or Nepal or India was that the US had come to Iraq. That made the oppression all the more real, the wounds all the deeper, and the victims all the more wretched. And there were lots of victims. In Iraq, tens of thousands of civilians[4] were being killed.

On a day in late March 2003, in the first few days of the invasion, I watched a 3rd Infantry checkpoint squad shoot dead an unarmed farmer who had driven up in a truck. The soldiers fired warning shots, but the man hadn't heard above the noise of his engine so when he was thirty yards away, eight men opened up on his cab. A single bullet entered the man's cheek, ricocheted down his spine and exited through his back.

The next day I spoke to one of the unit's commanders, Major Dean Shultis. Shultis was an intelligent and articulate man, and was one of the first in the US army to express concern at the mounting toll of civilian casualties and the effect that would have on the Iraqi attitude to US troops. He was trying to spread the word that approaching American checkpoints was dangerous. Talking to a group of Iraqi civilians, Shultis told them that US soldiers had fixed rules of engagement that they were obliged to follow. This meant that they would not hesitate to open fire if they were unsure of who was approaching. The Iraqis considered this. Then one man stepped forward and replied that Iraqis were following a different set of compulsions from the Americans. 'Look, we're hungry,' the man said. 'We're not going to stop coming.'

PART THREE

FOG

CHAPTER 9

FIRST CASUALTY

A bad jail wastes a body, and quickly. When I entered cell 6 at Gwanda police station, I was fit. But after five days in a concrete and iron-bar tank, with no food and only a few sips of water, my skin was flaking, my clothes were slipping off, my legs were shiny with mosquito bites and I had a constant migraine. The blanket I was given to lie on on the concrete floor had given me lice. The water I'd palmed from the rusty tap in the shower block had given me diarrhoea. Under a twenty-four-hour strip light, I hadn't slept more than a few minutes at a time. And I stank. So many men had passed through cell 6 that they had left their smell on the walls, and while I was making my own, the walls had also passed theirs on to me.

It took twenty-two hours and one interview to get arrested in Robert Mugabe's Zimbabwe. I flew into Zimbabwe's second city of Bulawayo in April 2007 and drove south to the gold fields of the Great Dyke. I was following tens of thousands of Zimbabweans who, as the economy collapsed around them, headed to the hills of Matabeleland hoping that the red earth might surrender something for them to live on. I expected to find a scene that would capture Zimbabwe's collapse.

My problem was that the regime was also keeping a close eye on the mines. As people and investment fled the country, it was holding on to every last ounce of wealth that remained, charging exorbitant fees for permission to mine and demanding to be sold all gold at a price it dictated. Since November 2006, it had arrested 25,000 illegal miners. Home Affairs Minister Kembo Mohadi was candid about the rationale behind Operation Chikorokoza Chapera: 'Each time there is a police blitz [government subsidiary], Fidelity Printers registers an increased flow of gold,' he told police magazine the *Outpost* in February that year.

Foreign journalists are routinely refused permission to enter Zimbabwe and I entered as a tourist. To maintain the pretence, I should have stayed north, close to Harare, the game parks and Victoria Falls. But Matabeleland was a microcosm of Zimbabwe's implosion. Thousands had died from disease brought on by malnutrition. Hundreds of thousands were surviving by trapping wild animals in the forest or mining with their bare hands. Millions had passed this way en route to South Africa or Botswana. And the area was simultaneously an opposition stronghold – Bulawayo had an opposition mayor – and a target for repression. The story was south. Driving into the small town of West Nicholson, I met Trynos Nkomo, a miner with several concessions. Unknown to me, he was also a police informer. During our ten-minute chat, he stepped out for a few moments. When I emerged from his bungalow, I was detained by two waiting plainclothes officers.

After five days in jail, I was taken to court, admitted a breach of sections 79 and 80, chapter 10:27, of the Access to Information and Protection of Privacy Act, 'working as a journalist without accreditation' and fined 100 Zimbabwean dollars, then worth around half a US cent.[1] It wasn't the first time I'd been in trouble. In 2001, I'd been publicly castigated by the Thai prime minister for questioning the sincerity of the government's crackdown on the sex industry. I was banned from Bangladesh in 2002 after writing about how the security forces had helped fugitive Taliban fighters returning home from Afghanistan. That same year, when I wrote a piece questioning the capacity of Indian Prime Minister Atal Bihari Vajpayee, who was old and increasingly infirm, I received death threats and narrowly escaped being deported.

Why do we get globalization so wrong? One reason has to do with the trouble it takes to get it right. Journalism is sometimes said to be the first draft of history.[2] But foreign correspondence is a very imperfect way of writing the history of the world. We send reporters into countries where they've never been, know no one, and don't speak the language – and expect them to capture the truth, in a maximum of 800 words, within hours. The demands of feeding 'live' technology have only shortened the time spent reporting.

What's more, to be a good foreign correspondent increasingly means putting yourself in danger. Reporters Without Borders says that in 2007 around the world, 83 journalists and 16 of their assistants were killed; a further 199 were imprisoned. That compared with 81 journalists and 32 of their assistants killed in 2006, and 52 kidnapped and 871 arrested that same year; and 63 dead journalists, 5 dead assistants and 807 journalist arrests in 2005. Those figures made 2007 the deadliest year for journalists since 1994, when 103 died – an exceptional toll explained by half of them being killed in the Rwandan genocide. Many of today's deaths occur in Iraq, which has proved more lethal for journalists that any conflict in memory. By the end of 2006, 157 journalists had died in just over five years of war in Iraq, approaching three times the number that died from 1955 to 1975 in Vietnam.[3]

That risk discourages good journalism. Most newspaper readers would be shocked to learn of the diminutive size of the Baghdad press pack, on many days down to a few dozen. And while the image of the fearless reporter dodging bullets may still hold true for some freelancers, staff of media corporations – overseen by managers who have a rising experience of the risk, and cost, of something going wrong – often find themselves forbidden to go. To give a few examples, despite the 2006 Ethiopian invasion, until March 2008, the BBC hadn't sent anyone to Somalia since the assassination of producer Kate Peyton in early 2005. The BBC was, however, the only corporation to place a permanent foreign correspondent in the Gaza Strip – until Alan Johnston was kidnapped and held for 114 days in 2007. Most of the big media houses refuse to send correspondents into Zimbabwe without accreditation – effectively making a ban out of official discouragement.

The golden rule for news managers around the world is that no story is worth dying for. And that's patently true. I've yet to come across the story that didn't pale in significance next to the body of the journalist who was trying to get it. But this is also a slippery slope. A rule that no story is worth dying for quickly becomes a rule that no story is worth risking death for. And that's demonstrably untrue. Imagine a world in which Iraq, Afghanistan, 9/11, Hurricane Katrina or the tsunami went unreported. Plus, those who think a story's not worth risking death for pretty soon start wondering if it's worth risking jail for or, worse, whether it's worth doing without accreditation. The point is: risk aversion has no place in foreign correspondence. Risk management does.

That, however, is a minority view today. To make matters worse, not only are fewer and fewer journalists going into danger zones, there's fewer of them available to send. Today only the BBC and the three main wires – Associated Press, Agence France-Presse and Reuters – maintain a comprehensive foreign staff, with a bureau or a correspondent in most significant countries around the world. Fifteen other English-speaking outlets, mainly American, maintain a meaningful foreign presence – CNN, National Public Radio, Voice of America, Al Jazeera, the *New York Times*, the *International Herald Tribune*, the *Washington Post*, the *Wall Street Journal*, the *Los Angeles Times*, the *Christian Science Monitor*, the *Economist*, the *Financial Times*, *Newsweek*, *Time* and the UN network, Irin (though the last confines itself to 'humanitarian' news from Africa, the Middle East and Central Asia). Most other newspapers limit themselves to stringers or wires, supplemented by a handful of their own foreign correspondents. A typical foreign deployment for a British newspaper, for instance, is one or two in Asia, one in Africa, one in the Middle East, two in the US, one in Europe and one in Moscow. A rough average of one correspondent per billion people in the developing world. (For some reason, Latin America is almost entirely ignored.) Most of these staff members will frequently be required to leave their nominal posts to patrol the beat that has become known by the acronym CRIBA – 'Countries Recently Invaded By America'. *Time* had one of the better international networks of correspondents. Even so, in India I was one of two staff reporters covering a sixth of humanity. In Africa, my patch – which I worked alone – ran to forty-eight countries. A British newspaper colleague in Delhi covered Kabul to Kiribati. A friend in Johannesburg for a terrestrial British television channel did the entire southern hemisphere. No story was worth dying for. But the bigger concern was: was foreign correspondence itself dying?

It's not just the danger. There are also sound business reasons for cutting back on foreign correspondents. We are expensive, in terms of flights, hotels and equipment, and in an era of declining circulation and advertising revenues, we're not cost effective. How much more efficient a deployment of resources to write several pages on the British royal family off the back of a single picture, than to send a correspondent to Sudan – which costs flights, hotels, car hire and other expenses – for a story that's never going to make the front page? Then there's the simple lack of reader interest. You can't expect people to be as gripped by events in a far-flung part of the world as they are at home. Newspapers logically deploy their diminishing resources in areas that maximize readerships. The most high-profile writers in the British press these days, for example, are restaurant reviewers.

But in the era of globalization, the slow death of foreign correspondence is also a paradox. As economies and cultures integrate and our world becomes one, we need more and more information on the world – not least because that process often throws up violent reaction. But that information is diminishing. At first glance, that appears illogical. You might think our knowledge would increase as the world becomes closer. For business in particular, you'd think it was paramount. And with cheap air travel exploding, you'd think hundreds of millions more overseas tourists every year would add to the world's knowledge of itself.

I've argued before that the reality of globalization is that it is a force for standardization, with a bias towards the more powerful. That tends to mean that Western systems of business and Western culture dominate, and alternatives, and the poor and powerless, are squashed and ignored. Now think of the generic five-star, four-restaurant, three-pool resort now found on the coast from Phuket to Namibia, or the all-but-identical shopping malls being erected from Cape Cod to Cape Town. Look at the effort that goes into insulating the tourist from the place he is visiting – from five-star hotels to the backpacker trail – to ensure he has all the amenities of home. It's hard to argue that you're seeing the world if you're merely visiting the same place in different locations.

Journalism is going through the same process of standardization. After all, why bother to get to know other parts of the world when, to the international traveller zipping between glass and steel airports and multinational hotel chains, they increasingly look like your own? Show-business provides one of the most striking examples. You might say the world has always shared the same celebrities, and that probably is true of North America and Europe, at least for the past half century. What is new is Paris Hilton's picture on the front of not just *People* magazine or *Paris Match*, but the *Papua New Guinea Post-Courier*. Sport provides another example. The world increasingly has one sport (soccer), one team (Manchester United) and one player (David Beckham).[4]

This 'flattening' process affects news too. You'd expect British newspapers to splash on train wrecks in London, or the US press to headline on fatal bridge collapses in America. But India's newspapers will also lead on the same stories, relegating twenty-word items about 'fatal mishaps' involving overcrowded Indian buses and Himalayan gorges to the inside pages. In the Philippines in 2001, I was astonished to see one national paper lead on the story of a Manila ferry disaster in which hundreds died and a rival splash on the story of four students who had been shot at a high school in the US. Hurricane Katrina was a story around the world. The story of Bombay's floods, in which many more died a month earlier, barely reached Pakistan. Many big stories – a war here, a shining beacon of hope there – are missed altogether. Our pool of knowledge is shrinking. And this narrowing of the world has a self-reinforcing effect. As people become less familiar with the world, they become less interested in it. One of the great paradoxes of globalization is that as the world becomes smaller and smaller, it knows itself less and less well.

The net result of this standardization in the media is this: globalization is spectacularly poorly reported. Mostly, it is covered by correspondents sitting in one part of the globe, the developed bit. That naturally induces a bias towards reporting globalization's effects on the developed world – detailed observation of the effect of 1.47 billion new workers in the global economy on jobs and wages in Britain, or the growth in New York's investments in emerging markets, or the fact that French supermarkets now sell exciting new products from Indonesia.

These are footnotes to the big story. The big story is explosive job and wealth creation in the developing world, the overnight appearance of cities such as Shenzhen, and the violent tension that throws up. It's the difference between reporting India's effect on a few thousand jobs in Silicon Valley, and the rapid emergence of a $36-billion Indian software industry and an army of Maoist rebels who want to smash it down.

In other words: to get globalization, you've got to go. After

September 11, many commentators seemed to think being attacked by al-Qaeda qualified them as authorities on Islam. It didn't. The catalogue of errors that followed – the idea of Islam as monolithic medievalism, the notion that freedom could be dispensed at the point of a gun, the ignorance of a well-documented animosity between Osama bin Laden and Saddam Hussein – was proof of that.

So it is with globalization. Documenting the outer ripples of globalization on London or New York does not capture the whole story. It's not that journalists or academics or business researchers or IMF and World Bank officials working those patches are mistaken about what they observe. It's that they need to get out more. With globalization, the truth is not within. It's out there. And that means real travel. Not to five-star hotels in Shanghai or business parks in Bangalore or the Africa debate at Davos. But to entirely new environments, places with relaxed attitudes to issues like plumbing and roofing.

Only a few do. Just a handful of Westerners have made the journey to see the Naxals. Only slightly more have poked around the causes of China's growing worker unrest. The most celebrated commentators on world affairs, the pundits, never do their own reporting, but gather their facts second-hand from CNN and Google. The journalists, academics and politicians who venture a little further – to the Bangalores and Shanghais – confine themselves to brief trips to the inner cities and mistake a tour of an elite shopping mall for a tour of the nation. That's like exploring New Orleans by visiting New York. It's how a couple of kilometres of Edwardian riverfront in central Shanghai came to be taken as a whole city, which was duly dubbed 'the Paris of the East'. And it explains how, on a 2006 state visit, George W. Bush hailed the 'new India' from a podium in central Delhi, apparently unaware he was looking out at a city where 10 million people had no toilet.

It's about perspective. You need to get close to see the detail. And you need to pull back to see the big picture. Too much of the former and the entirety of the object you're examining becomes obscured. Too much of the latter and everything looks – that word again – flat. Which is why, next time you hear someone say Bombay is the new New York, you should ask them how New Yorkers cope with all the cows in the street.

CHAPTER 10

THE MYTH OF ASIA

If the West doesn't know much about globalization, neither does Asia. Common sense dictates two nations with a combined population almost ten times the size of the United States wouldn't transform overnight. Even if China and India were to keep growing at their current rates, it would take fifty years for the average Chinese to match the living standards of the average American, a hundred years for the average Indian.

Yet if you believed the buzz, you'd think China and India had already arrived. One reason for that is that for many Asia watchers, prospects and growth are the point. Investment bankers say Chinese and Indian stocks are hotter than American because bankers bet on what they think is going to happen rather than the present. Similarly, foreign newspapers proclaim China and India as the coming economic superpowers because headlines about something new that might happen ('India – the Next Superpower') are more compelling than something old that already is ('India – Still Hot and Poor').

Inside China and India, there's been a surge in patriotic pride, which has nurtured a tendency to proclaim the arrival of a new Golden Age. And a little nationalistic euphoria is understandable. Both countries have endured centuries of deprivation and colonial subjugation, and decades of humiliation as other parts of the world left them in their dust. Why not celebrate the return of the good times?

Of course, in China, Mao took this to a whole new level. The Chairman always said his one great advantage over the nationalists that he defeated in 1949 was his understanding of the power of propaganda. That desire to control image and information is his most enduring legacy. As China's economy and influence grew, and the news of that boom attracted more investment which led to more growth, it became the propagandists' job to feed the best possible image of China into the equation. An even more important function was to try to control the domestic population and prevent them from demanding that political freedom accompany their new economic liberation. 'The government wants a stable society,' a senior twenty-seven-year-old Chinese journalist working for a state daily in Guangdong told me. 'The population is so big and not many people are well educated, so the people do not have a strong sense of judgement. They do not know what's right or wrong. So the government tries to tell them.'

Most of the workers' protests I reported never made the state-controlled Chinese papers. The subject of migrant workers' rights was downplayed and skewed: if it was reported at all, it was in the context of the government and the party coming to the workers' rescue. Certain subjects – the one-child policy, political discontent, religion, the Dalai Lama, domestic terrorism by Muslim Uighurs – were entirely off limits. Other news was subject to distortion by the censors. 'All major media outlets are supervised by the government,' said the journalist. Before publication, every edition had to be sent to the censors' office for review. Any changes they ordered would then have to be incorporated. 'The censors will never tell you what to print. They tell you what not to print.'

In the Internet age, the journalist didn't think such crude methods were working particularly well. 'The public is free to talk about anything,' she said. 'The government tries to keep the media under control, but with the new technology there's always a gap.' The Beijing Olympics drove a bus through that gap. The legacy of releasing tens of thousands of foreign journalists with no reason – such as the need to maintain a bureau or retain a work permit – not to report the truth will likely linger for years in China.

So China was learning subtler ways of finessing the country's image. The most effective took its lead from the zeitgeist of Shenzhen – ripping off the West. Counterfeiting was a massive industry for plastic surgeons, fakers of designer clothes and DVD pirates. It may have annoyed Western manufacturers, but it also fooled many a Western visitor into believing China was, essentially, becoming Western. 'Shenzhen is the window on China,' the migrant workers' lawyer Xiao Qing Jan had told me: 'It's the showcase. The Communist Party uses it to try to present an acceptable face to the international community.'

In the summer of 2007, Shenzhen took this facsimile approach to new heights. On 890 hectares of hills overlooking the ocean, it unveiled a new resort modelled as a replica of the Swiss village of Interlaken, to include three streets of what the developers excitedly called 'gingerbread houses', as well as 'the world's largest man-made waterfall', a 'Viennese ballroom', a 'Swiss village marketplace' and, for reception, 'a themed lobby lounge resembling a medieval European cathedral, with high-vaulted ceilings, gothic chandeliers and stained-glass windows – the "church" theme reinforced by an altar-style wine display behind the bar.' I had to go.

Finding a Swiss village in China was harder than it sounded. Shenzhen was growing so fast, no taxi driver could complete even the shortest journey without pulling over several times to ask for directions. Asking for 'Interlaken' also didn't help: it was only later I learned that in Shenzhen, the resort was known by the more prosaic 'Overseas Chinese Town East'. But once we were within 20 kilometres, the road was lined with posters extolling the charms of Shenzhen's latest attraction. One showed a row of Alpine chalets against green mountains and royal-blue skies. Another showed a white waterfall. A third showed the golfing bunker, surrounded by clipped green grass and blinding white mist. 'Interlaken Spa' appeared to be a half-sunken White House, the guests bathing between the pillars of the portico. And suddenly I realized where I was going. Across the world, from Beijing to Burma to Burundi, tacked to the wall above hotel receptions, stuck to the dashboard of a bus or framed in pride of place in modest living rooms, I had seen thousands of pictures of Switzerland. It was as if mankind had settled on a single vision of paradise, and it was an A-frame log cabin in a flowery summer meadow, cradled by snow-capped mountains. 'Interlaken,' I now realized, was that vision brought to gigantic, real life.

Except it wasn't. It would take an extraordinary pair of blinkers to ignore the reality around us. The sky wasn't royal blue, as in the posters, but diesel-fume grey. The hills weren't lush and green, they were scarred with yellow stone quarries. The sun wasn't bathing the gardens with a dazzling gold, it was covering them with a sickly orange. And the view was hardly Alpine. Next to Interlaken was a giant container port, its forest of cranes fading into the fog of pollution. Once inside the Interlaken Hotel, I was confronted by a dazzling, mammoth display in the giant foyer: plastic purple trees, gold plastic balloons, and a giant green plastic central tree, sprayed with fake snow and hung with plastic animals. Christmas in Saint Moritz, Made In China.

I'd arranged to meet one of the winners of China's boom at the coffee shop beside the fake lake. Billy Lee, thirty-nine, was the scion of a well-connected family that had seized its opportunity when China began opening up and built itself a fortune in hotels, power generation, importing heavy equipment for hotels, such as lifts and boilers, and, most recently, a lifestyle magazine. He was coy about his wealth, but he wore Prada glasses, a silk shirt, a silk jacket and a diamond stud in his left ear, and jetted between homes in Hong Kong, Beijing, Shanghai and Vancouver by private plane. When I asked him about the uneven pattern of China's boom, he was not as dismissive as government officials tended to be. Smart and articulate, he said he was aware of the 'very large' gap between rich and poor in China. But he seemed entirely unaware that this was brewing anger. 'I don't see any direct resentment of the pattern of growth,' he said. 'I don't see any fighting. The Chinese government is adopting policies to ensure a harmonious society.' He agreed that it would be difficult for every Chinese citizen to match his living standards, but he was confident 'the direction is right. This difference between rich and poor is temporary. The poor will catch up.'

Billy's confidence wasn't unassailable. Later in our conversation, he predicted that in twenty years Shenzhen would be 'like Hong Kong, like Singapore . . . if there is no turbulence, no social unrest.' He stressed the need for a strong government to hold the course while a country as large as China went through such a mammoth transition. And he admitted that his own lifestyle was constrained by fears for the future. 'There is a Chinese proverb,' he said. 'Live safely, but think of the worst. I save about thirty to fifty per cent of my income, just in case.' As the sun sank below the horizon and a speaker started up with 'On Top of the World', I asked Billy if he thought the propaganda and the glitz of places like Interlaken was blinding people like him to the reality of China's growing discontent. 'I don't think so,' he said. 'I believe China will be the country to benefit most from globalization.' For that to happen, however, democracy would have to wait. 'Democracy is no guarantee of economic development,' he said. 'The best political systems are based on the conditions in the country. What do people in China want? They want money. Food comes before their spiritual needs.' But what if it was precisely the strong government that he advocated that blocked their ability to earn a fair wage? Billy was convinced the authorities were benign. 'I think the Chinese government is more like a moderator, rather than a centralizer of wealth. If the government carries on as it is, I am optimistic that an equitable distribution of wealth will be achieved.'

Was it possible that rich Chinese simply didn't know about the worker unrest erupting across China? Were isolated projects like Interlaken fooling rich Chinese that their entire country was being transformed? One migrant workers' lawyer I spoke to told me that the efforts the authorities were making to even out China's yawning income divide were 'cosmetic' and were meant merely to present an 'image' of lifting the poor, rather than effecting any substantial changes. He added that in several big cases of worker protests, journalists from the state media had called him for details – and then no story had appeared. The point wasn't that the government had an addiction to lies. It was that it cared less about the truth of a report than the possible consequences or influences it might have. There was also the problem of striking a bum note when China was swelling with patriotism. 'Most of China simply does not want to hear about the miserable life of workers or poor conditions in the factories,' said the lawyer. 'Not now when the Olympics are coming and the country is so proud that we are the new power in the world.'

Myth was just as powerful in India. Not least because the media was in on it there too. The Indian advertising industry now makes TV spots in which modern Indian couples drive new SUVs up dramatic mountain roads, drink coffee in town-square cafes or shop in swish supermarkets, just as they do in Europe or the US. But while that might be India's dream idea of itself, the truth is that there are no smooth mountain roads or piazzas in India and only a handful of supermarkets. So what do the ad makers do? They shoot someone else's and cut and paste those foreign landscapes over Indian reality. Florence, London and Singapore are just some of the cities regularly standing in for Delhi, Bangalore or Bombay. Bollywood also increasingly shoots abroad: New Zealand stands in for war-torn Kashmir and Mauritius for litter-strewn Goa, while a whole host of plots feature expatriate Indians beating the world at its own game in New York, Sydney and London. Newspaper food columnists, writing for magazines with names like *Aspire* fill their pages with articles on the joys of truffles and deli-counter olives, neither of which are available in India. Motoring journalists review cars that are not on sale. I once heard a Delhi housewife brag that whatever you can enjoy 'over there' is now available in India. It took a rare gift for imagination to say that over glasses of warm Thums Up cola mixed with Bagpiper whisky during yet another week of power cuts.

It would be a mistake to think the media was a mirror of a transformed India. Like all media, they're reflecting their market. In the West, that's the majority. In India, it's the rich. TV, newspapers and magazines in India, particularly those publishing or broadcasting in English, reflect the lifestyles of the privileged few, because that's their readership. The vast majority of Indians don't earn enough to qualify as a consumer market. The truly poor don't even read.

But in India, I was surrounded by friends who fervently believed the entire country had made it. I met scores of bright young Indian graduates who had returned from colleges in the US and Britain to take part in the latest happening economy. Academic acquaintances were releasing books with titles like 'India Unbound'. And as I travelled around India, from high tech campus to blighted cornfield and rebel stronghold, I began to wonder whether there was a more fundamental reason for this blinkered self-belief. I was a stranger in India. But maybe India was a stranger to itself too.

The idea made some sense. For one, India's too big, an artificial patchwork of kingdoms and fiefdoms stitched together by the British, with little central coherence outside of times of war or cricket. From the Christian fisherman of Kerala to vegetarian Hindu herdsmen of Gujarat to pygmy tribesmen in the Andamans, India's people have thousands of identities.

It would take more than a lifetime to know all India. I'd lived in India for nearly five years and had barely scratched the surface. A paucity of data also means there is no short-cut summary. There is no reliable population figure for any of India's cities, for instance. The government doesn't even know how many people it employs. Finance Minister P. Chidambaram once told me that the best approximation he could find for the number of people in his pay was 750,000 to 1,500,000.

I also knew most Indians didn't try to get to know their country. For centuries, India has been divided into communities segregated by caste and religion. The new divide between rich and poor has only reinforced those walls. Inside their self-contained world, rich Indians extrapolate their own lives into talk of a booming nation, when they're really talking about their own bulging wallets. And it's not only Indians that are fooled. In a place the size of India, an elite can equal the population of a small European country. Foreign investors and journalists return home convinced they have seen a nation transformed, when they have merely mixed with thousands of affluent Indians in upmarket parts of Bombay or Bangalore.

The power of myth in India should come as little surprise. Hinduism is founded on it. In more modern times, India built an entire cinematic tradition – Bollywood – that outdoes Hollywood for formula escapism. Boy meets girl (songs of joy!), boy leaves girl (songs of sorrow!), boy meets girl again (joy!) and leads a cast of hundreds in a leaping, ululating, face-achingly joyous finale in a meadow outside Zurich.[1]

But myths have limits. When the ruling nationalist Bharatiya Janata Party, or BJP, told India a sense of 'feel-good' was sweeping the country during its doomed India Shining campaign in 2004, it crossed them. Telling people who spend their lives fighting disease and malnutrition that they've never had it so good was, unsurprisingly, a vote loser.

But nobody seemed to read the message in the BJP's defeat. The air of collective delusion continued. It spawned some remarkable moments, such as the publication of a book by the builders of the Delhi metro – when they had built just four stations and estimated their completion date as 2029 – which was subtitled 'How We Did It'.

Then in May 2006, after tripling in three years, India's stock market plunged 30 per cent in weeks – 10 per cent in two hours at one point – wiping out billions of dollars. Despite the fall, Indian companies remained 20 per cent overvalued compared with other markets. And yet international investors proclaimed India was still the best market in the world. *Time*'s Asian edition quoted a well-respected emerging markets investor called Mark Faber. 'If someone put a gun to my head and said, "You have to put all your money in India or all of it in the US,"' he said, 'I'd choose India.'[2] What had persuaded him of India's wealth? Those same 'chic restaurants, hotels and stores' that had sprung up around the tiny elite. It was bizarre. If the investors were recommending specific companies or saying that after the crash was a good time for bargain-hunting, that was one thing. But they weren't – they were endorsing the entire country. Indian stocks had just popped, a sure sign of a bubble. But nobody seemed to have noticed. Faber argued that 'India's infrastructure and housing are ripe for improvement' and 'gaps in development provide opportunities for growth'. That was true. But in the context of infrastructure as poor as India's, that was also like saying that famine creates an appetite for supermarkets. It does, but that's not really the point. Sure enough, in October 2007, India's market popped again – dropping 9 per cent in a day – and once more on 11 January 2008, losing 7 per cent and a further 21 per cent over the next three months.

Nothing illustrated India's efforts to pretend it was something it wasn't than its desire to change its skin. In the West people spend billions of dollars trying to create a café-au-lait tone. But Asia, from its geishas to its Ganesha gods, has always longed to be pale. In Shenzhen, the desire is an industry. In India, it is a national obsession. You see it in the personal ads, which range from the general ('Wheatish girl invites match') to the pinpoint specific ('Suitable alliance invited for 28.11.1972 (7.45 a.m.), 160 cms, fair, smart, well-educated only daughter having advanced training in footwear moulds designing'), but which consistently mention the aspirant's light skin. You see it in pharmacies selling Fair and Lovely whitening soaps and creams and – new in 2005 – Fair and Handsome. And you see it in TV and newspaper commercials, where India's top two models, Katrina Kaif and Yana Gupta, are, respectively, English and Czech.

Fairness is also big business. Fair and Handsome's maker, Mohan Goenka of Calcutta-based Emami, says the whitening-cosmetics market has grown by two thirds in the past five years to an annual $250 million. India's 60,000 beauty salons do an estimated $400-million-a-year trade bleaching faces and blasting skin with tiny sand blowers. They even made a soap opera about it. When I met the star, Rajashree Thakur, on a set outside Bombay, she seemed badly miscast as an ugly duckling. Her face was a flawless ochre, punctuated by ebony eyes and framed by jet-black hair that tumbled to her waist. In the light of the setting sun, she glowed. Rajashree was playing the lead in *Saat Phere* ('Seven Steps', the name of a Hindu marriage ritual), which, between riveting digressions into the lives, loves and astounding secrets of a Rajasthani family, was the tragedy of Saloni, whose unfortunate looks banish all hope of love. 'It's not that Saloni isn't beautiful,' clarified Thakur, a former model. 'It's that she's dark. Because of her complexion, her family thinks no one will marry her.' At the shoot I was visiting, Saloni sought solace at a Hindu temple after another trying day of dusky humiliation, only to be lectured on the virtues of fairness by a fat, ivory-skinned boy. 'Ah, Saloni,' grimaced Thakur. 'She goes through hell.'

Everyone had their own theory for the origin of this fascination with white skin. Thakur and Goenka pointed to pale-faced conquerors from Britain and central Asia who brought architecture and order, as well as military power, and forcefully instilled a reverence for white outsiders. Cultural conservatives complained that Bollywood was pushing aside Indian heroes in favour of Western stars all too ready to display their pale flesh. Some sociologists argued that in a country where most people still farmed, dark skin was associated with lowly labour in the outdoors.[3] Deciding to tap an expert, I arranged to meet Cory Wallia.

Cory is Bollywood's top make-up artist and a man whose cautionary – and perhaps apocryphal – tales on whitening include the time the mother of a bride insisted he slap on so much white foundation that the young girl somehow turned blue. (The punchline? The mother approved.) He believed the real reason for the fairness craze is more troubling than most care to admit. While no one suspects that Westerners seek tans to 'change' their ethnicity, Indians, he said, are motivated to do just that. 'Indians are more racist with other Indians than any American ever was with his slaves,' Cory said. 'The desire for whiteness has very little to do with beauty. It goes right back to our foundations, to the Aryans that settled here 3,500 years ago, and to our castes and gods. The highest Brahmins are the Shuklas and the first word of the invocation of Vishnu is Shukla. And what does Shukla mean? "White One".' Light skin, in other words, marks out an Indian as above and apart from the rabble.

After speaking to Cory, I wondered whether India might not also be trying to give itself a makeover. It seemed to explain the fervent, outlandish patriotism. In 2003, the Pew Global Attitudes Project confirmed India was by far the proudest country on earth. Four out of five Indians believed Indian culture was innately superior; almost the same proportion thought large parts of neighbouring countries belonged to them. It also accounted for the wilful ignorance – the *Maya* – that would prompt an educated and worldly woman like Simi Garewal to cut me off when I mentioned poverty.

Simi and others told me of the shame they felt during the 1960s and 1970s when they travelled to London or New York and were treated with patronizing sympathy. Now India had begun to change and they were sensing a different attitude on their foreign trips. Billy's experience was almost identical. 'In the 1990s, when I went to Canada and the US,' he said, 'I could feel that Chinese people were not welcome. At that time, most Chinese people were working in manual jobs. Now it's a completely different story. Chinese are businessmen, managers, we even have a mayor in Australia. When I go abroad now, people's attitudes are less cold. That's because China's image has improved.' Having tasted a new status, rich Indians and Chinese were impatient for the transformation to be done. They wanted to be equal to anyone in the world. They wanted to be better. Today. This would also account for their prickly defensiveness. In their hearts, the cheerleaders probably knew they were overstating their case.

The most egregious example of national delusion occurred in the aftermath of the 2004 tsunami. Of all the thousands of kilometres of coastline that the waves devastated around Asia on 26 December 2004, the Andaman and Nicobar Islands in the Bay of Bengal were some of the worst hit. Bus conductor Antony Victor, thirty-four, told me he realized it was 'definitely, certainly' Doomsday when the Nicobari island of Katchal, a few hundred kilometres north of the earthquake epicentre, split open beneath his feet and seawater began spurting 'like a fountain' from the fissure. A moment later, after watching a whirlpool carry off babies, wide-eyed cows and whole buses full of people, Victor found himself trapped between surges bearing down on him from either side. 'I closed my eyes and surrendered to the waves,' he said. Somersaulting in the current, Victor was swept on to a hill with several hundred of his neighbours. From there, he watched the sea withdraw, dragging 5,000 of the 8,512 islanders with it. As Jaya Kumar, a thirty-one-year-old government surveyor from the main island of Car Nicobar, said: 'It was the end of the world.'

The islands' indigenous tribes, including En-mei, survived. But many of the settler towns were obliterated. The Nicobars' feeble infrastructure of jetties, a few roads and one runway was largely gone. A week later, Indian air-force pilots flying relief into the area reported difficulty orienting themselves as their maps no longer bore any relation to the geography beneath them. The waves had devoured whole islands, such as the hamlet of Bamboka. It smashed others, like Trinket, home to 500 people, into pieces. The boundaries of India had also moved several kilometres north: its southern tip, Indira Point, vanished, while new volcanoes of hot ash and mud were erupting along the archipelago.

For many survivors, the horror was just beginning. Maya Rajsekhar, thirteen, saw the ocean swallow her mother and father and, after floating at sea for two days on a wooden door, washed up on a Car Nicobar beach that was swarming with poisonous snakes. Newspapers wrote of refugees in Great Nicobar fending off crocodiles as they trekked through the jungle in search of water. And a rescued port official who did not want to be identified even claimed that on one small island, Kundul, 'people are looking for bodies to eat. What else can they do?'

It wasn't as if the government could be blamed for Armageddon. Nevertheless, the administration's first instinct was to dissemble. At daily press briefings, the islands' chief administrator, Lieutenant Governor Prof. Ram Kapse, described the mood of the 41,227 refugees in 111 camps as 'happy'.

More insidious than this clumsy propaganda was how the administration eliminated 18,000 refugees from its relief effort at the stroke of a pen. In the first few days of the disaster, the island authorities estimated the total population affected by the tsunami at 60,000. This took account of all residents and 20,000 unregistered migrant labourers from the mainland, many of whom worked on government infrastructure projects. Then, without explanation, Kapse's administration reverted to an official population figure of 42,068, taken from the 2001 census, excluding all migrants and cutting by a third the number of people for which it was responsible.

This was fantasy taken to dark and lethal depths. A Delhi-based Western relief expert who was kept in Port Blair almost for the duration of the relief effort fumed: 'India doesn't see itself as a developing society with its begging bowl out any more,' she said, 'and it doesn't want others to see it that way either.' Hence the government paid scant attention to its own disaster zone, while trumpeting its dispatch of India's own relief workers to other countries in the region, such as Sri Lanka. The Indian government was aware of the real situation. An internal memo dated 31 January was from Car Nicobar relief officer Ajit Srivastava and complained 'medical supplies are quite insufficient'. A foreign aid worker stationed in Port Blair reported an 'eight-day hiccup' in Indian government relief reaching many areas, something which he said 'probably resulted in thousands more deaths'. And yet India refused all offers of foreign aid, and congratulated itself when the US sent a message of appreciation at its decision to stand on its own two feet.

I uncovered the full scale of the administration's efforts to downsize its relief duties in a raft of confidential official documents I obtained from outraged government officers. One was an internal assessment of the situation on one heavily populated island, Car Nicobar, signed by relief officer Ajit Srivastava and dated 27 December. It spoke of a population of 30,000 in 11 of the island's 15 villages of which '50 per cent' were dead – that is 15,000 people. These figures were also backed by the Red Cross, witnesses and local relief groups. Shortly afterwards, using the official 2001 population for Car Nicobar of just 20,292, the authorities pronounced a Car Nicobar death toll of 812. The same statistical sleight of hand was applied across the islands.

Enterprising administrators found another way to cut the death toll: list people as missing. A second document I was handed concerned the island of Katchal and was dated 16 February. This was a full fifty-three days after the disaster, and yet only 344 people were described as dead, a status which qualified their relatives for relief. A full 4,310 people, however, were 'missing', a description which qualified for none.

Thus the islands' administrators systematically and deliberately underrated the disaster, and held on to relief funds. Relief workers were outraged. The International Red Cross conservatively estimated a death toll of 30,000 from an original 60,000 people living in the Nicobars. To this day, the administration claims the tsunami killed just 1,330, and lists another 5,750 as missing.

To Aisha Majid, tribal leader of the island of Nancowry, the government's actions were outrageous. 'When the government can help other countries, why are they letting us down?' Said fellow survivor Aslam Majid, twenty-two, who went five days without water: 'People aren't dying from the tsunami. They're dying of thirst and hunger.' Islanders and relief workers began to suspect that, steeled in a culture of incompetence and inertia, the bureaucrats simply decided to pretend everything was fine. On Car Nicobar, Mus village head Thomas Philip alleged on 27 December sailors forced him to sign a receipt 'for rice, dhal, sugar, medicine, Nescafé' while delivering none. On 2 January, in another internal document, the Delhi-based Central Relief Commissioner SK Chattopadhyay castigated the island administration for still not knowing the 'full picture' of what had happened. Things did not improve. It wasn't until 28 January that a committee coordinating state and voluntary efforts met for the first time and not until 16 February that villagers in Chonghua on Kamorta island received their first tent. Even after two months, relief workers said hundreds of bodies remained unburied.[4]

Lieutenant Governor Ram Kapse denied his officials had

tried to downplay the calamity. I caught up with him months later as he visited Delhi – bundling into the back of his car for a quick interview between his presentations of his near-perfect rescue operation to government leaders. At first he insisted his figures were 'absolutely correct'. Pressed, he admitted that most missing people were likely to be dead, adding that there may have been some mistakes. But the relief operation had gone smoothly, he said. 'I think people should congratulate us.' Of all the individuals I met in Asia, Kapse had perhaps the most highly developed ability to see black as white. When I asked after the Jarawas and their cousins the Sentinelese – a Palaeolithic tribe with a population of just thirty-nine that lived on their own island – Kapse replied that the tribesmen had shot arrows at a passing coastguard helicopter. 'They were in a very cheerful mood,' he remarked.

CHAPTER 11

LEADERSHIP

As his servants left us with a series of silent bows and closed the door, it became clear King Gyanendra of Nepal spent his days in the company of ghosts. Outside his window, a pale sun was setting over the Himalayas, the staff was emptying in a hushed file through the western gate and a flock of hundreds of ravens was settling noisily into the firs. The light faded, the birds ceased their cawing and a funereal calm settled like a frost on the royal gardens. Nothing stirred in the dimly lit palace. Not even the cacophony of rickshaws and battered buses in the streets outside penetrated the palace walls. 'It is lonely,' said Gyanendra, drawing deeply on a cigarette and flicking ash casually on to a tiger skin at his feet. 'I miss my brothers and sisters. I am a human being after all.'

When I first met Gyanendra, it was early 2004 and two and half years since 1 June 2001 when his thirty-two-year-old nephew Crown Prince Dipendra shot his way through Narananhity Palace in a Shakespearean massacre that briefly gripped the world. Dipendra had been enraged by his mother's refusal to let him marry his girlfriend, a woman of higher caste than she who would have usurped her place in the palace order. A palace inquiry found that, numbed by whisky and hashish and armed with an M-16 Colt assault rifle, an MP-5 submachine gun and an Austrian Glock revolver, Dipendra strode wordlessly in full combat dress into his grandmother's house inside the palace compound and opened fire on his assembled family. By the time he turned his revolver on himself, Dipendra had shot and killed his parents – Queen Aishwarya and King Birendra – his brother, a sister, an aunt, two uncles, two cousins and injured several others. Gyanendra, Birendra's brother, was away in western Nepal. But Gyanendra's wife, Komal, who had taken her children to spend the evening at the palace, was hit several times. She survived, losing six pints of blood and a lung. Gyanendra's son Paras, who became the crown prince, escaped with his sister after pleading for their lives.

Dipendra blew away almost everything his uncle had ever known. Gyanendra lost most of his family, and in an instant went from low-profile chain-smoking businessman to king, and Vishnu incarnate. Dipendra also killed off popular esteem for the royal family. Gyanendra soon became the subject of lurid – and entirely fictional – conspiracies alleging lethal ambition and murder, gossip that would have felt positively sacrilegious only a few days before. The royal family's reputation was further damaged by Paras, whose frequent rampages through Kathmandu's nightclubs – on which he was generally accompanied by bodyguards all too ready to dispense violence on Paras's orders – had long filled the newspapers. To Nepal's horror, Paras was now heir to the throne.[1] And if murder, suspicion and outrage weren't already enough, in November 2001, the Maoists began some slaughtering of their own.

I met Gyanendra in his office in the palace, a stone's throw from where the killings took place. The room was plush, filled with tiger skins and gold-trimmed furniture. Gyanendra, plump, chinless and dressed in the traditional jacket, breeches and *topi* – a multicoloured Gandhi cap – seemed relaxed. He was by the fireplace. An empty chair next to him indicated where I was to sit. It was the first time the Nepalese royal family had spoken publicly about the palace killings. It was Gyanendra's first interview, and my first encounter with a living God.

Asked if he knew any more about the massacre, Gyanendra replied: 'I wish. I was not here.' He continued: 'I left this palace thirty years ago when I got married and I never thought I would have to occupy it again. It is difficult, but we do the best we can. It's people that change a house into a home and that's what we've been trying to do.'

Even to those who did not meet him, it was apparent that Gyanendra's isolation at the top of the world had increased since he took power. Nepal's politicians had proved an abject failure since democracy's arrival in 1990, squabbling over power and doing little to address the aching poverty and discontent from which the Maoists drew their support. Gyanendra seemed to feel the disappointment more keenly than most. In October 2002, barely a year after taking power, he sacked Prime Minister Sher Bahadur Deuba and, apparently as impatient with democracy as the Maoists, replaced him with his own appointed government. As a result, Gyanendra was in a stand-off with both Nepal's political parties and the Maoists. Meanwhile a tide of republican student protests was sweeping the country. Demonstrators were smashing cars and shops and setting up barricades of burning tyres in the streets. 'The smell of burning tyres on the streets of the capital reeks of democracy in decay,' wrote *Nepali Times* columnist C.K. Lal. 'Fears of anarchy are real again.' One of Gyanendra's friends told me that, for a king, family was the only true confidant. Without one, Gyanendra was cut off from the world. 'You can have friends, advisers, all the experts you want,' he said. 'But without family, monarchy is a very lonely place. If you look at Gyanendra, he's really on his own.'

Gyanendra did little to dispel that idea. He admitted that with a crumbling civil service, his main source of strength was the overstretched 83,000-strong army. 'There is a vacuum,' he said. He realized he had to somehow reconstitute an alliance with the political parties – 'The future of Nepal, yes, lies in constitutional monarchy and multi-party democracy' – but given their dismal performance, he refused to leave the country in their hands. 'The days of royalty being seen and not heard are over,' he declared.

He also acknowledged that sacking Deuba risked looking autocratic. But 'had I not acted as I did, I think Nepal would be in a worse situation than today. If I step on people's toes, I'm sorry.' He returned to the subject later. 'My fear is that we might be heading for a ditch. Some of the basic things gelling the country together have been trampled.'

Gyanendra lit another cigarette, and returned to the subject of his image. He admitted he was aware of the conspiracy theories: that he was a lethally ambitious autocrat, and had assassinated his family to take back the throne and return Nepal to divine rule. '[The theories] are nonsense, a wild goose chase, and cruel and offensive.'

He said he showed little emotion after the massacre because 'I had to conduct myself in a proper manner. There is a human face to every king – but that does not mean he has to flaunt it.' He grew defensive when asked about loneliness. 'What makes you think I don't have friends?' he asked.

Towards the end of our talk, Gyanendra said he dreamed

of a time when 'all of Nepal should have the opportunity to progress irrespective of colour, caste and creed.' He added: 'You know, there is a saying here: if the people are happy, the king is happy.' The odds of Nepal pulling back from the brink were slim enough. The chances of Gyanendra finding personal happiness seemed to me to be smaller still. But he could still take a joke. What was it like being a living God? 'I've been waiting for you to ask this,' he laughed. 'On the living God thing, let me interpret it this way: we were given the personification of Vishnu and Vishnu is the preserver of all things. And I'm glad that my role, the role I have to play, has been spelled out like that.' He puffed on his cigarette and smiled again: 'I'm a pragmatic and practical person. I've never said I'm God.'

When I met Gyanendra a little over a year later in March 2005, I wondered whether he hadn't changed his mind. After sacking Deuba, he had sacked his replacement, appointed and sacked two more prime ministers, before finally taking absolute power with the military's support in February. He was thinner. He dressed in a dark green military uniform. He declared sternly that power 'must be my destiny. So be it. I will not shy away from responsibility.' The isolation had increased even more – machine gunners sat in crows' nests around the walls of the palace. Asked once more about loneliness, he replied: 'Religion gives me solace. I meditate. One does not have to go berserk or into a state of depression, as we hear happens in your cities.'

Gyanendra was enjoying power. He relished the tough times ahead. He had become an orator, with a fondness for alliteration. 'The army will do whatever is required,' he told me. 'Coerce, comprehend, coordinate, cooperate.' Since he never spoke in public, I imagined him practising in the mirror. 'We have chosen a path strewn with many, many thorns and there is a long way to go,' he declared. 'Extreme situations require extreme measures. Perseverance, honesty and moral values must be part and parcel of our daily lives. A little law is required. We have to be austere and stand on our own two feet. But with determination, discipline and diligence, Nepal will move forward.' He had also been giving some thought to the conduct becoming for a king. 'For me, power is patience and gentleness. And there are three origins of power: wealth, strength and talent. The combination, wisely used, will give you what you seek.'

Later Gyanendra's friend told me he saw even less of the king. Among the few people Gyanendra did meet regularly were the men who had helped him take power, his generals. 'These are people who tend to see things in black and white,' said the friend. As if to underline how separated he was from the country he ruled, Gyanendra didn't even leave the palace to announce his 1 February coup, but broadcast a message to the nation from a television studio he had built expressly for the purpose inside the grounds. Said the friend: 'To lose his family in one go, to have nearly lost his wife, and then to assume the throne when it's facing annihilation, no one can imagine how lonely that is. Who does he go to for advice? The queen's never been interested in state affairs, his mother's very old and the palace secretariat is just a bunch of file-pushers. He found himself talking more and more to the generals. And they surrounded him and cut him off.'

But something was bothering Gyanendra. He was disappointed by international condemnation of how his army strode into newspaper and radio offices, rounded up thousands of students, politicians and human rights activists. There were frequent accusations that it was executing suspected Maoists. Gyanendra thought this was unfair. Just as the Maoists said they were ultimately fighting global capitalism and the US, Gyanendra believed he was manning one of the frontlines in a global war, defending the US and globalization against terrorism. 'What was our objective?' he asked. 'This is clearly to fight for democracy against terrorism. Our friends must come and tell us whether this objective is incorrect, or help us in this cause.'[2] The problem was his anti-democratic methods, I said. Who was the US to criticize that? he replied. 'Think of Guantánamo, Iraq.' He returned to the subject of ends justifying means later: 'We can go on arguing about methods [and] asking: was it necessary to go so far? But less might have yielded no result. And have no doubt: this is about the survival of the nation.' He went on to defend the curtailing of civil rights in language that seemed to borrow much from George W. Bush. 'No law-abiding citizen should feel pain. But those who do not abide by the law, the law-breakers, they will feel pain.'

Gyanendra felt he had a natural ally in a pugnacious White House. He felt spurned when he was ignored. And the more I thought about it, the more I realized he was right. Gyanendra's position in Nepal was the same as Washington's position in the world. Most of Nepal's difficulties (backwardness, poverty, war) stemmed from the inequality that still prevailed in the kingdom, and Gyanendra was the one who benefited most from that uneven system. Substitute the world for Nepal and the White House for the king, and the same broad logic held true. Many of the world's problems (backwardness, poverty, war) came from inequality, and the US was the country that benefited most from that uneven system.[3]

Gyanendra was intelligent and ambitious. He recognized a

God King in the twenty-first century was an anomaly. He knew he was the problem. But he enjoyed power and genuinely believed he could help his people. Talking with his enemies wasn't going to improve his position. Talking could only mean talking it all away. So he chose to fight.

Were these same impulses guiding the West? If they were, it would explain why our leaders' responses to globalization often appeared to be so inappropriate. And there was some evidence to suggest that Western governments did realize that they, or at least the comparative richness of their economies, were the problem, and one that related to violence. What were the trillions of dollars spent by the West on overseas aid in the developing world, if not an implicit acknowledgement that the system of global income distribution was unfair? What was the deployment of hundreds of civil affairs specialists among the 800 Special Operations soldiers at the US antiterrorist base in Djibouti, if not a Pentagon admission that Africa *lacked* and that, if unaddressed, such yawning deficits produced unrest?[4] What were the billions of dollars spent on reconstruction of Iraq and Afghanistan, if not an acceptance that quenching the fires of insurgency took wealth as well as war?

Like Gyanendra, the White House would never talk to terrorists. But beyond the old objection that talking to terrorists only encouraged others, was there another reason: that negotiations could only mean weakening the Western position? Again, there was evidence to suggest so. Look at Bush administration intransigence on climate change. Or the European Union steadfastness on preserving unequal terms of trade with Africa. Or look at the war on drugs, or the war on terror. Those seemed to show a preference for fighting, rather than diplomacy. In the late years of the Bush administration, critical American newspaper columnists disinterred an ancient word to describe this overconfident, uncompromising, often damaging stance: hubris. That sounded a lot like Gyanendra.

Thirteen months after our final talk, I watched Gyanendra's last stand from Bodriganal's rooftop in central Kathmandu. I was edging along a backstreet when a student with lanky brown hair who lived on the top floor of a three-family building leant over his balcony to tell me it wasn't safe and that I should come up. Sure enough, minutes after I joined Bodriganal, five protesters sprinted around the corner to his street and tried to leap a barbed-wire fence into an onion garden, quickly followed by thirteen Nepalese riot police in full battle gear. One of the fleeing demonstrators, a teenager in a white shirt, caught the bottom of his jeans on the wire and fell, tangled, to the floor. Seven or eight of the police crowded in and started to beat him, swinging their canes down from behind their backs like peasants threshing hay.

Bodriganal's roof was four storeys up and on a corner, so we could see into another street. There shouts alerted us to ten more policemen caning a passer-by, ramming him into a metal shutter, dragging him by the T-shirt and cracking their sticks over his head. We looked back to the first demonstrator. He seemed unconscious, but the police, who were as young as he was, were still beating him. A woman on the terrace of her house three floors above screamed and threw a pail of water over them. The police responded by picking up bricks from the ground and throwing them through two of her windows. Then they dragged the protester's body away, and walked back down the lane towards us, laughing. One of them spied me and my notepad and shouted: 'Do not write, motherfucker.' Bodriganal sighed. 'It's been like this for fourteen days,' he said. 'There's no human rights here. If that guy's dead, you'll never find the body. And if he's alive now, believe me, he's dead anyway.'

In April 2006, after what was then ten years of civil war and just over a year of Gyanendra's one-man rule, Kathmandu erupted in something like its own *intifada*. Facing a collapsing economy, a future as the laggard of Asia and an intransigent king, 'popular anger exploded', said British ambassador Keith Bloomfield. Mass demonstrations were taking place in every major Nepalese city. Nineteen people were killed by the police, although the protesters claimed the security forces had carted off many more bodies, as they had outside Bodriganal's apartment. The violence was centred on Kathmandu. There, when I arrived, young Nepalese had been fighting police and soldiers for two weeks along a ring road surrounding the city, hurling bricks, burning barricades of tyres, and dodging tear gas, baton charges and the occasional live round.

The protesters' target was the king. Instead of reinvigorating democracy as he promised, Gyanendra had gutted civil society. He almost revelled in his disdain for public opinion. 'H.M. King Gyanendra does not seek cheap popularity' read a propaganda billboard in central Kathmandu. The parties and the Maoists were not popular either – the politicians were despised for graft and incompetence, the Maoists for cruelty – but they were smart enough to co-opt this new 'movement' as it was called. All walks of life were declaring their allegiance to this ill-defined force. Police arrested lawyers in Kathmandu and professors in the resort town of Pokhara who came out in support of it. In the capital, twenty-five civil servants at the

Home Ministry shouted slogans at their desks demanding the king be ousted. Even a gay rights group pledged its support to popular change. On the street, 'the movement' was largely represented by teenage or twenty-something kids in Nirvana and Metallica T-shirts. Rohit Bhandari was one. He had a good job as a technician in a Kathmandu medical laboratory and was the son of a bureaucrat and mid-level leader for Nepal's pro-monarchy Rashtriya Prajatantra Party. And yet Rohit, twenty-six, found himself in a mob of thousands shouting, 'King Gyanendra, leave the country or we will kill you.' Rohit wasn't sure why he was risking his life, beyond a belief in 'freedom' and a conviction that Nepal's leaders were keeping the country's riches to themselves and their people in the dark ages. 'Everybody feels Nepal is being left behind,' he said, as a RNA helicopter buzzed overhead. 'This is the twenty-first century.'

A few days later, Gyanendra capitulated, giving up almost all his powers, restoring parliament, and allowing constitutional change to prevent him seizing power again. The Maoists saw a power vacuum, and filled it. Within months, they had joined the government. In September 2007, they resigned and forced the postponement of a general election, which they later won in April 2008. It was a demonstration of their power. Few doubted they would soon abolish the monarchy. Gyanendra had taken a stand, and had lost. What was the eventual fate of the US in its war?

What was clear was that Gyanendra's unilateralism – his hubris – added fuel to the fire in Nepal. It had been the same for the Bush administration in Afghanistan, Iraq and Somalia. Not all Americans saw the world in the same way, however. First among those taking a different approach to the world was the man who, until Warren Buffett finally beat him to second place in 2008, was the nation's richest son.

When in 2002 Bill Gates announced $100 million to fight AIDS in India, he might have expected thanks from a nation that at the time could find only $5 million a year to protect its billion people. Instead, when the Microsoft founder quoted what were then widely shared predictions that the number of Indians infected with HIV and AIDS would top 20 to 25 million by 2010 – a trajectory that would double what was then the world HIV/AIDS population and shift the epidemic epicentre from Africa to Asia – the Indian government castigated him for 'spreading panic' and 'completely inaccurate data' damaging to 'safety and security'. 'It was definitely a mixed situation,' Gates later remarked of his trip to India.[5] 'The prime minister met me [but] there were other people trying to downplay the whole size of the problem. They didn't like the figures.'

At first glance, Bill and Melinda Gates would appear to be the answers to many of India's prayers. Rich, efficient, guided by a single word – 'inequality' – and prepared to spend billions, they should have been a big help keeping India's progress on track. As Gates recognized: 'India's really on the rise, there are great things happening – and other than a war or something, this is the only thing that could stand in the way of them achieving that potential.'

But the Gates rub India all the wrong way. One newspaper editor told me: 'They're foreign, they're richer than Lakshmi Mittal and they *will* keep talking about disease.' As S.Y. Quraishi, director general of the National AIDS Council, put it: 'Generosity can be an offensive word.' The hostility increased the more money the Gateses gave. And they gave a lot of money. By 2005, the Bill and Melinda Gates Foundation had committed another $100 million to fighting AIDS in India.

Complaints over the Foundation's India campaign (called Avahan after the Sanskrit word for 'clarion call') centred on suspicions that the Microsoft founder's munificence was a sweetener for his corporate ambitions in India. The sentiments of Purushothaman Mulloli, head of the Joint Action Council Kannur – an Indian charity involved in AIDS-related work – were as widely shared as they were ill-informed. 'Gates's interest in HIV projects in India is not meant for charity but to protect his billions of dollars of investments in pharmaceutical companies interested in conducting field trials in India,' he said. If they didn't hear this sort of thing so often, Foundation staff would laugh. Said one executive: 'If it were a PR thing, we'd do something warm and fuzzy with kids. Can you think of anything you'd less like associated with your brand than sex work, anal sex, drug use and sexually transmitted diseases?' Avahan's Delhi-based head Ashok Alexander added: 'Doing good in India, and getting away with it, can be very, very difficult. Indians don't like to be in a begging-bowl position. Everyone suspects ulterior motives. The question is always: "Why are you really here?"'

Bill Gates Snr., seventy-eight, a former lawyer who is now Foundation director, says the story of his son's conversion from corporate titan to social justice campaigner is straightforward. He says Bill Jnr. was on his private jet returning to Seattle in 1999 when he happened to read a comparison of international healthcare in the *New York Times*. 'My son was a pretty sophisticated man who had been around the world,' says Bill Snr. 'But the manner in which the article presented this most egregious type of social disparity, such a vivid comparison between the care his own children were getting and other parts of the world, it came through with a seriousness that had not occurred to him before.' At home, in the kitchen, Gates showed the article to his wife. Bill Snr. says the same 'insatiable need to understand' that as a boy drove Bill Jnr.'s interest in computers, now honed in on world health. Melinda says the 'strong volunteer ethic' in which Bill Snr. raised his son also came into play. 'It was a surprise to Bill that even curable, preventable diseases were not being taken care of in the rest of the world,' she said. 'Bill said: "Hey, we can have an effect here."'

So they did. Five years later, that decision had led the world's richest woman 12,000 kilometres from billionaire's row in Seattle to the bare floor of a Calcutta slum where I was watching her sit cross-legged and holding hands with some of the world's poorest, trying to remember the words to a civil rights anthem. 'We shall overcome,' chanted fourteen AIDS-outreach workers squatting around her. 'We shall overcome, we shall overcome, some day . . .' The singing stopped for a moment and Melinda Gates tried to stand, but the singers had a firm grip on her and there were four more verses. 'Oh, we are not alone,' they started again, pulling a laughing Melinda back down to the floor. 'We are not alone, today . . .'

A moment of connection can hardly bridge the divide between a preppy multi-billionaire and paupers with holes in their shoes. But the degree of commitment the Gateses demonstrate – Melinda spends weeks at a time visiting projects and her husband is giving up his day job to concentrate full time on philanthropy – is almost unheard of among India's own financial elite. Most Indian billionaires seem barely aware of the poor, too blinded by their own dazzling riches to see the big picture. Avahan's Alexander remarks that the only time the Indian rich would enter a slum is 'if their drivers are lost'.

This lack of concern has serious consequences. A constant complaint of Indian charities is that the well-developed Indian sense of duty to family and religion extends no further. It's the same nonchalance that sets the stage for environmental collapse. It also gives justification to Maoists and Islamists for their use of violence – what choice do you have, say the guerrillas, when no one listens to your words? Warren Buffett's decision in 2006 to add $31 billion to the Gateses' original $29 billion only highlights the stinginess of the richest Indians. 'Where is philanthropy, where is civil society?' asks Alexander. 'Why is big business doing nothing about AIDS?' Melinda says giving money away is 'who Bill and I are'. Quraishi says it's just not who rich Indians are. 'I had one CEO tell me that millions dying in Africa was very sad, but why should he worry about ten or twenty deaths in India? There are millions of AIDS victims in India! Frankly, the corporate sector isn't interested, and doesn't understand.'

And yet the question remains: why spend your life building up the world's biggest fortune, only to give it all away? This is an old scepticism. In the sixteenth century, the English poet Nicholas Breton called philanthropy 'to fish for honour with a silver hook'. Breton was talking about the first golden age of giving, a time of revolutionary exploration when London merchants made staggering fortunes from international trade, and then funded projects to eliminate poverty. A second age came in late-nineteenth-century America, when robber barons such as Andrew Carnegie and John D. Rockefeller, who had made fortunes from industrialization, competed in giving endowments to the arts, education and the poor. We are now in the third age of philanthropy, in which men like Gates and Buffet who accumulate unprecedented riches from a third economic revolution – global technology and global finance – choose to redistribute.

And, just as the Elizabethan merchants of London and America's early captains of industry appeared to realize the pendulum had swung too heavily in their favour, so the same appears to be happening today. Research by the Centre on Wealth and Philanthropy at Boston College shows that the bigger the fortune, the higher percentage of it goes to charity.[6] In November 2007, Buffet even suggested he ought to pay more tax.[7] As Richard Tomkins, a frequent writer on globalization, puts it succinctly in the *Financial Times*, 'a pattern emerges. A social and economic revolution occurs; some people make enormous fortunes from it; the gulf between rich and poor grows to the point where it becomes as great as society can bear; and the newly rich defuse the crisis by surrendering some or all of their wealth. Seen in that light, philanthropy could be said to act as a safety valve or even a form of social control: a mechanism adopted by the rich (if only subconsciously) to maintain the existing order at times of great change and extremes of inequality.'[8]

There are exceptions to the Indian tight-and-mighty rule. Azim Premji, boss of Wipro and worth $12 billion, flies economy, drives a twelve-year-old car and has ploughed millions of his own money into education. Narayan Murthy has gone one step further by quitting his day job to work full time on inequality. And one Indian business house foresaw the need for philanthropy from the year it was founded, in 1868.

*

The son of a Parsi trader from Bombay, Jamshet Nusserwanji Tata knew how to turn a profit. But he also had a patrician vision of spreading wealth and lifting a nation. In a 1902 letter to his son about building a workers' city around his Tata Steel works, he rejected the squalor he had witnessed in England's industrial towns and anticipated what would become standard for future urban planning. 'Be sure to lay wide streets planted with shady trees, every other of a quick growing variety,' he wrote. 'Be sure that there is plenty of space for lawns and gardens.' After his death in 1904, the city took his name (becoming Jamshedpur) and continued his legacy under the direction of Fabian Society leaders Sydney and Beatrice Webb. In this obscure corner of eastern India, Tata Steel introduced a series of worker benefits that would become standard only much later in the West, such as the eight-hour working day in 1912, maternity benefit in 1928 and profit-sharing in 1934.

Today Jamshedpur, with free housing, free hospitals and free schools, sports stadiums, clean streets and the only drinkable tap water in India, remains the envy of the country – an island of social justice in a state, Jharkhand, that is otherwise awash with Naxal violence. The city is an oasis of well-tended parks and litter-free pavements. Among its other achievements, Jamshedpur is single-handedly trying to correct India's poor sports record, training athletes, footballers, archers and even a Special Olympics squad. The contrast as you leave Jamshedpur and cross into that other, government-run India beyond is as wide as traversing the boundary between South and North Korea. In 2004, the UN chose Jamshedpur alongside the likes of Melbourne and San Francisco as one of six showpieces of the Global Compact Cities Pilot Programme.

J.N. Tata's founding ideals also live on in the way the business is run. Tata Sons, the holding company that manages the group, is 65.8 per cent owned by eleven charitable trusts, which spent $379.2 million on social causes in 2003–4. In 2004–5, Tata companies themselves gave away a further $97.8 million. Beneficiaries range from a host of Tata educational, health and scientific institutes that dot India to 225,000 women graduates in 102 years to the giant mahseer fish, saved from extinction in the Ganges by a Tata-funded breeding programme. Stockbroker Rakesh Jhunjhunwala, owner of 8.5 per cent of Tata subsidiary Titan Watches, says one of his golden rules for stock picking is squashing all sentiment. 'But when you talk about the Tatas, I get very emotional,' he says. 'That spirit. Those values. That integrity.'

The group's corporate piety extends to the boss's pay. Though the business house carries his name, chairman Ratan Tata merely draws a salary from Tata Sons. And he takes personal modesty seriously. Tall, guarded and retaining the outsider's accent he picked up in an earlier life as a trainee architect in the US, he is famously private. He lives with his two German shepherd dogs, Tito and Tango, in the same second-floor apartment in Bombay that he has kept for twenty years. He is one floor below his stepmother, and neighbours say they have never known him to throw a party. His one indulgence apart from his dogs – he is frequently spotted muddying his pinstripes as he plays with them in a park near his home – is a collection of cars. Apparently embarrassed by the extravagance, in a 2006 interview he excused his interest as stemming from a love of design, not show. 'I drive them periodically,' said the sixty-eight-year-old at his office in Bombay House, the elegant Edwardian group headquarters on the southern edge of India's business capital, 'and then back to the garage.' Indeed, he drives a cheap Tata estate car to work. You wouldn't expect the head of India's biggest business house to say being rich is boring, and he didn't. But Ratan Tata came close. 'I've never had the desire to own a yacht, to flaunt,' he said. 'It's not really the point.'

What's truly fascinating about Tata – and the reason why the group should serve as a model for other Indian companies, and anyone doing business in the developing world – is how the group is able to combine profits and philanthropy.[9] This is not the rape-it-and-repair-it model of charity as practised in the West. This is enlightened economics, gainful selflessness. When Ratan Tata said wealth didn't interest him, he was not just talking in terms of personal taste but customers too. Look at the excitement over China and India, said Tata. Look at the attention given to the new rich. The reality was that consumption, as it is understood in the West, was still a dream for all but a fraction of their combined 2.5 billion population, just as it was for 3 billion more in the developing world. The spare million in a few fat wallets, he said, was not enough to excite a truly global company – it's only good pickings for niche, luxury brands. Far more attractive, he said, was the spare change in a billion slim ones. How much more profitable if you target the very bottom of the income pyramid – a lot of people with a little, rather than a few with a lot? Put another way: how do you make consumers out of the truly poor, people whose disposable income, while real, is considerably less than the average American child's pocket money?

One of Tata's answers was the Tata Nano – a four-door, 33-horsepower, rear-engine runaround that he designed himself and which launched in early 2008 with a price tag of 100,000 rupees ($2,500). Another was the Ace, a 700cc truck that retails for less than $5,000 and which, since its launch in southern Indian in May 2005, has accounted for two thirds of all trucks sold there. Purchases of both of these were supported by low-debt consumer credit from Tata Finance and they were marketed as taxis and public transporters as much as private vehicles. Following the same model, Tata's hotel chain was building 200 hotels across India under the brand Ginger, offering rooms with wireless Internet, air conditioning and attached bathrooms for 1,000 rupees ($22) for the budget business traveller, at least a fifth of the typical cost today. Ratan Tata said he was also eyeing property. 'Today people are being venal in terms of what they are offering,' he said. 'So can you break that barrier, and provide affordable good housing? The other builders would want to kill you. But it's something I've often felt we could do more effectively.' The idea is to make a market of people who weren't in any before. 'Everyone is catering to the top of the pyramid,' said Tata. 'The challenge we've given to all our companies is to address a different market. Pare your margins. Create new markets.' Or as stock trader Jhunjhunwala said: 'The future business of the world is about the man who earns $1 a day.'[10]

For the same reasons, Tata loves Africa. In South Africa, the group has investments in mining, tourism and motor manufacturing and uses the country as its gateway to the continent. By the end of 2005, there was an instant coffee plant in Uganda, a bus factory in Senegal and a phosphate plant in Morocco. Tata Africa's revenues had risen from $37 million in 2003–4 to $112 million in 2004–5 to $210 million in 2005–6, on an investment of $100 million. Other Tata companies were also investing. Tata Steel was building a $100-million ferrochrome smelter at Richards Bay, South Africa; Indian hotels were putting $180 million into hotels in Johannesburg, Cape Town and Durban; and telecoms operator VSNL was planning a $1-billion African phone and Internet system. 'We look at countries where we can play a role in development,' said Tata. 'Our hope in each is to create an enterprise that looks like a local company, but happens to be owned by a company in India.' Tata Motors managing director Ravi Kant said cutting the ribbon on the Senegal bus factory showed him how powerful that plan can be. 'It was a very small plant making 450 buses a year,' he said. 'But it had a ripple effect across all of West Africa. The president came. Prime ministers from four neighbouring countries came. A crowd of 100,000 showed up. It was a big deal. We were participating in improving the quality of life.' As a result, he smiled, Tata was well placed in West Africa to take advantage of the moment at 'around $1,000 per capita GDP' when 'car ownership explodes'.

None of which would be more than mildly interesting if Tata were unimportant. But the group is not only India's biggest conglomerate, it has also grown exponentially since it started following Ratan Tata's radical philosophy. By the end of 2006, the group comprised ninety-six companies, including the world's largest tea company; Asia's largest software company; a steel giant; a worldwide hotel chain; and a motor arm that runs from a bicycle factory in Zambia to a tie-up with Fiat to make trucks. Since Ratan Tata became chairman in 1991, he has multiplied Tata group revenues seven times to an annual $21.7 billion. Between 2000 and 2006, the group's market capitalization jumped eighteen times to $49.8 billion. At the same time, Tata has been on a $1.9 billion shopping spree that has netted Britain's Tetley Tea, South Korea's Daewoo Commercial Vehicles and Singapore's Natsteel. At the end of 2006, it took over Anglo-Dutch steelmaker Corus, valuing the firm at more than $8 billion and in March 2008 it bought Jaguar and Land Rover from Ford for $2.3 billion.

Tata's success is a revelation to the business world. Contrary to conventional thinking, Ratan Tata has proved that a philanthropic approach also can be highly profitable. He described a virtuous circle: good karma is good business, is more good karma, is more good business. Little surprise, then, that Ratan Tata is widely cited as the most influential businessman in Asia.[11] Sometimes it seemed like he wanted to single-handedly restore the image of business itself. 'Why does business carry a connotation of being bad?' he asked. Because being 'very hard-nosed and very tight on what you want to do' often leads to 'being branded as a tremendous exploiter'. And that's bad business. Nodding at mention of Enron, WorldCom, Parmalat and Tyco, he said: 'A number of companies, who were applauded a few years ago for how sharp they were on what they returned to their shareholders, do not exist today. They skated too close to the edge.'

That was not to say Tata was a soft touch. 'We are not in anything for charity,' said the chairman. Nor is life always sweet in Tata-land. In 2003, police arrested six top managers at Tata Finance, accusing them of embezzling more than $4 million. In January 2006, Tata Steel's plans for a mill in the eastern Indian state of Orissa took a horrific turn when police opened fire on protesters accusing local politicians of short-changing them on the deal, killing twelve. But other unpleasantness is skilfully avoided. When Tata Steel laid off 40,000 people at Jamshedpur, it gave departing workers a proportion of their salary until retirement. Initiatives like these have ensured seventy-nine years without industrial action.

But aside from figures like Murthy Narayan and Azim Premji, and the Mahindra conglomerate, which was founded by one of J.N. Tata's former managers, few follow Tata's example in India. 'People say this is baggage we are carrying,' said Ratan Tata. 'They still believe this really isn't the smartest thing to do.' Tata's refusal to pay bribes also means they are 'scoffed at'. 'It takes all kinds of people to make the world happen,' is Tata's comment.

I asked Tata how, if he had no interest in riches, he spent his spare time. He replied that on his rare evenings off, he took a half-hour ride across Bombay harbour to a small, scruffy beach house. 'It seldom had power, so I had to put in a small generator,' he said. 'It's quiet and away from everywhere. There is a town and there are neighbours, but I go quietly on my own. I walk the beach and I read and I think about what I should do.' He sounded more like a philosopher than a tycoon. I think that was his point.

Gates, Buffett, Tata. All titans of global business. All forging a new path that acknowledged the world was iniquitous and reckoned the gap was so dangerous, they had to use their riches to try to fix it. Western business has begun to do the same. Their efforts may be less dramatic than Gates or Buffett, but today no sizeable multinational corporation would think of doing business in the developing world without a robust corporate social responsibility programme. In March 2008 De Beers, founded by the arch-imperialist Cecil Rhodes, and for decades one of the most rapacious and secretive companies working in Africa, signalled the new mood sweeping businesses in the developing world when it moved its diamond sorting and valuing operation to Botswana in a move it said it hoped would create 3,000 jobs. Meanwhile, one of the big pharmaceutical companies, Merck, has ploughed more than $50 million into an HIV/AIDS prevention and treatment programme in Botswana, which has one of the highest infection rates in Africa. In a few years, 82,000 of the 110,000 infected Batswana were receiving anti-retroviral drugs and the HIV/AIDS infection rate among fifteen- to forty-nine-year-olds fell from 37.4 per cent to 32.4 per cent. Merck has also ploughed millions into projects to treat river blindness across the continent.

Jeff Sturchio, Merck's vice president of external affairs, says the big picture is an implicit admission that what is good for a global giant like Merck is not good for everyone. 'Globalization has not been good for people around the world,' he says. 'It's not that globalization is not a good thing. It's that its benefits are unequally distributed. That's what's wrong with the world.' Sturchio says some people will always be 'cynical about big corporations' and many will doubt 'we're doing this because it's the right thing to do'. But like Tata, there is also a benign commercial logic to Merck's social programmes. 'You could say that one reason we do this kind of work is that in the long run healthy people boost economic development which will create robust markets for Merck products,' he says. 'That's true – there is a long-term benefit to our business. Health leads to wealth.'

PART FOUR

POST MORTEM

CHAPTER 12

IS WAR GOOD?

Gold rushes have a history stretching back to Columbus's wayward attempts to find a western passage to India. They happen when blind faith outweighs normal commercial considerations. In 2006, the business world decided India was the hot destination of the moment and, for at least a year or two, that was to hold true whether or not ground reality matched up. As a senior American media executive remarked when I enquired after his week-long fact-finding trip: 'Looks like a marvellous place to lose $300 million.'

China had been a marvellous place to lose billions for years. A Hong Kong investment banker, who had steered funds into a variety of Chinese industries for eight years, told me that when a country 'arrived' investors often paid scant attention to the details in the scramble to jump on board. In China, many saddled themselves with state partners who added little and soaked up profits. Others found themselves in distinctly alien environments. The media executive told me how he and his rivals had poured money into China, ignoring such plainly insurmountable obstacles as China's lack of English and freedom of expression. Now, after a decade in which they made not a cent and had eventually given up, they were switching to India. Why? It was the hot destination.

The investment banker speculated there would probably be even less caution in India. Why? Those who had failed in China now had an even greater incentive to find Shangri-La in India, she said. 'People piled a fortune into China,' she explained. 'No reason they wouldn't do double in India.'

I couldn't help wonder whether these people were a little unwell. Some certainly exhibited signs of fever. Mark Faber, the man who believed no infrastructure spelled opportunity, published an Asian financial newsletter which he called *The Doom, Gloom and Boom Report.* So which was it?

The truth is that China, probably, is going to make it. It will have a much rougher ride than is commonly understood. Worker protests and civil violence will escalate. Corruption, counterfeiting and product quality scandals will continue. Crime and pollution will worsen. But whatever the failings of its local government, China's central government gets it. At the 17th National Congress of the Communist Party in October 2007, President Hu Jintao had his concept of 'scientific development' – his term for a more socially equitable and sustainable approach to economic growth – written into the party's constitution. Migrant workers 'mainly work in construction, mining, cleaning and catering industries, or the kind of jobs usually labelled "dirty", "hard" and "low-paid",' said the *People's Daily* in a report in the run-up to the Congress. '[The] wealth gap is also one of the key issues for Chinese leaders to address at the National Congress.' It quoted Hu as saying: 'Vigorous efforts will be made to raise the income of low-income groups, gradually increase poverty-alleviation aid and the minimum wage, and set up a mechanism of regular pay increases for enterprise employees.'[1]

Crucially, few of the workers' rights activists I met were contemplating extra-legal means. Rather, they saw their job as making the existing channels for their discontent more responsive and forcing the government to live up to its responsibilities. It wasn't about changing the government. It was about trying to reform it from underneath, and applying the existing law. The biggest threat of violence came from the bosses. One lawyer told me of a rash of stabbings of labour activists by mafia goons in Shenzhen, three in a fortnight in November 2007. I asked him if he had any overarching political ideals. 'That's all a little bit too big for us,' he replied. 'We're just trying our best to do something for the migrant workers, to achieve some practical improvements. We don't have any higher ambition.' I asked him if he thought globalization was to blame. 'Maybe,' he said. 'But I think globalization is broader than just economics. It entails the introduction of common standards in democracy, the exercise of power and legal rights.' That was already happening in China, he said, to the benefit of the workers. Membership of groups such as the International Standards Organization and the World Trade Organization was forcing Chinese companies to meet international norms. A freer flow in information was also educating workers, who were becoming more aware of their rights. 'There are radicals emerging' in the ranks of labour activists, said the lawyer. But his prediction was for incremental progress, such as a new workers' rights law that was coming into effect in January 2008, and that 'social unrest will lessen and radicalism will decline'.

India looked a lot shakier. By the end of 2007, there were signs the days of the boom might be numbered. One effect of the demand for outsourcing had been to push up wages of the top graduates in India by 20 to 30 per cent a year and, in Bombay and Delhi, raise rents beyond rates seen in London or New York – eroding India's competitive advantage and the whole raison d'être for its offshoring industry. That added to a catalogue of existing troubles. Companies like Infosys had begun hiring American graduates to make up for India's skills shortage. Almost nothing was being done to fix the infrastructure, or the red tape, or the corruption. The government faced vehement opposition from India's communist party over a win-win nuclear energy deal with the US, periodically threatening its survival. Then there was the Islamic bombing campaign in the cities, and the Naxal revolution in the countryside. Proof of the difficulty of India's business environment came in the actions of CEOs like Ratan Tata and Lakshmi Mittal, who were on an acquisition spree abroad, rather than trying to expand at home.

Like China, India's leaders were aware of the problems. The big difference between the two countries is that India's government was incapable of doing much about them. China's totalitarian government was proving more or less equal to the forces of globalization. It could contain the unrest. It could smooth the starker inequalities. It could use the new money to build infrastructure. China was protected from the vicissitudes of globalization precisely because its government was not globalizing: China's Communist Party, by refusing to adopt the global norms of democratic governance, had reserved for itself the strength to handle globalization.

India's democratic government, on the other hand, was swamped. It was ineffectual against the Naxals. It was unable to control its billionaires – of which it had more than China – or demand that they redistribute their income. It seemed unable to build new roads or sewers or airports to any reasonable timetable. India's government was just too weak.

It had a tiny budget, no authority and was hamstrung by inefficiency and kleptocracy. For China, the future looked contentious, but prosperous. For India, trouble loomed.[2]

And yet. Driving back from the eastern Indian city of Jamshedpur – Tata town – I'd rolled across a series of flat dusty plains in eastern India. There was the occasional wood shack by the side of the road. And my driver, worried about Naxal attacks, was showing his nerves, anxiously glancing up at the cliff-tops when we passed through a gorge. It felt like a cowboy movie. And the more I thought about it, the more the comparison seemed appropriate. This was a land of bank robberies, jail breaks and shoot-outs with lawmen. India wasn't the new America. But maybe it was the old America.

The parallels between today's India and late-nineteenth-century America are striking. Travel back to the late 1800s and the US has just concluded a civil war over slavery. Today, central India is just starting a civil war over the rights of the poor. In the America of 130 years ago, the Wild West was the land of the gun. Today, so is India's Wild East.[3] Both countries have also, within living memory, won independence from Britain by revolution.

The UN Development Report of 2005 predicted it is going to take a century for living standards in India to catch up with the United States. And India today and the US a hundred years ago are both at early stages of industrialization. In 1860, 16 per cent of the US lived in cities and manufacturing made up just under a third of national income. Today, 25 per cent of Indians are city dwellers and industry makes up just more than a quarter of GDP. In 1913, Henry Ford launched the first mass car, the Model T. In 2008, Tata Motors the Tata Nano. America, before their conversion to philanthropy, had its robber barons, like the banker J.P. Morgan, the oil baron John D. Rockefeller, the steel magnate Andrew Carnegie. India has its doubles in figures like Lakshmi Mittal, Vijay Mallya and Mukesh Ambani. Meanwhile, adjusted for inflation and purchasing power parity, the national per capita income for the US in 1880 was $3,379. In India 2005, it is $3,300. And even though inflation and purchasing power parity erode the accuracy of absolute comparisons, it is arresting nonetheless that labourers in modern-day India and turn of the century America are paid precisely the same – $2 a day.

Social conditions also bear comparison. Both countries are divided by race. Dark skin counts against you as much in new India as old America, as do indigenous genes. (In an inflection that neatly encapsulates Columbus's poor geography, tribes in America are called Indians, while in India they are called tribals.) Slavery, while illegal, also lingers on in both in the form of indentured labour. And there are the slums. Consider this description. 'In unaired rooms, mothers and fathers sew by day and night. Those in the home sweatshop must work cheaper than in the factory sweatshops. And the children are called in from play to drive and drudge beside their elders . . . Nearly any hour . . . you can see them – pallid boy or spindling girl – their faces dulled, their backs bent under a heavy load of garments . . . Is it not a cruel civilization that allows little hearts and little shoulders to strain under these grown-up responsibilities, while in the same city a pet cur is jewelled and pampered and aired on a fine lady's velvet lap on the beautiful boulevards?' It could be a contemporary account of life in Bombay's garment mills. Actually it's an account of New York in 1907, written for *Cosmopolitan* magazine by the poet Edwin Markham.[4]

Surely India's rebels set it apart? Surprisingly, no. One of the most compelling similarities between today's India and nineteenth-century America emerges when you uncover how socialist militants were once as common as cowboys in the US. Rather than Russia or China, it was Europe and the US that left-wing agitators saw as the great hope of proletarian revolution. The late 1800s saw hundreds of violent uprisings in America, regular bloody street battles between workers and policemen, and the birth of a series of mass anti-establishment movements such as the Knights of Labor, the Grange Movement, the Populists, the Progressives and the Wobblies – more formally known as the International Workers of the World. 'What do you think of the workers of the United States?' Marx asked Engels in a letter during the US railroad strikes of 1877. 'This first explosion against the oligarchy of capital . . . can very well form the origin of an earnest workers' party.'[5] Rebellion continued well into the twentieth century. There are still those alive today who can recall April 1914, when the National Guard opened fire on striking miners in Ludlow, Colorado, and killed fourteen – just as police fired on the crowd outside the proposed Tata Steel in Orissa in January 2006. Or the summer of 1916, when two left-wing radicals killed nine people in a bomb attack on a parade in San Francisco.

Earlier in this book, I argued that there is more than one way to develop. The idea that the rest of the world just needs to get with the programme, and specifically a Western one, was, I argued, a nebulous if widespread misperception. China's success is proof of that. Despite its acceptance of economic globalization, no one would argue that China is following a Western path to development.

But India is. And one more arresting parallel between India

today and the United States a century ago is that both are places of violence and insurrection. America didn't improve much on that score. The twentieth century started out with a large part of America trying to hang on to segregation, and with poverty rubbing abrasively up against wealth, and moved on to a world war, a crash, a depression, another world war, the Cold War, Korea, Vietnam and Cambodia, Nicaragua, the Gulf War, race riots in Watts and LA, Waco, Columbine and 9/11. Twentieth-century America was more than merely violent. It defines our notions of violence, from gangster movies to gangsta rap.

But the twentieth century was also when the United States became the richest nation on earth. Violence had accompanied progress. That raises several possibilities.

The first is that violence is an incidental and awkward by-product of development. This is best summarized by the analogy of growth as a rocket. Just because a nation's trajectory is jet-powered, don't forget that a rocket is a bumpy ride.

But can it be that violence is an integral, albeit unfortunate, adjunct to progress? Looking at their smooth graphs of rising prosperity, economists can be tempted to say that development is always unequal, inequality is an old story, revolution is a sideshow, and none of it should distract us from the big story of globalization, which is development itself. The starving thousands of Africa, the malnourished millions of India, the unhappy billions earning less than $2 a day, all are unfortunate but predictable bystanders caught in the back-draught of progress. Never mind that history's tendency to repeat itself is a poor reason to ignore it, this book presents the counter-argument to that idea: that inequality and violence are not footnotes to globalization, but part of the same story. No one would seriously suggest a single line on a graph represented a complete account of American history. Similarly, telling the story of globalization without mentioning its losers is like telling the story of the Bush administration's plan to democratize the Middle East without mentioning Iraq. You can't take the bang out of the boom. Rising prosperity – development – is only half the story, the happy half. As HSBC's chief economists, Stephen King and Janet Henry, write: 'Globalization isn't just a story about a rising number of export markets for Western producers. Rather, it's a story about massive waves of income redistribution, from rich labour to poor labour, from labour as a whole to capital, from workers to consumers and from energy users towards energy producers. This is a story about winners and losers, not a fable about economic growth.'[6]

It is important to note that if violence is integral to advancement, it also doesn't necessarily harm it. Despite all that turbulence, US incomes did go up. Exponentially. Look at Japan's recovery after Hiroshima and Nagasaki. It can take a lot to throw a nation off course. That leads us to a third possibility. What if violence is not just integral to progress, but necessary for it? We have seen how globalization is violent. Development can destroy. Progress can kill. It's the old phenomenon of omelettes and breaking eggs. But if turmoil generally accompanies change, and change is good, is violence good? Is it necessary? Was America successful *because* of violence? Is killing a sign of progress? Is war good?

We certainly enjoy violence. 'The day of mourning is at hand,' wrote the *Economist* in its Lexington column on 7 June 2007. 'On June 10th, after eight years, 86 episodes and innumerable garrottings, gougings, beatings, decapitations and chain-assisted drownings, "The Sopranos" comes to an end, and with it arguably the best hour on American television.'[7] We also like to use violent language. In business, we talk about battles, hostile takeovers, blood on the streets. In sport, we talk about attack and defence, winners 'slaughtering' the opposition and losers being 'crushed'. I'd begun my own love affair with violence at Qala-i-Jangi. Watching bravery and cowardice, chaos and error, casual murder and giddy fear, I had never felt more sick, nor more alive. Within a few months, I had been to Sri Lanka to see Asia's bloodiest civil war, to Nepal to see its newest, and back to Afghanistan for Operation Anaconda, the single largest action of that war. A year after Qala-i-Jangi, one of my editors remarked someone had died in the opening paragraph of every story I had written since. He was only half joking.

So: we enjoy violence. But do we also believe in it? Maybe. Violence often goes hand in hand with heroism. Our idols are frequently violent doers, achievers, men of action, beaten down but returning with violent, righteous fury to score a final triumph in a physical test of will. The legends of early America, stories of gunslingers and the Wild West, would have us believe the country was built on righteous violence. That continues today. Look at action movies or television police dramas or video games.

Thomas Jefferson was one supporter of violence. 'I hold it that a little rebellion now and then is a good thing,' he said in 1780, right after the violent birth of America and just before France – where he was stationed as ambassador – exploded in revolution in 1789. 'It is a medicine necessary for the sound health of government. God forbid that we should ever be 20 years without rebellion. The tree of liberty must be refreshed from time to time with the blood of patriots and tyrants. It is its natural manure.'[8] Those sentiments were shared by Chairman Mao in his *Little Red Book*, published in 1964. 'When it moves to the peaceful years, I hate it,' wrote Mao. 'Not because I love chaos, but because a time of peace is not good for the development of the people. It is unbearable.'[9]

Most of us might find it uncomfortable to agree with a man who sacrificed 40 million people in the name of leaping forward. But how many more of us, faced with a gang war on our doorstep, would not endorse the kind of zero-tolerance policing seen in New York in the 1990s or, a more extreme case at the same time, the series of killings-by-cop Bombay. In his Sunday column, *Hindustan Times* executive editor Vir Sanghvi made police encounters one of his pet subjects. He is blunt about how, given a dysfunctional judiciary, police executions are an unfortunate, but crucial tool for India's advancement. 'We do not think this is a perfect situation,' writes Vir. 'But in common with the rest of the middle class we have come to the regrettable conclusion that there is no real alternative.'[10]

In the aftermath of one of Sri Lanka's many suicide bomb attacks, a European diplomat told me: 'Killing is Sri Lanka's way of doing politics.' I began thinking: maybe it was everyone's way. With 9/11, did al-Qaeda lift our taboo on mass murder? Or did it actually remind us that killing was a way to get things done? History showed we were always killing each other. We killed for God, we killed for empire and sometimes, such as in the Hundred Years War between England and France, we killed just because we always had done. From the Roman Empire to the execution of Saddam Hussein, murder and violence was often how we got results.

This is not mindless violence. At the root of most conflicts were fundamental disagreements over how best to progress. The Nazis believed totalitarian dictatorship and ethnic cleansing were the true way. The Soviets thought Western capitalism was evil. Ronald Reagan believed the opposite. But no matter which side they were on, our forefathers considered their bedrock beliefs – what they meant by civilization, how they wanted to live, who they wanted to lead them along what road – to be worth dying and killing for. A Taliban survivor at Qala-i-Jangi, asked by a reporter why he had fought, replied without hesitation: 'We fought for an idea.'

Today, the prevailing Western view is that little is worth dying for. And as our lives grow more comfortable and secure, we become more obsessed about keeping them that way. We treat every unnatural death as a national tragedy that speaks to some imminent social disintegration. We turn every new disease into a health scare. We accuse ourselves of inadequate responses to natural disasters whose occurrence and effect are entirely beyond our control. Progress has made us fearful strangers to death.

But was that an aberration? Maybe 9/11 was a giant wake-up call, a bloody reminder that mankind had not, could not move beyond violence. Maybe we were incomplete without it. Humanitarian may be what we aspire to be. Human is what we are. As Carl Jung famously said: 'I would rather be whole than good.'

The dominant view of war is also that it is an economic bad. An October 2007 Oxfam International report calculated that the twenty-three wars that raged in Africa from 1990 to 2005 cost the continent $284 billion by shrinking economies by an average of 15 per cent a year.[11] But this is a specious calculation. Who knew how much Africa would have grown without war? Who knew whether war economies were less prosperous than peaceful ones? From Afghanistan to Darfur, I'd met young men who had been grateful to war for offering them a wage as a gunman as opposed to a life staving off starvation by subsistence farming.

Even if you could measure the cost of war, how could you measure its benefit, the manner in which it hones a spirit of action and creativity? In *The Fruits of War*, historian Michael White argues that most modern technology, 'many of the things we take for granted in our everyday lives', owe their origins to war and weapons development.[12] 'Our aggression is linked inextricably, many psychologists suppose, with human creative energy,' writes White. 'It is the evil twin born from the same seed as our creative urge, the urge that motivates us to learn, to explore.'[13] He quotes the American historian William H. McNeill as writing: 'Anyone looking at the equipment installed in a modern house will readily recognize how much we in the late 20th century are indebted to industrial changes pioneered in near panic circumstances when more and more shells, gun-powder and machine guns suddenly became the price of survival as a sovereign state.'[14] White goes on to explore how war spurred advances from medicine to nuclear power to credit cards.

And then there's Darwin. From an evolutionary point of view, the global economy is the ultimate Darwinian experiment – a fight between all mankind to find the fittest of the species.[15] The logic of Darwin means that the more turbulence, the more intense the struggle, the greater evidence of can-do hustle and ambition. If the developing world was convulsed by violence, perhaps that was a good sign. War, per se, is not good. But neither are we. And if war is integral to us, an expression of what it is to be human, then war, for mankind, is a sign of life.

*

If you accept a Darwinian view of human nature, then the arguments for and against globalization are diminished. Globalization becomes inevitable. And since fighting is who we are, globalization, as a meeting ground for all mankind, will also be extremely messy. The anti-globalization argument is reduced to mitigation. It becomes about trying to control ourselves, behaving better than our base nature, being good-natured – humanitarian as opposed to human.

It's not all bad news for the anti-globalizers, however. If you accept that mankind is essentially disagreeable, then globalization can never achieve its goal. The chances of 6 billion people ever agreeing to live by the same set of standards and becoming a vast, dull monolith are slim to non-existent. More likely is that we'll keep on fighting.

This can sound depressing. It doesn't have to be. It provides an answer to the End Timers, for one. The last few years have seen a rise in a diverse set of cults who believe Armageddon is around the corner. There are Hindus who think we are in the Age of Kali – a final, imploding stage of man that ends with Kali cleansing the earth with sword and fire. There are Christians who believe in the End of Days, and fundamentalists on both sides of the Christian–Muslim divide who believe in the clash of civilizations. A few years ago, programmers put a technological twist on this imminent Doomsday when they told us to fear the Y2K bug at the turn of the millennium. Many of these cults take their evidence from the chaos and violence in the world around them – a dark suspicion that the reverse to inevitable progress holds true, and that we are swiftly and helplessly plunging to our doom. These are scary times after all.

The answer to the End Timers is: it's always been like this.

In our interconnected world, the links of live media and cheap jet travel make an event like 9/11 more immediate, more shocking, and are witnessed by many more of us. But imagine how horrifying it would have been to watch the Normandy Landings, Dresden or Nagasaki live, up close and personal. There is nothing new about bloodshed. It's always scary times.

There is also some hope here. If a current of darkness runs through even the brightest human life, maybe a current of light runs through the dark. Something often missed about war zones is that they are frequently exceptionally beautiful. Nepal's countryside is a picture of bucolic paradise, rivalled perhaps only by the blossoms of Afghanistan's northern mountains in spring. Cambodia's civil war raged against a backdrop of the awesome architecture of Angkor Wat, while the graves of 70,000 Sri Lankans are lush jungles of palms and ponds alive with kingfishers, green parrots and black and yellow longtails. Sierra Leone is a tropical paradise. The coastal cities of Croatia are Venetian wonders. Downtown Mogadishu, that tropical Dresden, is like any work of painstaking craftsmanship: breathtaking.

Perhaps the most beautiful war zone of all is Kashmir in March, as the snow pulls back through the damp pine forests and ponies wander through flower-filled grasslands. In Kashmir, I'd generally stay at Ghulam Butt's houseboats on Dal Lake, on the edge of the summer capital Srinagar. There each morning Abdul would be up at dawn, padding around the houseboat's living room, fussing, making cardamom tea. A golden sun would be breaking over the Himalayan foothills to the east and its rays reflecting off the placid, grey waters into the cabin, playing on the sandalwood panel walls and the outsize chandelier. Through the carved window frame, swallows would be swooping over the lilies, black ducks diving in the shallows and kingfishers preening themselves on the veranda. There'd be a nip to the air, not a cloud in the sky and no sound but birds and the occasional distant splash from a leaping carp. Somewhere, not so far away, there was a war on. But at Butt's houseboats, for $40 a night, I'd rarely felt greater peace.

It was a short trip from Butt's to the house of my friend Omar Farooq, the *mirwaiz* of Kashmir. Farooq was the young spiritual leader to 5 million Kashmiris, a leading moderate and one of the first people I'd met after arriving in India. One day sitting outside his home in Srinagar under a bright-blue sky in a garden full of sunflowers and red lilies, I remarked on the picture-perfect scenery. Farooq sighed. 'Sometimes you wish it was just a little less pretty,' he said. 'Maybe then not so many people would want it.'

Farooq was making a profound point. Wars are rarely fought over dumps. New York–Madrid–London–Bali sounds like a delightful round-the-world-trip. It's also a list of war zones. Seven years later, despite everything that has happened since, New York is still the bloodiest spot in the war on terrorism. To think of New York or Madrid or London or Bali solely as a place where blood has been spilled, however, would require the tightest set of blinkers.

The point is: we need to stop thinking of war as a place apart. War is not 'zoned'. It is not some unusual, grainy, distant place removed from the rest of the planet. War, like love, is all around.

So is peace. War correspondence, like all journalism, is the edited highlights of horror. No war correspondent is going to write a story that begins: 'Rebels today slaughtered thirty-one women and children in a savage attack beside a babbling brook in a meadow of wild irises, daisies and tiny pink anemones.' But that, actually, would be more accurate. Baghdad is not in a state of continuous and cacophonous war. The Iraqi air is not filled with lead. The Iraqi soil is not carpeted with shrapnel or mines. Even a bomb site is peaceful the day before the explosion goes off, and the day after.

Farooq thought Kashmir's magnificence intensified the fighting. It did. But it nurtured hope too. Killers I met on both sides of the Kashmir conflict murdered without conscience. But they became lyrical when they spoke about the landscape they were fighting over. I took heart from that. The dreamy pride some Kashmiris took in their smashed and cratered homeland was at once odd, and oddly comforting. It spoke of souls behind battle-narrowed eyes, victims and murderers whose dearest wish was for a family picnic by the lake.

Kashmir is one of the bloodiest and enduring wars on the planet. Its position on the frontline of one of the most intractable conflicts – where militant, separatist Islam clashes with secular, inclusive Indian – means it will be years before the militants and the soldiers lay down their arms, and generations before the divide heals. But war is just one of the things that happens in Kashmir. There is hope for all the world in the notion that when a Kashmiri thinks of peace and beauty, he thinks of home.

The Himalayas turned out to be a good source of such global wisdom. Gyanendra hadn't proved especially shrewd. But he had neighbours who had. In Bhutan, King Jigme Singye Wangchuck's family had ruled Bhutan since Britain appointed his great grandfather king in 1907. The present king has been carefully moving the Himalayan Buddhist kingdom from a hermit existence into the global age. He has tried to abolish his own unilateral power – eventually prevailing against popular royalist sentiment by holding a March 2008 general election that, nonetheless, saw a landslide victory for the most pro-monarchy party. And he has opened the Land of the Thunder Dragon to tourists and allowed television and the Internet – though installing the country's first traffic light in the capital Thimpu was deemed a step too far and the king had it removed. In his careful blending of tradition with modernity, the king declared that in an age where globalization would erode culture and identity as well as raise incomes, his country would not be measured by mere money, using the standard calculations of Gross Domestic Product. Rather, Bhutan would adopt a more ethereal measure: Gross National Happiness.

There was another Himalayan sage who, all his life, had felt the crushing weight of foreign power. Discovered as the 14th incarnation of Tibetan Buddhism's high priest at the age of two and enthroned at four, it was after he fled Chinese troops invading Tibet for northern India at nineteen that Tenzin Gyatso became a world leader. Since then politicians, celebrities, refugees, hippies and Chinese spies had flocked to McLeodganj to hear the Dalai Lama dispense insight from his cottage among the steep forests in the old British hill station. I met him there, in his modest living room, on a crisp autumn morning in 2004.

When he talked about Tibet, the Dalai Lama could have been describing almost any developing nation facing the assault of globalization. Mongolia, Xinjiang and Manchuria had been assimilated into China, he said. Those cultures had been lost. 'That danger is very alive for Tibet. The threats to our cultural heritage, religious freedom and environment are very serious. [Then there is] the big gap in China proper, between rich and poor. The whole picture, it almost looks hopeless. That's why we are trying to gain meaningful autonomy.'

The answer was not to fight the superior power, he said, but to negotiate. 'Meeting face to face and having friendly discussions is very, very important, very helpful to build mutual trust. In 1973 or 1974, China was still in the Cultural Revolution. But in this very room, on that seat, we decided that sooner or later, we had to talk to the Chinese government. We decided we had no alternative. It was the only realistic way. Now, some Tibetans accuse me of selling out their right to independence. My eldest brother is for complete independence and my second brother [even] worked with the CIA.'

The fundamental issue was freedom. 'We love freedom. Even animals love their freedom.' This irresistible need to be free meant that even the most authoritarian regimes were eventually self-correcting, he said. Freedom was the touchstone to which mankind would always return. Even China would have to respond to 'the will of its own people'. Many of the rebellions happening around the world today could be explained by the process of how our desire for freedom always, and 'naturally', counters repression. 'If you look at the Tibetan situation locally, then it's hopeless,' said the Dalai Lama. 'But from a wider perspective, it's hopeful.'

The key, said the Dalai Lama, was never to see the world in absolutes. 'Much depends on how you look. You have to look [at things] from a wide perspective. You can't say this is white or this is black, absolutely positive or negative. Everything is, you see, mixed.' Good mixed with bad; development mixed with inequality; violence with progress. 'Some people,

I notice in the West, are fond of clear cuts. [If the situation is] positive, [they are] very happy. Little negative, very unhappy. This is unrealistic.'

He paused. I wanted to ask him more. The Dalai Lama was talking about Tibet. But much of what he was saying had a much wider application. I felt as though I'd stumbled into a grand discussion with one of the world's great minds, who might finally give me some answers to the big questions that had dogged me since Qala-i-Jangi. Was war endless? Would this mix of conflict and progress ever resolve itself? Were we locked forever into a bloody contest for advancement? What was the future for mankind?

But he was tired and, apparently sensing the deluge of questions welling inside me, he cut me off by raising his palm. Then he stood, held out his hand, on to which an attendant laid a white silk scarf, which he wrapped gently around my neck. He held me by the shoulders, beamed at me and, still smiling, showed me the door. 'These are my last words on all this,' he said as we parted. 'The future? Not bad.'

ENDNOTES

PROLOGUE

1. Much of the information on the Jarawas comes from Madhusree Mukerjee, *The Land of Naked People* (New Delhi, Penguin Books India, 2003): 2.
2. Thanks largely to the remarkable patience and vigilance of my friend and fixer on the islands, Denis Giles. Twice I flew to the islands to track En-mei down. Twice, I failed. Finally, eight months after my second trip, I left a list of questions with Denis. After eight more months of waiting, Denis received word that En-mei had emerged from the jungle, jumped into his car with the sheets of questions I had scribbled down and drove all night to meet him and put my questions to him before he disappeared back into the jungle.

PART 1

CHAPTER 1

1. Rashid Ahmed, *The Taliban: Militant Islam, Oil and Fundamentalism in Central Asia* (I.B. Tauris, 1 March 2001): 56.
2. US soldiers have a non-negotiable code for the corpses of the fallen – 'Leave No Man Behind'. This accounts for the ongoing operation to recover the bodies of dead American servicemen in Vietnam, and anywhere else US servicemen are still listed as missing in action.
3. Satellite communications.
4. JDAMs: Joint Direct Attack Munitions, a guidance kit that converts dumb bombs to smart bombs by combined use of an internal targeting system and the Global Positioning System (GPS).

5. MIA: American military acronym for missing in action. More serious still is KIA, killed in action, which was Spann's true status.
6. Dodge, Damien and Oleg all later won awards for their work at Qala-i-Jangi. Damien and Dodge shared the Rory Peck freelance cameraman award for the footage they shot inside the fort. Oleg's remarkable pictures ran in almost every newspaper, earning him a clutch of prizes.
7. The Alliance said two US soldiers had died. In Washington, spokesmen for the Pentagon – who at this time were also denying Spann's death on the pretext that the former Marine was not a Defense Department serviceman but a CIA paramilitary, and would do so for forty-eight more hours until forced to relent by his family – said that there had been no military deaths but that five US service members had been seriously injured and evacuated to Landstuhl Regional Medical Centre in Germany. Four British soldiers were also reported wounded, though British officials – who never comment on the SBS – would not confirm. From the Alliance, there were as many as thirty dead and fifty injured.

   Three months later Najib and I returned to the fort and met the same junior commander who had tried to turn us away. Perhaps because of a large Christmas bonus I had given him, Najib had decided he preferred journalists to soldiers by then and was deploying all his wiliness in my cause. 'I've got this really annoying journalist with me,' he told the commander in Farsi as I stood next to him. 'He keeps insisting that two big American commanders were killed here in that bomb strike.' The commander fell for it immediately. 'What a moron!' he replied. 'It was just two low-ranking soldiers. Do these journalists ever get their facts right?' He then told Najib he had personally helped in the operation to extract the two men's bodies and their effects from the tons of earth thrown up by the bomb – an operation that took weeks and was overseen by Tyson.
8. For a full account of the battle, see Alex Perry, 'Inside the Battle at Qala-i-Jangi', *Time* (10 December 2001: 22–9). www.time.com/time/nation/article/0,8599,186592,00.html
9. There were other stories to emerge from Mazar. One that stood out was whether Qala-i-Jangi, bloody as it was, had been a distraction from the true slaughter going on nearby. The first I heard of hundreds of Taliban prisoners suffocating in sealed freight containers after their November 2001 surrender at Kunduz was three months after the events at Qala-i-

Jangi. I was visiting Dostum's main jail at Shiburghan, two hours to the west of Mazar, where I met Abdul, a Pakistani jihadi. Of 300 men in his container, Abdul said he alone survived. Over the next few months, reports emerged of a mass grave at Dasht-i-Laili, west of Shiburghan. Villagers complained of a sickening stench blowing in from the desert. And in May, United Nations experts and scientists from the Boston-based Physicians for Human Rights announced that preliminary autopsies suggested the prisoners were suffocated, executed or buried alive. Dostum admitted to 200 bodies, the UN estimated 960, but the numbers of missing – 8,000 Taliban surrendered and only 3,000 reached Shiburghan – suggested a mass slaughter. Then, returning to Shiburghan once again in September, I met Najib's cousin, also called Najibullah Quraishi. And he told me about the videotape.

The second Najib explained that Dostum's other videographers had recorded the great victory at Kunduz and the prisoner surrenders. Three scenes from a 1-hour-and-40-minute film made a particular impression. 'In the first, you can hear Taliban prisoners shouting and screaming for air,' he said. 'So an Alliance soldier just fires his AK-47 into the container.' Later the convoy arrives at Shiburghan jail, the doors are opened and a slippery crush of bodies and dying men spills into the courtyard. Finally the trucks (now reloaded) arrive at Dasht-i-Laili. Again the containers are opened and disgorge their grisly cargo. Dostum's fighters then walk among the cadavers, methodically shooting anyone still alive. I asked about the twelve American Special Operations soldiers attached to Dostum. Najib said the key question of exactly how much they knew about what went on, whether they were there, was answered in full, unmistakable Technicolor. Looking at him, it was difficult to doubt him. He had a yellow bruise over his eye, a purple graze on his cheek, his lip was split, his arm was in a sling and he walked with a stiff limp. Two weeks earlier Dostum's men had caught him trying to copy the videotape. They beat him unconscious and tried to throw him down a well. After lying low, he was escaping to Kabul and London.

By the time the tape resurfaced in late January 2003, Dostum's killers had tortured and murdered two men – a convoy driver and a taxi driver who saw blood pouring from a passing container – for speaking to British documentary maker Jamie Doran. But the tape had survived and its owner, a Mr 'Ati Kola', was trying to sell it to Doran. With Doran, I arranged a pick-up team to meet the owner just over the Afghan border in Uzbekistan: video technicians Maxim and Nikolai, security expert Jim and my Uzbek fixer Mohammed.

At precisely twelve noon on the agreed day, we pulled up at the grey Intourist hotel. Nikolai stayed with the cars while Jim, Maxim and I skirted the icy puddles and made for the double doors. Mohammed was already inside in an upstairs room, where he'd been waiting nervously since 9 a.m. to alert us if the seller checked in. 'Nothing,' he'd said on the phone. No 'Mr Ati Kola' and no other Afghans. As we reached the entrance, Jim braced against the wall, snapped open a steel butterfly knife and slipped it handle first up his sleeve.

Inside, a sullen 'nyet' from the Uzbek receptionist confirmed no one had arrived from over the border. Thirty minutes later, we'd been joined in the lobby by two policemen in dirty camouflage jackets and fur hats, who idled in front of the doors, smoking and pretending not to watch us. They weren't our only observers. Jim said a minivan of 'heavies' had pulled up at the back while a woman in a fur coat and a man in a white tracksuit were out front. Plus, if the seller was this late, he'd either been caught or he'd changed his mind. The call eventually came at 1 p.m.

'Leave now,' came Doran's voice. 'You understand? Right now.'

Once past the checkpoint on the edge of Termez, we switched the Ladas for two fast saloons and sped north to Tashkent. I called back. 'The seller was taken,' said Doran. 'Check in with me every few hours from the road.' Another man was arrested, perhaps dead. And we hadn't even seen the tape.

Back in Tashkent, Doran told me that Uzbek border guards had stopped and searched the seller as he crossed the bridge from Afghanistan to Uzbekistan. They took the tape and sent him back. Dostum's men were waiting. The man, a member of the warlord's inner circle, hadn't been seen since. Later, diplomat friends said we'd been watched from the moment we arrived in Uzbekistan. What happened to the tape is unclear. What was certain was that hundreds and perhaps thousands of men were dead and three more who tried to tell their story had joined them.

10. Joseph Stiglitz, *Making Globalization Work* (Penguin, London 2006): 9.
11. Joseph Stiglitz, *Globalization and its Discontents* (Penguin, London 2002): 6.

12. The al-Qaeda movement itself presents an interesting paradox. Its actions are those of anti-globalizer: striking a more powerful foe in a guerrilla war, railing against the dominant Western way of life. But its ambitions – to impose a vast Muslim caliphate on the world – are those of a globalizer.
13. John Gray, *Al Qaeda and What it Means to be Modern* (Faber, London, 2003): 3.
14. Ibid: 3.
15. Joseph Stiglitz, *Making Globalization Work* (Penguin, London 2006): 9.
16. World Commission on the Social Dimension of Globalization, *A Fair Globalization: Creating Opportunities for All* (International Labour Office, Geneva 2004): 44.
17. Take the world's biggest economy. In the first quarter of 2006, US company profits hit an all-time high as a proportion of GDP. According to the US census bureau, the top fifth of American households received 50.4 per cent of all household income in 2005, the largest share since those records began in 1967 – and the biggest gains were made by those at the very top. In 2005, the average pay of a CEO of an S&P 500 company was 411 times that of an average worker, up from 107 times in 1990.[1] A 2005 analysis of US tax returns by Emmanuel Suez at the University of California and Thomas Piketty at the Paris School of Economics found that only twice before over the past century has 5 per cent of national income gone to the top 1/100th per cent of the US – 15,000 families with incomes of $9.5 million or more a year – and that was in 1915–16, and in the 1920s just before the Wall Street crash. Suez and Piketty also found 21.8 per cent of US national income went to the richest 1 per cent in 2005 – a level not seen since 1928. The pattern is the same around the world. In Britain in 2005–6, for example, directors' pay jumped a full 28 per cent from the previous year.

    1. Daniel Gross, 'Why the Rich are Getting Richer', *Newsweek* (12 November 2007): 33–9.

18. George Wehrfritz, 'The Death of Social Mobility', *Newsweek* (12 November 2007): 40–2.
19. Richard Freeman, *The Great Doubling: America in the New Global Economy*, Usery Lecture, 8 April 2005. Georgia State University, *What Really Ails Europe (and America): The Doubling of the Global Work-*

force, *Globalist*, 3 June 2005. http://www.theglobalist.com/StoryId.aspx?StoryId=4542

20. 'The current expansion has a chance to become the first sustained period of economic growth since World War II that fails to offer a prolonged increase in real wages for most workers,' wrote Steven Greenhouse and David Leonhardt in the *New York Times*.[1] Western middle-class salaries were largely stagnant in 2006, or at best experiencing the sort of rises you would expect in a recession. US labour data shows the median pre-tax inflation-adjusted wage grew just 11 per cent between 1966 and 2001, compared to 58 per cent for incomes in the 90th percentile and 121 per cent for those in the 99th. Greenhouse and Leonhardt found the median hourly wage for American workers had declined by 2 per cent since 2003 in real terms, and that wages and salaries made up the lowest share of Gross Domestic Product (GDP) since the government started recording the data in 1947. A Goldman Sachs research note on the US economy in 2006 stated that several factors had contributed to a situation in which 'as a share of GDP, profits reached an all-time high in the first quarter of 2006 . . . [But] the most important contribution to the higher profit margins over the past five years has been a decline in labour's share of national income.'[2] Again, it was the same picture in the UK. British median weekly wages, adjusted for inflation, actually fell by 0.4 per cent in 2005–6,[3] while in July 2007 the Joseph Rowntree Foundation published a survey that found inequality in the UK was at its highest for forty years and that the numbers of poor had risen over the previous fifteen years and now accounted for more than 25 per cent of the country.[4]

    1. Greenhouse and Leonhardt, 'Real Wages Fail to Match a Rise in Productivity', *New York Times*. http://www.nytimes.com/2006/08/28/business/28wages.html?pagewanted=2&hp&ex=11568240 (28 August 2006).
    2. Ibid.
    3. Richard Tomkins, 'What's in it for Them', *FT* Magazine, 23–4 September 2006: http://us.ft.com/ftgateway/superpage.ft?news_id=fto101320060924420805&page=2
    4. Daniel Dorling, Jan Rigby, Ben Wheeler, Dimitris Ballas, Bethan Thomas, Eldin Fahmy, David Gordon and Ruth Lupton, *Poverty*,

Wealth and Place in Britain 1968 to 2005, The Policy Press (17 July 2007).

21. For sourcing and further explanation, see p. 68.
22. He Jianwu (Development Research Centre) and Louis Kuijs (World Bank), *World Bank China Research Paper No. 7: Rebalancing China's Economy – Modelling a Policy Package*, September 2007: http://www.worldbank.org.cn/english/content/working_paper7.pdf
23. The weight of statistical evidence of this growing inequality is becoming undeniable. Today the combined wealth of the world's three richest *people* is greater than the Gross Domestic Product of the forty-eight poorest *countries*. And inequality has increased as globalization has progressed. In 1998, the United Nations Development Programme found that in 1960, the average income of the richest 20 per cent of the world's population was thirty times higher than that of the poorest 20 per cent, but by 1995 this had become eighty-two times greater. Similarly, it found that in 1970 the gap between the per capita GDP of the richest country, the USA ($5,070), and of the poorest, Bangladesh ($57), was 88:1. In 2000, the gap between the richest, Luxembourg ($45,917), and the poorest, Guinea Bissau ($161), was 267:1. Inequality has also risen within nations. A study of seventy-seven countries with 82 per cent of the world's population showed that between the 1950s and the 1990s inequality rose in forty-five and fell in sixteen. The International Monetary Fund also finds that in 1980, 18 per cent of the world's population lived in developed countries and enjoyed 71 per cent of the world's income. In 2000, 16 per cent lived in developed countries, enjoying 81 per cent of world GDP. So in 1980, 82 per cent got 29 per cent of the world's income cake, while in 2000, 84 per cent had to share out 19 per cent. Defenders of globalization argue that all incomes have risen around the world due to the greater integration of markets. This is true. But the incomes of the rich have risen faster. (Achin Vanaik, New Delhi, *On Global Inequality*, 2005; Brian Barry, *Why Social Justice Matters*, Polity Press, 2005.)
24. This widening disparity has often been actively assisted by governments. In Russia, the corrupt privatization of natural resources created overnight billionaire oligarchs. The same pattern of vast individual enrichment occurred with state enterprises in China. In the Arab world, the

last forty years have seen the ruling elites accumulate untold wealth while their people moved little or even backwards under tyranny and stagnation. One of the world's wealthiest men is Mexican Carlos Slim, whose former state telecoms company Telmex was maintained as a monopoly by the government. In South Africa, former anti-apartheid African National Congress activists Cyril Ramaphosa and Tokyo Sexwale used their party connections to be reborn as private equity magnates.

25. Largely unfavourable ones, apparently. A series of strikes and workers' protests has plagued construction in Dubai since 2006. In March of that year, about 2,500 labourers at the site of the Burj Dubai – set to be the tallest building in the world – rioted over conditions which led to Human Rights Watch calling on the United Arab Emirates' government to 'end abusive labour practices'. The government subsequently announced it was mulling over a minimum wage.
26. Brian Love, *OECD jobs report shows darker side of globalization*, Reuters, 19 June: http://www.reuters.com/article/ousiv/idUSL193680420070619
27. Daniel Gross, 'Why the Rich are Getting Richer' *Newsweek*, (12 November 2007): 33–9.
28. The campaign itself was notable for being the first Indian campaign to adopt sophisticated marketing techniques. Instead of the usual cheap posters with cut-out and superimposed pictures of the candidates, the BJP spent $90 million on a high quality press campaign which featured eye-catching and well-crafted photography. Most impressive, Vajpayee recorded a short message about his vision for India which was then sent to every mobile phone in the country. Millions of Indians who could afford mobiles were stunned and delighted to hear their prime minister's voice on the line. The hundreds of million who could not took this as another sign that the BJP was an elitist party.
29. I am indebted to Thomas Friedman for first alerting me to this startling passage. Friedman, *The World is Flat* (Penguin Books, London 2006): 235–6.
30. Mark Twain, *Following the Equator: A Journey Around the World* (first published 1897; reprinted by Dover Publications, Mineola, NY 1989): chapter 43.

CHAPTER 2

1. Alex Perry, 'Crossing the Line', *Time* (7 May 2001): 18–21.
2. Ibid.
3. Ibid.
4. Ibid. Reliable estimates are hard to come by with so much illegal migration, but this was the lowest.
5. Moisés Naim, *Illicit* (Random House, London, 2007): 12.
6. UN Office for the Coordination of Humanitarian Affairs, Small Arms: 528.
7. Peter Reuter and Edwin M. Truman, *Chasing Dirty Money: The Fight Against Money Laundering* (Washington DC, Institute for International Economics, 2004): 13.
8. I spent months trying to get on the inside of the international sex trafficking rings in Shenzhen, but to no avail. One of the city's main sources of child sex slaves was South East Asia, particularly Thailand and Burma. Eventually I gave up on Shenzhen and flew to Bangkok, then up to Mai Sae, on the border of northern Thailand and Burma. There I met British photographer Jonathan Taylor, who spoke Thai and had constructed a special rucksack through which he could secretly video. We ended up buying a couple of sex slaves – Tip (whose name means 'heavenly light') and Lek (meaning 'small') – and smuggling them back into Burma to try to reunite them with their families. Our attempt did not have a happy ending. For a fuller account, and a package of stories exploring Asia's trade in child slaves, see: Alex Perry et al, 'The Shame', *Time* (4 February 2002): 23–9.
9. *Mingbao*, 23 July 2007. http://epochtimes.com/gb/7/7/23/n1780581.htm. Translated by the *Epoch Times*: http://en.epochtimes.com/news/7-7-28/58111.html
10. 'Rural Unrest in China: Worries about Poverty and Instability in central China', the Economist Intelligence Unit. http://www.economist.com/daily/news/displaystory.cfm?story_id=8864384
11. *Blue Book of China's Society*: 'Analysis and Forecast on China's Social Development', Social Sciences Academic Press, Beijing, 2005.
12. 'Migrant workers striving for better life as Hu vows to tackle widening

income gap', *People's Daily*, 21 October 2007. http://english.peopledaily.com.cn/90002/92169/92188/6287565.html

13. Yu Jianrong, 'Social Conflict in Rural China', China Security, Washington DC, Spring 2007, Vol. 3, No 2: 2–17. http://www.wsichina.org/cs6_1.pdf
14. Ibid., 11.

CHAPTER 3

1. Statistics and rankings of the world's mega-cities vary widely, due to the chaotic nature of these vast conurbations and the difficulties of demarcating different, connecting urban sprawls. Here I have used Brinkhoff: 'The Principal Agglomerations of the World', http://www.citypopulation.de, 30 September 2007.
2. Bombay was officially renamed Mumbai in the mid 1990s. The new name is not, as many Westerners think, simply the Hindi rendition of Bombay or the original, non-Portuguese name. Rather, it is an entirely new name, thought to be derived from the city's famous Hindu Mumba-Devi temple. The choice of an exclusively Hindi name reflects the chauvinist views of the ruling political party of the time, the Shiv Sena, one of whose core beliefs was a virulent anti-migrant, anti-Muslim stance called Bhumiputra, or 'Son of Soil'. Most Bombayites, and most Indians, still refer to the city as Bombay, which is more in keeping with its cosmopolitan and multi-lingual character.
3. National Association of Software and Science Companies (NASSCOM), *Strategic Review*, 2007.
4. UN Population Reference Bureau Report, 2005. Only 19 per cent of India lives on more than $2 a day, which is the common threshold definition of poverty used by the UN and World Bank.
5. NASSCOM, Indian IT industry fact-sheet, 2007.
6. UN Population Reference Bureau Report, 2005. Though overall poverty rates are falling when measured by both the World Bank and the government, India may miss a target set by the UN as part of the Millennium Development Goals to halve the number of people living on less than $1 a day from 1990 levels by 2015, according to a October 2007 report by the UN and the Asian Development Bank. The

country has also achieved less than half its targets to halve hunger, according to a study by the US-based International Food Policy Research Institute.

7. UN Development Report, 2006. India accounts for 2.4 million of the annual 4.4 million child deaths.
8. Ibid.
9. Ministry of External Affairs Report, 'Industry and Services: Infrastructure (Health)', 2002.
10. In February 2008, the Indian government announced its most ambitious project to tackle poverty ever – a nationwide National Rural Employment Guarantee Scheme (NREGS), which aims to provide 100 days of minimum wage employment – 60 rupees a day – each year to tens of millions of rural poor in public works like ditch-digging. The government said it would fund the programme with $4 billion in 2008, adding it would waive $15 billion in loans to small farmers.
11. The unit was eventually disbanded in 2005, amid allegations that some officers were colluding with the gangsters.
12. Mike Davis, *Planet of Slums* (Verso, London, 2006).
13. See Amin Jaffer's account of the period *Made for Maharajahs: a Design Diary of Princely India*, New Holland, London, 2006.
14. Gurcharan Das, *India Unbound: From Independence to the Global Information Age* (Profile Books, London, 2002).
15. Government figures show around 6,500 women are killed in India every year in dowry crimes – either by the groom's family, unhappy at what they see as insufficient gifts, or by their own, embarrassed by their own penury.

PART 2

CHAPTER 4

1. Bertil Lintner, *Blood Brothers: Crime, Business and Politics in Asia* (Palgrave Macmillan, London, 19 March 2003).
2. The Centre publishes weekly, quarterly and annual reports on piracy worldwide. See http://www.icc-ccs.org.uk/main/publication.php
3. Somalia eclipsed Indonesia for pirate attacks in 2007. Nevertheless, over

the past few years, the waters off Indonesia are consistently the most dangerous in the world.

4. Violent crime has become so bad in South Africa, and such an embarrassment to the state, that the South Africa Police often refuse to release statistics, particularly regional breakdowns, and are often also accused of tampering with the real figures. As a result, the statistical picture is incomplete, prone to inconsistencies and sometimes relies more on anecdote than official tallies. The murder rate, for instance, varies from 19,200 a year – the police number for 2006 – to 33,000, South Africa's Medical Research Council figure for 2000. The figures I use in this section are largely taken from *The Social Contradictions of Organized Crime on the Cape Flats*, a paper by one of South Africa's foremost crime researchers, André Standing. (Institute of Security Studies, Johannesburg, Paper 74, June 2003.)
5. André Standing, *The Social Contradictions of Organised Crime on the Cape Flats*, Institute for Security Studies, Pretoria, June 2003: http://www.iss.co.za/pubs/papers/74/paper74.html
6. Antony Altbeker, *A Country at War with Itself: South Africa's Crisis of Crime* (Jonathan Ball, Johannesburg, September 2007).
7. A good illustration of this is India's caste system. Being born into a caste removes all ambition and expectation. Improvements are left to the next reincarnation. The anti-globalization movement is largely about the disappointment the poor feel on discovering that they are expected to compete on equal terms with players who have more than an equal share of resources. In that sense, for India's authorities the caste system is a handy tool to control social unrest.
8. I am indebted to Mark Gevisser for unearthing this telling comment in his comprehensive biography: Mark Gevisser, *Thabo Mbeki: The Dream Deferred*, Jonathan Ball, Johannesburg, 2007): xxxi.
9. Standing, 'The Social Contradictions of Crime on the Cape Flats'.
10. Benjamin Joffe-Walt, 'Riots Engulf South Africa's Townships' (*Daily Telegraph*, London, 5 June 2005): http://www.telegraph.co.uk/news/main.jhtml?xml=/news/2005/06/05/wsafr05.xml&sSheet=/news/2005/06/05/ixworld.html
11. 'Keep the Borders Open', *Economist*, 5 January 2008, Leaders: 9.
12. For examples, see the 2006 Zambian general election campaign, where China's presence became the central issue; South African President

Thabo Mbeki's December 2006 warning that Africa needs to guard against 'a colonial relationship' with China; the murder of Chinese oil workers in Nigeria (2005) and Ethiopia (2007).

13. Figures from the Somali Association of South Africa.

CHAPTER 5

1. Nicholas Shaxson, *Poisoned Wells: The Dirty Politics of African Oil* (Palgrave Macmillan, New York, 2007): 2.
2. John Ghazvinian, *Untapped: The Scramble for Africa's Oil* (Harcourt, New York, March 2007): 12.
3. Widely shared. See Shaxson, Ghazvinian, the US State Department.
4. Paul M. Lubeck, Michael J. Watts and Ronnie D. Lipschutz, *Convergent Interests: US Energy Security and the 'Securing' of Nigerian Democracy*, The Center for International Policy, Washington, DC, February 2007, http://www.ciponline.org/NIGERIA_FINAL.pdf
5. Sachs, Stiglitz, Humphreys, *Escaping the Resource Curse* (Columbia University Press, New York, 23 April 2007).
6. Shaxson: 5–7.
7. Bunkering also frequently results in horrific fireball accidents, which incinerate hundreds a year.
8. Shaxson: 3.
9. IMF, 'Regional Economic Outlook, Sub-Saharan Africa', April 2007.
10. UNDP, Human Development Report, 2006.
11. Ibid.
12. New America Media, 'Lure of Resources Bring Great Powers Back to Africa', Michael Klare interviewed by Brian Shott, 24 November 2006: http://news.newamericamedia.org/news/view_article.html?article_id=d17cc8681a1a7d3914a16a96ae53b6e0
13. In 2007, the International Energy Agency predicted China would become the world's emissions leader by the end of the year. The Netherlands Environment Assessment Agency said China had already passed that level.
14. CNA Corporation, 'National Security and the Threat of Climate Change': http://securityandclimate.cna.org/report
15. George Monbiot, 'In This Age of Diamond Saucepans, Only a Recession Makes Sense', *Guardian*, 9 October 2007: http://politics.guardian.co.uk/economics/comment/0,,2186730,00.html
16. National Environment Trust.

CHAPTER 6

1. BBC, 13 February 2006: http://news.bbc.co.uk/1/hi/world/south_asia/4707482.stm
2. Ass, 'Promoted from Boleros and Pajeros', *Nepali Times*, 7–12 April 2006: http://www.nepalitimes.com/issue/343/Backside/13394
3. Bruce Loudon, 'Gays are a Capitalist Pollutant', *Australian*, 6 January 2007: http://www.theaustralian.news.com.au/story/0,20867,21016174-2703,00.html. The Maoists weren't the only ones to hold this view. Iranian President Mahmoud Ahmadinejad told an audience at Columbia University in New York in September 2007: 'In Iran, we don't have homosexuals, like in your country. In Iran, we do not have this phenomenon, I don't know who has told you that we have it.'
4. The death toll eventually hit 14,000 by the time a ceasefire was agreed in November 2006.
5. Asian Human Rights Commission, 'Nepal Drowning in a Madness of Barbarity with No Rule of Law', Hong Kong, 20 January 2005: http://www.ahrchk.net/pr/mainfile.php/2005mr/129/
6. International Crisis Group, 'Nepal: Dealing with a Human Rights Crisis', Asia Report No 94, New York, 24 March 2005: http://www.crisisgroup.org/home/index.cfm?id=3337&l=1
7. Human Rights Watch, 'Nepal: Danger of 'Disappearances' Escalates', *Human Rights News*, New York, 9 February 2005: http://hrw.org/english/docs/2005/02/09/nepal10152.htm
8. Alex Perry, 'A Kingdom in Chaos', *Time*, 2 February 2004: 14–16: www.time.com/time/magazine/article/0,9171,501040202-582486,00.html
9. Ibid.
10. Dr Thomas A. Marks, 'Insurgency in Nepal', Strategic Studies Institute of the US Army War College, Carlisle, Pennsylvania, USA, 1 December 2003: http://www.strategicstudiesinstitute.army.mil/pubs/display.cfm?pubID=49
11. Communist Party of Nepal (Maoist), 'Common Minimum Policy & Programme of United Revolutionary People's Council, Nepal (URPC)', Item 75, Worker, Issue 8: http://www.cpnm.org/worker/issue8/urpc.htm
12. Watchlist, 'Caught in the middle: Mounting violations against children in Nepal's armed conflict', New York, 26 January 2005: http://

www.watchlist.org/reports/nepal.report.php. Also see South Asia Intelligence Review, 'Nepal: Arming the Children', March 2004: http://www.satp.org/satporgtp/sair/

13. He spoke to the BBC a few months later.
14. 'Inequality in Latin America: a Stubborn Curse', *Economist*, 6 November 2003: http://www.economist.com/world/la/displaystory.cfm?story_id=2193852#subscribe
15. David de Ferranti, Guillermo Perry, Francisco H.G. Ferreira and Michael Walto, 'Inequality in Latin America & the Caribbean: Breaking with History?', World Bank, 7 October 2003. http://lnweb18.worldbank.org/LAC/LAC.nsf/ECADocByUnid/4112F1114F594B4B85256DB3005DB262?Opendocument
16. Mac Magolis, 'How Brazil Reversed the Curse', *Newsweek* 3 November 2007: http://www.newsweek.com/id/67850/output/print
17. Jorge Castanada, 'Latin America's Two Left Wings', *Newsweek*, 9 January 2006: www.newsweek.com/id/47471
18. Chávez's descriptions of the 2000–2008 US president include 'killer', 'madman' and the 'world's only terrorist'. Perhaps most famously, at the 2006 UN General Assembly in New York, the Venezuelan president said of his American counterpart: 'The devil came here yesterday. It still smells of sulphur today.' The 2006 Assembly was a festival of anti-Americanism and rallying cries against US domination. Chávez went on to denounce the US for promoting 'a false democracy of the elite' and a 'democracy of bombs', while Bush spoke 'as if he were the owner of the world'. A day earlier Iranian President Mahmoud Ahmadinejad accused the UN of being a tool of the US. 'As long as the UN Security Council is unable to act on behalf of the entire international community in a transparent, just and democratic manner, it will neither be legitimate nor effective.' And Afghan President Hamid Karzai even took an oblique shot at US military-heavy methods in its war on terror, arguing military action alone would not stop terrorism.
19. The figures were collected from various issues of *Accidental Deaths and Suicides in India*, National Crime Records Bureau (NCRB), Ministry of Home Affairs, Government of India. Prof. K. Nagaraj of the Madras Institute of Development Studies (MIDS) drew his date from issues from 1997 to 2005. See also: P. Sainath, '1.5 lakh farm suicides in

1997–2005', *India Together*, November 2007: http://www.indiatogether.org/2007/nov/psa-mids1.htm The deaths follow an almost identical pattern – small landowners who dream big and borrow money at extortionate rates from illegal lenders to rent more land, who then find themselves unable to make the payments and kill themselves by drinking the last of their investment, the pesticide.

20. See the South Asia Terrorism Portal for estimates on the Naxals' strength: http://www.satp.org
21. Two months later in the same area, rebels abducted fifty villagers suspected to have cooperated with Indian security forces. Thirteen bodies were later found deep in the forest, their throats also slit. The other villagers were never seen again.
22. World Bank, 'Country Strategy for India 2005', Introduction: http://siteresources.worldbank.org/INTINDIA/Resources/Introduction.pdf
23. All the statistics in this section are Government of India figures.
24. South Asia Terrorism Portal: http://www.satp.org/satporgtp/countries/india/terroristoutfits/CPI_M.htm
25. Ibid.
26. A second symptom was the violence against migrants. A third was the rainbow of separatist ethnic rebel armies that dot India's north-east, such as the United Liberation Front of Assam (ULFA), which was periodically staging bloody attacks and trying to shut down the tea industry. A fourth symptom was the new Luddite movement sweeping Bangalore. The group, an alliance of local Kannada speakers who oppose the transformation (by outsiders) of Bangalore, and all foreign or out-of-state influence, staged two days of riots in the Indian tech capital in April 2006. It achieved its first significant victory the following November when it changed Bangalore's name to Bengalooru, a corruption of Benda Kaluru, the city's original Kannada name, which means 'place of boiled beans'.

CHAPTER 7

1. IMF, 'World Economic and Financial Surveys, Regional Economic Outlook, Sub-Saharan Africa', October 2007: 43. http://www.imf.org/external/pubs/ft/reo/2007/AFR/ENG/sreo1007.pdf
2. Transparency International Corruption Perceptions Index 2007: http://www.transparency.org/policy_research/surveys_indices/cpi

3. The report can be found at: www.wikileaks.org/wiki/KTM_report.pdf
4. UN Human Development Report 2005, 'International cooperation at a crossroads: Aid, trade and security in an unequal world'. http://hdr.undp.org/en/reports/global/hdr2005/
5. UN Department of Economic and Social Affairs, 'Report on the World Social Situation 2005: The Inequality Predicament', 25 August 2005: http://www.un.org/esa/socdev/rwss/index.html
6. Transparency International Corruption Perceptions Index 2007: http://www.transparency.org/policy_research/surveys_indices/cpi
7. See S. Hussain Zaidi's *Black Friday* (2002) for a full account. The book has also been made into a film, but Indian censors nervous at its incendiary subject matter held up its release. Dawood Ibrahim, the gangster behind the attacks now thought to be living in Pakistan, personifies the link between poverty, inequality and terror. Born poor and Muslim in India, he took to crime to even the score – and then became India's most wanted terrorist, and a hero to many of India's disadvantaged Muslims, with the bombings.
8. Aakar Patel, editor of Bombay's afternoon tabloid *Mid-Day*, told me the growth of the Muslim middle class in cities like Bombay had fostered fundamentalism. 'They are extremely well educated and more aware of their faith and their adversaries,' he says. 'Particularly in Bombay, the Islamists see the way India is heading, a sort of Western consumer model of development, they don't like it and they have the imagination and wherewithal to do something about it.' This was later confirmed by the police officer tasked with hunting down the bombers. Deputy police commissioner Pradeep Sawant told me: 'Of the twenty-one we've caught and charged, two are doctors, six are computer specialists and two or three more are university graduates in other disciplines.' His boss, joint commissioner Ahmad Javed, himself a Muslim, described it as ominous 'when people who are so qualified choose a path which means throwing everything away. It tells us that there is a new sort of thinking circulating in the community.'

   Indeed, outside Bombay, police across India had arrested newly formed or newly active cells of Muslim militants in India's IT hub of Bangalore as well as in prosperous cities like Madras, New Delhi and Hyderabad, all featuring a high proportion of professionals and university graduates. The extent to which terrorism's old hands are capitalizing on the new fury among well-educated Muslims becomes only too apparent in the written confessions of the men arrested for the Bombay blasts. Seven of them describe how, as young, smart, affluent Muslims, they were specifically targeted by militant recruiters who offered them high-paying jobs in Dubai, mostly as software engineers. Once in the Middle East, under the auspices of a man called Nasir Bhai and a Saudi-based Indian expatriate called Abu Hamza, they were gradually introduced to the principles of fundamentalism and given basic weapons and bomb-building training before being sent back to India. Sawant says his colleagues across India who have also made terrorist arrests in recent months have noticed the same new pattern of recruitment.

Sawant also told me about how, when he went to the wealthy Muslim suburb of Borivili to arrest a forty-four-year-old suspected of being the ground commander in the bombings, he and his officers were forced to withdraw by a crowd of 300 people. Days later, Sawant's men found two AK-56s, four pistols, four revolvers and 250 home-made bombs hidden in the local well. 'I fear this is only the beginning,' predicted Sawant accurately. Javed agreed. 'We will have more strife and the situation will get more difficult.' But as a Muslim, he insisted: 'There is hope for Muslims in India. There has to be. If Muslims lose hope, then what?'

9. I knew several hundred fugitives from Afghanistan had sailed around India to Muslim Bangladesh at the end of 2001 (Alex Perry, 'Deadly Cargo', *Time*, 21 October 2002: 22–5), but at the time I took Omar's statement as bravado. Months later, however, a European intelligence operative based in Delhi confirmed Omar's story to me. A far greater number of Taliban and al-Qaeda fighters had travelled overland from Afghanistan to Kashmir and beyond, said the operative.
10. For an excellent account of how political Islamists were overtaken by the nihilist, millenarian militants of Osama bin Laden et al., see Jason Burke's *al-Qaeda* (London, Penguin Books, 2004).
11. The Bombay police later tried to blame Pakistan for the bombings. This was disingenuous. SIMI has connections with other militants in Pakistan, and Omar told me SIMI would take help from anyone who offered, including radical Islamists inside the Pakistani security services. This did not make the Bombay blasts a Pakistani plot, any more than 9/11 was a Saudi plot, or the London bombings were a Dewsbury, West Yorkshire, conspiracy.

12. The 2001 national census, whose results on Muslims were released only in August 2006, found 44 per cent fewer Muslims completed high school and only 1 in 101 Muslim women was a graduate, compared to 1 in 37 non-Muslim women. Prime Minister Singh convened a commission to investigate. It found Muslims were over-represented in one state institution – prison.
13. Hindu riots over the last two decades in India have cost the lives of more than 6,000 Muslims, yet only a handful of Hindus have been convicted. Indeed, an indication of which way the courts are leaning in three other Gujarat massacre cases – in which the death tolls were 89, 42 and 38 – can be found in the release of all but 10 of the 114 alleged murderers, rapists and arsonists on bail.
14. Aryn Baker, 'Beyond Faith', *Time*, 13 August 2007: 22–9. http://www.time.com/time/specials/2007/article/0,28804,1649060_1649046_1649032,00.html
15. Ibid.

CHAPTER 8

1. Richard Kerbaj, 'My son has joined al-Qaeda', *Australian*, 1 October 2007: http://www.theaustralian.news.com.au/story/0,25197,22509826-601,00.html
2. Eritrea split acrimoniously from Ethiopia in 1993 and the neighbours fought a border war in 1998–2000 in which tens of thousands died. The border dispute is unresolved, and periodically threatens to flare up again.
3. Joseph Stiglitz, *Globalization and Its Discontents* (Penguin, London, 2002): 274.
4. In October 2004, the British medical journal the *Lancet* released a survey that estimated 100,000 Iraqi civilians had died in the eighteen months since the invasion. Two years later, the Johns Hopkins Bloomberg School of Public Health published another estimate: somewhere between 426,369 and 793,663 civilian deaths, and probably just over 600,000. In November 2006, Iraq's Health Minister estimated civilian deaths at 100,000 to 150,000. The lowest figure was from the Iraq Body Count project: that estimated 68,495 to 74,927 civilian deaths up to 1 August 2007.

PART 3

CHAPTER 9

1. For a full account of my trip to Zimbabwe, see Alex Perry, 'Land of Chains and Hunger', *Time*, 23 April 2007: 20–3.
2. A grandiose description, perhaps, but fair in my experience. Most journalists prize a combination of accuracy and speed, rather than painstaking meticulousness. Nevertheless, collectively as a profession, they know the world better than almost any other. I meet plenty of other journalists in the field, but rarely anyone else – with the notable exception of staff of Human Rights Watch and Médecins Sans Frontières. Many academics seem to think a Google trawl is as good as meeting people on the ground. And I am always shocked by how rarely, despite fleets of 4x4s, aid agency staff leave their secure compounds.

   Perhaps most shocking are the failings of the CIA in the lead up to and aftermath of 9/11. These are well documented elsewhere. I had some first-hand experience of the agency's failings. There was Qala-i-Jangi, where Mike Spann and Dave Tyson attempted interrogations without being able to speak Farsi, or even having an interpreter. There was the CIA station officer in New Delhi who I arranged to meet once to discuss the Tamil Tigers – and for whom I had to locate on a map and spell out the southern Indian state of Tamil Nadu (population 80 million). And there was Gary Berntsen. In 2005, Berntsen published an adrenalin and righteousness-fuelled book called *Jawbreaker*, written with Ralph Pezzullo, in which he described himself as 'the CIA's key commander coordinating the fight against the Taliban around Kabul'. Imagine my surprise on reaching Chapter 16 to find this passage:

   'Shortly after 10 a.m. additional Special Forces soldiers and eight men from the 10th Mountain Division arrived in trucks. Two Special Forces soldiers armed with radios and an all-important SOFLAM inched their way along the northern parapet. 'Be advised,' said one soldier over his radio as he watched from below, 'you're dangerously close. You're about 100 yards from the target.'

   'I think maybe we're a little too close,' replied the spotter. 'But we have to be to get the laser on line.'

SF spotter: 'Be advised we have new coordinates, north 3639996, east 066558866. We're about ready to pull back.'

Pilot: 'We're ready to release.'

Spotter: 'Two minutes.'

There are two more similarly extensive passages taken from my work and odd descriptions cut and pasted in elsewhere. These were my descriptions. These were events only I had witnessed. These conversations only I had. When Berntsen talked about a blast blowing open doors ten miles away, he was writing about my door. Berntsen's book carried a tag on the cover that read: 'The book the CIA doesn't want you to read!' Maybe the CIA was less worried about what secrets the book revealed than about what plagiarism said about the knowledge and competence of senior CIA officers in the field.

Gary Berntsen, with Ralph Pezzullo, *Jawbreaker* (New York, Crown Publishers, 2005): 255–67.

3. These figures are from Reporters Without Borders, the Paris-based international press freedom NGO. See www.rsf.org
4. For the eight years until Beckham left Manchester United in 2003, it was possible to cover world sport in one story, as a glance at newspaper back pages from this period around the world will confirm.

CHAPTER 10

1. Switzerland again, though for Bollywood, Switzerland is generally a stand-in for Kashmir, judged as too dangerous for a location shoot.
2. William Green, 'How to Ride the Elephant', *Time* 18 June 2006: http://www.time.com/time/magazine/article/0,9171,1205357–2,00.html
3. Which also might explain why India produces legions of office-bound doctors and engineers but, outside cricket, few sportsmen.
4. In some places, desperation turned to anger. On Great Nicobar, a crowd of settlers kidnapped the island's top civilian official and his deputy when, after walking through the rainforest for four days, living off coconuts and rainwater, they arrived at the capital Campbell Bay to find the pair sitting down to a lunch of biryani. And on 30 December, the crew of relief boat MV *Sentinel* mutinied when their captain refused to pick up 200 refugees from the island of Camorta.

CHAPTER 11

1. Whether he would accede to the throne was another matter. Late one night after a long dinner in Kathmandu, a friend of the royal family told me that Paras would never sit on the throne. 'Look me in the eyes,' he said. 'If Gyanendra dies, Paras will not be king. You understand me? Paras will never be king.'
2. Other autocrats adopt the same argument to justify their rule, notably Pakistan's President Pervez Musharraf, Uzbekistan's Islam Karimov and even China's Communist Party, which had cracked down on Muslim Uighurs on China's western fringes.
3. There was another connection. Gyanendra and George W. Bush both took power in disputed circumstances, found their feet in the patriotic boost after their enemies attacked, then became steadily more unpopular.
4. The US military presents one of the clearest manifestations of how the US tacitly acknowledges that the new global war has roots in the new global inequality. Under the Bush administration, the US military was restructured to be faster, leaner and deployed to more forward bases for quick reaction. The idea was to be on site along the 'arc of instability' that stretched from Africa through the Middle East to Asia. But the arc of instability closely maps the arc of globalization. The US military is being restructured to be close to those spots left out of globalization. That was the thinking behind JTFHOA at Djibouti. Around half the 800 Special Operations personnel at JTFHOA at Djibouti were civil affairs specialists. While the Pentagon was deploying expert killers to deal with the extremists spurred on by global disparity, it also was deploying military aid workers to dilute the disparity itself. It was fighting 'the war on terror' with development as well as guns.
5. To my editor, Michael Elliott, in interview, Davos, 2005.
6. For this and other illuminating work on philanthropy, see: http://www.bc.edu/research/cwp/
7. NBC, 'Warren Buffett and NBC's Tom Brokaw: The Complete Interview': http://www.cnbc.com/id/21553857/
8. Richard Tomkins, 'What's in it for Them', *FT* Magazine, 23–4 September 2006: http://us.ft.com/ftgateway/superpage.ft?news_id=fto101320060924420805&page=2
9. For much of its history, Tata would have been the last business group

you'd have turned to for radical thinking, or even owning anything abroad. For the first half of the last century, the Indian business establishment *was* Tata. J.N. Tata was a nationalist. While his ideas were imported from abroad, his business plan was wholly domestic, driven by the idea of a strong, self-reliant India. He gave India its first steel plant, first hydro-electric plant, first textile mill, first shipping line, first cement factory, first science university, even its first world-class hotel. His successors – among them J.R.D. Tata, India's first pilot – created the first airline, first motor company, first bank and first chemical plant. What's more, after Indian independence in 1947, the group came to symbolize all that was bad about Indian business. It lost its airline and insurance arm to nationalization. To avoid giving up more to the Congress Party socialists who ruled India for half a century, J.R.D. Tata emphasized individual companies over the group, keeping the group stakes small and demanding little coordination. In addition, shielded by a wall of state protectionism and the restrictive bureaucracy of the 'licence Raj', Tata's companies bloated. Ratan Tata took over in 1991, as India began its process of economic reform. He raised the group's stake in all its companies to a minimum of 26 per cent. And he ordered each to meet a set of targets – to be first or second in its industry, and to meet scores of indicators such as leadership, innovation and agility – or be sold. Most shaped up. 'The Tata group's relationship with its employees changed from the patriarchal to the practical,' reads the Tata Code of Honour, which sets group-wide standards of conduct. Subir Gokarn, chief economist at Crisil ratings agency, says Ratan Tata correctly read the runes of change. 'He survived the bloodbath,' he says of the rash of failures that followed reform. 'Those who made no changes became extinct.' After nine years of consolidation and streamlining, in February 2000 Tata signalled a new prominence for the emerging Asia conglomerate when the most Indian of brands bought one of the most English, Tetley Tea. The deal was groundbreaking. At $435 million, it was the biggest in Indian history. More significantly, it prefigured a wave of international expansion from other Indian or Chinese business houses like Mittal Steel and Lenovo. (And nationalist grumbles in the British press were a premonition of the opposition such Asian upstarts would face.) Later acquisitions included Tata Motors' takeover of Daewoo's heavy truck maker ($102 million), Tata Steel's purchase of Natsteel ($486 million), Indian Hotels' purchase of the Pierre in New York and telecom provider VSNL's purchase of Tyco in the US.

10. For a full discussion of this idea, see Coimbatore Krishna Rao Prahalad, *The Fortune at the Bottom of the Pyramid* (Wharton School Publishing, Penn., 5 August 2004).
11. See *Fortune* Magazine's Power 25, 2005–7.

PART 4

CHAPTER 12

1. 'Migrant workers striving for better life as Hu vows to tackle widening income gap', *People's Daily*, 21 October 2007: http://english.peopledaily.com.cn/90002/92169/92188/6287565.html
2. On the other hand, revolution is a far more serious challenge in places where government is big. One reason why worker unrest in China is watched so closely by the authorities and Western intelligence agencies is that in China, the Communist Party government *is* the country, a claim it legitimizes by lack of dissent (albeit enforced). To challenge the Chinese government is to challenge the nation. A Naxal-type revolution in China would be catastrophic not only to the Communist Party, but to how all China works. In India, lack of resources means many parts of the country are virtually ungoverned. This causes huge problems, crippling India's ability to build infrastructure or redistribute wealth. But it has one big advantage when it comes to rebels. By being small, government presents less of a target. In areas where the Naxals operate, there are no roads, no schools and no administration, not even a dam to blow up, and teachers and policemen have fled. Revolution does not represent such a direct challenge to the state for the simple reason that the state is not there. You can't defy a mirage. And a government can't really be hurt if it's not even in the fight. By being small, to some extent the Indian government dodges the bullet.
3. See the 2006 study by Oxfam, Amnesty and the International Network on Small Arms, which found India was home to 40 million of the world's 75 million illegal arms.
4. Edwin Markham, 'Labour Force: Children', *Cosmopolitan* Magazine (January 1907), reprinted in *Out of the Sweatshop: the Struggle for*

Industrial Democracy, Leon Stein, ed. (New York: *New York Times* Book Company, 1977): 24.

5. Howard Zinn, *A People's History of the United States, 1492–present*, 3rd Edition, (Harlow, UK, Pearson Education Limited, 2003): 250.
6. Stephen King and Janet Henry, 'The Return of the Political Economy', HSBC Global Economics, Q4 2005: 1.
7. Lexington, 'Bada Bing!', *Economist*, 7 June 2007: http://www.economist.com/world/na/displaystory.cfm?story_id=9304030
8. Thomas Jefferson, letter to James Madison, (Paris, 30 January 1797): http://www.earlyamerica.com/review/summer/letter.html
9. Mao, *Quotations from Chairman Mao Tse-Tung* (China Books & Periodicals Inc, 1990): Chapter 5.
10. Alex Perry, 'Urban Cowboys', *Time*, 13 January 2003: 25
11. Oxfam, 'Africa's missing billions: International arms flows and the cost of conflict', October 2007: http://www.oxfam.org/en/policy/briefing papers/bp107_africas_missing_billions
12. Michael White, *The Fruits of War: How Military Conflict Accelerates Technology* (London, Simon and Schuster, 2005): 346.
13. Michael White, *The Fruits of War: How Military Conflict Accelerates Technology* (London, Simon and Schuster, 2005): 2.
14. Ibid.
15. Narayan Murthy agrees. 'At its most basic, globalization is about making the world more competitive with itself,' he says.

ACKNOWLEDGEMENTS

A correspondent is nothing without a good fixer. These transcend that inadequate description: Kassahun Addis in Addis Ababa, Denis Giles in Port Blair, Sanjeev Kumar in New Delhi, Mohammed Ibrahim Mohammed ('Fanah') in Mogadishu, Najibullah Quraishi in Mazar-i-Sharif, Padam Shahi in Nepalganj, Campbell Spencer and Yubaraj Ghimire in Kathmandu, S. Hussain Zaidi in Bombay and David and Ali in Shenzhen, who due to Chinese discomfort with their work must unfortunately remain semi-anonymous.

For their help and guidance, I am indebted to: Aravind Adiga, Faizan Ahmed, Peter Apps, Max Askew, Aryn Baker, Phil Benedictus, Sandeep Bhaumik, Subir Bhaumik, Dodge Billingsley, Keith Bloomfield, Laura Blue, Richard Brown, Matt Bryden, Spencer Campbell, Phil Chetwynd, Chris Chivers, Matt Cooper, Chris Cottrell, Jamie Doran, Jean Dreze, Zoe Eisenstein, Jumana Farouky, Omer Farooq, Peter Foster, Deborah Fowler, Willie Frater, Jim Frederick, Bobby Ghosh, William Green, Karl Greenfeld, Ghulam Hasnain, Nick Holland, Farid Hossain, Talat Hussein, Syed Amin Jafri, Yusuf Jameel, Hola Jiwa, Daisy Jones, Deborah Jones, Jitendra Joshi, Wendy Kan, Parag Khanna, Laura A. Locke, Zamira Loebis, Simon Long, Andrew Marshall, Julian Marshall, Jeannie McCabe, Capt. Christopher McKinney and Sgt. Eddie Heater of the 101st, Katrin MacMillan, Sgt. William Mitchell and the men of Charlie Rock, Michael Moriarty, Oleg Nikishin, M.P. Nunan, Christina and Richard Nutter, Chris Otton, Andrew Perrin, Colin Perry, Sara Rajan, Gautam Rana, Simon Robinson, Josh Ruxin, Ajay Sahni, Dave Savage, Elaine Shannon, P.P. Singh, R. Bhagwan Singh, Rick Stengel, Lee Teslik, Sankarshan Thakur, Josh Tyrangiel, Achin Vanaik, Lasantha Wickrematunge and Adam Zagorin. Because of the nature of the work, many of the sources in this book are anonymous. Many thanks to these many men and women for making themselves available, and entrusting themselves to my confidence.

Much of the work reported here was originally undertaken on assignment for *Time*, and some chapters contain excerpts of articles that appeared in the magazine. My thanks to Michael Elliott and Adi Ignatius at *Time*, New York, for graciously giving permission for that work to be reproduced here. An incalculable debt, naturally, is owed to *Time*, and all my editors there, for engaging so thoroughly on the issues of globalization and war, and for granting me so many opportunities to pursue the stories that gripped us all. The team at *Time* is, in my opinion, the best in the business, and one of the last to comprehensively cover the kind of issues that concern me here. The magazine's reputation for excellence, fairness and accuracy was instrumental in unlocking so many of the doors I needed to access in the course of my reporting, and this book would not exist without it. In a few instances, my research was assisted by other *Time* correspondents. My thanks also to them – I have acknowledged that help where appropriate by crediting them in the text.

At my agency Gail Ross, I am indebted to Howard Yoon, who took on this project at a very early stage with enthusiasm, wisdom and skill, and to Gail herself, who put all her considerable energies in steering it to publication. They were assisted ably by Arabella Stein at Abner Stein, who worked her magic in London.

My publishers, Peter Ginna at Bloomsbury USA in New York and Georgina Morley at Pan Macmillan in London, proved precise and patient editors, handling my jet-lagged appearance at meetings and long absences in the field with impressive grace.

Photographers and travel companions who graciously agreed to let me reprint their work here include Damien Delguelde, Tomas van Houtryve, Benedict Kurzen, Prashant Panjiar, Per-Andres Petterson, Dominic Sansoni and Sven Torfinn.

Finally, my eternal love and gratitude to Tess, Katya and Grace. Life as a foreign correspondent is often great; life as the family of a foreign correspondent forced to accommodate long absences frequently less so. Their forgiveness and support is remarkable, and an inspiration.

INDEX

INDEX

INDEX

INDEX

1 Battalion 501 Brigade 101 Division